W9-AQB-064

Religion *in* Hip Hop

For Tuesday, April 30th:
Bun B on religion &
hip hop (124)

For Thursday, May 2nd:
Zombies in the Hood (183)

BLOOMSBURY STUDIES IN RELIGION AND POPULAR MUSIC

SERIES EDITORS: CHRISTOPHER PARTRIDGE AND SARA COHEN

Religion's relationship to popular music has ranged from opposition to "the Devil's music" to an embracing of modern styles and subcultures in order to communicate its ideas and defend its values. Similarly, from jazz to reggae, gospel to heavy metal, and bhangra to qawwali, there are few genres of contemporary popular music that have not dealt with ideas and themes related to religion, spiritual, and the paranormal. Whether we think of Satanism or Sufism, the liberal use of drugs or disciplined abstinence, the history of the quest for transcendence within popular music and its subcultures raises important issues for anyone interested in contemporary religion, culture, and society.

Bloomsbury Studies in Religion and Popular Music is a multidisciplinary series that aims to contribute to a comprehensive understanding of these issues and the relationships between religion and popular music.

Christian Metal, Marcus Moberg
Sacred and Secular Musics, Virinder S. Kalra

Religion *in* Hip Hop: Mapping the New Terrain in the US

**EDITED BY
MONICA R. MILLER,
ANTHONY B. PINN AND
BERNARD "BUN B" FREEMAN**

**PREFACE BY
MICHAEL ERIC DYSON**

Bloomsbury Academic
An imprint of Bloomsbury Publishing Plc

B L O O M S B U R Y
LONDON · NEW DELHI · NEW YORK · SYDNEY

Bloomsbury Academic

An imprint of Bloomsbury Publishing Plc

50 Bedford Square	1385 Broadway
London	New York
WC1B 3DP	NY 10018
UK	USA

www.bloomsbury.com

BLOOMSBURY and the Diana logo are trademarks of Bloomsbury Publishing Plc

First published 2015

© Monica R. Miller, Anthony B. Pinn, Bernard "Bun B" Freeman and Contributors, 2015

Monica R. Miller, Anthony B. Pinn and Bernard "Bun B" Freeman have asserted their right under the Copyright, Designs and Patents Act, 1988, to be identified as Editors of this work.

All rights reserved. No part of this publication may be reproduced or transmitted in any form or by any means, electronic or mechanical, including photocopying, recording, or any information storage or retrieval system, without prior permission in writing from the publishers.

No responsibility for loss caused to any individual or organization acting on or refraining from action as a result of the material in this publication can be accepted by Bloomsbury or the editors.

British Library Cataloguing-in-Publication Data
A catalogue record for this book is available from the British Library.

ISBN: HB: 978-1-4725-0743-3
PB: 978-1-4725-0907-9
ePDF: 978-1-4725-0601-6
ePub: 978-1-4725-0722-8

Library of Congress Cataloging-in-Publication Data
A catalog record for this book is available from the Library of Congress.

Series: Bloomsbury Studies in Religion and Popular Music

Typeset by Deanta Global Publishing Services, Chennai, India

*To Hip Hop, Hip Hop Intellectuals, and the life,
work, and memory of Dr. Greg Dimitriadis*

Contents

Illustration

Contributors

Monica R. Miller is an assistant professor of religion and Africana studies and director of Women, Gender, and Sexuality Studies (WGSS) at Lehigh University.

Anthony B. Pinn is currently the Agnes Cullen Arnold Professor of Humanities and Professor of Religious Studies at Rice University, founding director of Rice's Center for Engaged Research and Collaborative Learning and director of research for the Institute for Humanist Research (Washington, DC).

Bernard "Bun B" Freeman is better known by his stage name Bun B who rose to fame in the influential rap duo UGK, has won numerous awards, and has been nominated for a Grammy.

Michael Eric Dyson is University Professor of Sociology at Georgetown University.

Julius Bailey is an associate professor in the Department of Philosophy at Wittenberg University.

Elonda Clay is an archivist and digital librarian (Philander Smith College, USA) and a PhD candidate, Theology and Religious Studies, VU University Amsterdam (The Netherlands).

Greg Dimitriadis is a professor in the Department of Educational Leadership and Policy in the Graduate School of Education at the University at Buffalo, SUNY.

Maco Faniel is a native Houstonian and currently a doctoral student in history at Rutgers University.

Biko Mandela Gray is a PhD candidate in religious studies at Rice University.

Margarita Simon Guillory is an assistant professor of religion at the University of Rochester.

Daniel White-Hodge is the director of the Center for Youth Ministry Studies and assistant professor of Youth Ministry at North Park University in Chicago.

John L. Jackson, Jr. is dean of the School of Social Policy & Practice and Richard Perry University Professor at the University of Pennsylvania.

James Peterson is the director of Africana studies and associate professor of English at Lehigh University.

James W. Perkinson is a professor of social ethics at the Ecumenical Theological Seminary and a lecturer in intercultural communication studies at the University of Oakland (Michigan).

Joseph Winters is an assistant professor at UNC Charlotte in the Religious Studies department.

Acknowledgments

We are grateful to the numerous individuals and contributors who have, since the inception of this project, offered their sustained support for *Religion in Hip Hop: Mapping the New Terrain in the US*. We would especially like to thank Commissioning Editor for Religious Studies at Bloomsbury Press, Lalle Pursglove, whose enthusiasm and eagerness to see this work through helped to make this volume possible. We deeply appreciate the close attention to and sustained support of this work; we appreciate much your patience and conscientious and meticulous diligence throughout the publication process! We are grateful for the time, energy, and support offered through Bloomsbury's ongoing commitment to publishing at the intersections of religion and popular culture over the last several years. Additionally, we are grateful to the Series Editor(s) who took an interest in this project; we are more than pleased that this work has found a fitting home in the Religion and Popular Music Series. We would also like to thank the volume's contributors, who enthusiastically supported this project from the start, despite demanding schedules and multiple commitments that come with various career stages in the academy. To everyone involved in the project on the publishing end, your support and energy has made this project enjoyable.

Our deepest thanks to The Center for Engaged Research and Collaborative Learning at Rice University, including Maya Reine, assistant director for programming and administration, and the graduate students associated with the African American religious studies PhD concentration at Rice. Over the years, CERCL has done much to solidify southern hip hop's contribution to the academic arena. Today, these efforts provide blueprints for engagement now used across the country. We would also like to specifically thank Rice PhD candidate Biko Mandela Gray, who kindly agreed to interview coeditor Bernard "Bun B" Freeman for this volume, and to Dr. Christopher Driscoll, graduate of Rice's African American Religious studies program and now visiting assistant professor at Lehigh University, who assisted with nearly every aspect of this project and offered substantial feedback on various portions of this work. We appreciate both of their generous efforts. We also thank both of our institutions, Rice University and Lehigh University's CAS, Religion and Africana Studies, for providing space, resource, and collegial support as this project unfolded.

We cannot thank enough Dr. Michael Eric Dyson for his scholarship, insight, and intellectual genius over the years at the intersections of religion and hip hop culture and for enthusiastically agreeing to participate in this project from the start. Finally—we would like to give a huge shout-out to hip hop and the many constituents who've helped to make this growing area of study a palpable reality in the academy, classroom, and beyond. We hope *Religion in Hip Hop: Mapping the New Terrain in the US* demonstrates our celebration of critical engagement, love for hip hop culture, and ongoing commitment to the theory, method, expansion of data, and the sights, voices, times, and spaces that gave the world this thing we call hip hop culture.

Monica R. Miller
Anthony B. Pinn

Preface

Turning nothing into something is God Work': Holiness and hurt in the hood

Hip hop didn't invent the word, although one of its earliest benedictions radiates literary aspiration: Word. Some linguists argue that language burst on the human scene a hundred thousand years ago through a single chance mutation in one individual that spread like a verbal prairie fire to others in the breeding circle. Other linguists say that language evolved over long stretches of time and circumstance and emerged in *Homo sapiens* less than two hundred thousand years ago. If you believe biblical scribes, The Word stretches all the way back to God and the beginning of time and space and the universe. In the beginning was the word. In religious genealogy, then, grammar begets gravity, so to speak. Literally.

Neither did hip hop invent the beat; if it doesn't quite have the celestial bragging rights of speech, rhythm's origins are hardly less primitive, tucked inside our bodies where our hearts measure our existence one beat at a time. Blending word and beat as part of hip hop's own creation myth means that an art form that dates back just to the seventies connects to the creation myth of the universe itself.

Depending on how you view hip hop culture, such a belief is heady, arrogant, or delusional, or a brazen remix of all three. From the start, hip hop has been unwilling to settle for anything less than cosmic significance and global influence, even when it could barely make it from its Bronx bedroom to a train stop in Brooklyn, much less travel from Long Island to London. Hip hop's reach often exceeded its grasp, or else what's a cipher for? All of its bombast and outsize boasts seem to flow in the traffic between hood saviors and their divine inspiration in project flats that doubled as modern birthplaces for artistic gods.

If that comparison seems far too self-important and spiked with hyperbole, then consider this equally ambitious parallel: At least one holy book declares that God got his start on earth as the son of a single mother who got knocked up by someone out of the picture, leaving a brave man to step in and love the mother and raise the boy who would be delivered in harsh circumstances among the poor because the establishment barred them from comfortable birth.

Jesus meet Jay-Hova. Nazareth meet New York. Manger meet Marcy. Mother Mary meet Afeni Shakur. Swaddling clothes meet Underoos. Scripture meet scribbling in note pads. Missing years between adolescence and adulthood learning to bear the weight of the world as the messiah meet missing years between high school and rap career spent pushing weight before saving hip hop. Overturned tables in the temple meet the temple of hip hop and its turntables. Forty days in the wilderness meet no church in the wild. The list of such similarities could literally go on, if not ad infinitum, then at least ad nauseam.

Like sacred texts and the spiritual figures they reveal, the speech, rhythms, and representatives of hip hop battled mighty opposition to forge artistic triumph and commercial dominance. Hip hop has endured significant ridicule because the primary makers of its talk and beats are black. Black art has been relentlessly mocked as a hodgepodge of inferior form and puerile content. Thomas Jefferson savaged the artistic pedigree of black music; before him David Hume denied the existence of black arts at all. Black art was widely viewed as a black mark on what little humanity and intelligence black folk were said to possess.

The initial thorns in hip hop's flesh grew from the same bush-league criticism that has always dressed down black culture while its opposition is dressed up as highfalutin' theory or scientific analysis. It is chilling to recall, for instance, that the same society that in the name of science sponsored the Tuskegee experiment and allowed disease to spread in three hundred black men without treatment is the same society that tried to convince us that Tupac's meditations on black manhood were morally diseased. The Tuskegee experiment ended in 1972; 'Pac's life began in 1971. There is no relation between the two dates, except the relation forced on random events in history by human beings out to do harm or to relieve suffering through their words and actions. In a world where the Tuskegee experiment could exist to hurt black men, their sometime noble artistic defender Tupac had to be born.

That may be putting the proverbial sociological cart before the artistic horse. Hip hop has rarely had the freedom to just be, as Common allusively suggests in the title of one of his greatest albums, because it got dragged so quickly into political arguments about its right to exist, and because hip hop is widely viewed as the soundtrack to black pathology. Perhaps the condition of its emergence had something to do with how the shadow of politics has cloaked the roots and rise of hip hop culture. The messiah in a manger, metaphor aside; hip hop's birth is no less miraculous for taking place in crushing social, political, and racial conditions.

Hip hop got its start less than a decade after a defining and cataclysmic event: The death of Martin Luther King, Jr. King's death rocked our culture like few deaths ever have – Lincoln's death shook the nation of course, and so did the death of the Kennedy brothers, but all of them were presidents or politicians who had the blessing of the state and the resources of government at their call. King magnetized the needle of America's moral compass as a private citizen and quite literally as a minster without portfolio. King challenged America's musty racial views through vibrant social struggle, and like the hip hoppers who came after him he moved the crowd through the power of his melodic speech.

King's death cast a pall of deep grief on black America and led many folk to question whether the nation was willing to genuinely support ideals of fairness and equality that it paid lip service to but steadily undercut. The racial miasma that triggered King's assassination briefly gave way to fleeting black empathy before hardening into white backlash. As the civil rights movement sputtered, the black power movement picked up steam to proclaim the beauty of blackness and the need for more aggressive resistance. On the cultural front the Black Arts Movement (BAM), sparked by the tragic death in 1965 of another seminal black leader, Malcolm X, had already begun to fight the power of white superiority by painting the canvas of history and aesthetics in bold black strokes.

By the time BAM reached its end in the mid-seventies, the battle against white resentment and, later, the fight over affirmative action would reenergize the civil rights movement. Together the waning black power movement and the revived civil rights movement flooded the ballot boxes of northern cities to elect black mayors in Newark and Detroit in the early seventies after successfully electing mayors in Cleveland and Gary, Indiana, in the year of King's death. The South and West got on board with black mayors in Atlanta and Los Angeles. At the same time black folk flexed their electoral muscles at the polls to sweep into office many more black members of congress.

If black folk gained on the political front, they continued to knock down barriers in television, film, and radio, and in sports and entertainment as well. Bill Cosby and Diahann Carroll integrated the small screen while Sidney Poitier continued lighting up the big screen. And the original Foxy Brown—Pam Grier—torched the local Cineplex with her erotic charisma before Blaxploitation symbolically burned it down. The expansion of FM in the seventies garnered a bigger audience for black radio and its corps of spirited DJs. The ranks of major league baseball swelled with black players less than a quarter century after Jackie Robinson ended apartheid on the diamond. And black basketball players eclipsed white athletes in the NBA in the mid-seventies, but not before the New York Knickerbockers were derided as the New York "Niggerbockers." The NFL got a lot more color too, paving the way for a league that today is nearly 70 percent black.

Motown and Philadelphia International Records bestrode the culture as recording colossuses, and R&B artists began to break free of commercial ghettos and cultural constraints. Marvin Gaye brought conscience to black pop with the groundbreaking *What's Going On?*, a theme album meditating on war, spirituality, the ecology, God, and the salvation of children. Disco stars Donna Summer and Sylvester gave spirited voice to an art form that unapologetically traded on raucous female energy and gay bravura. Aretha Franklin amplified her sixties' cries for respect at home and in society and returned to her spiritual roots with the landmark *Amazing Grace*. Stevie Wonder pled for universal love, cosmic enlightenment, social justice, and black equality on the monumental *Songs in the Key of Life*. And Michael Jackson released *Off the Wall* in 1979, a sonic harbinger of the eclecticism that made him the dominant musical artist of the 1980s and the greatest entertainer in the world.

In the same year, on September 16, a single dropped that forever changed the musical landscape: The Sugarhill Gang's "Rapper's Delight," the first hip hop recording to popularize an art form that later won international acclaim. In the meantime, "rap"—the talking part of hip hop culture—was largely viewed as a temporary musical trend that would eventually disappear like dolphin earrings and K-Swiss sneakers. But the music and the culture that supported it struck a nerve with youth in New York City and then around the country. For better and worse, males created hip hop and it is still a *testosterocentric* affair often booming with patriarchal ambitions. Hip hop culture can therefore be heard and seen through four metonyms that relate the artist to the accoutrements used to craft his art: Man and mat, man and machine, man and marker, and man and microphone.

Man and mat—referring to the *breakdancer*—conjures the cardboard mats used by breakdancers on the streets to cushion their acrobatic moves as they spin on shoulders or heads in sync with the break beats isolated and looped on sound recordings. Man and machine—referring to the *DJ* and then the *producer*—images of the DJ's turntables that were central in the early sound of hip hop and, later, the machines used by hip hop's sonic architects to produce and perfect sound. Among the recent favorites are the Auto-Tune voice processor preferred by T-Pain and Lil Wayne and famously bashed by Jay-Z on "D.OA. (Death of Auto-Tune)." Of earlier vintage is the Roland TR-808 drum machine which, along with Auto-Tune, is used by Kanye West on his fourth studio album and even cited in the title of that searing reflection on love, loss, and loneliness, *808s & Heartbreak*—a seething musical stew of electronica, synthpop, R&B, electropop, and hip hop. Man and marker—referring to the *graffiti* artist—pictures the magic markers and other utensils employed by graffiti artists to scar the tissue of public space while inscribing their existence. And man and microphone—referring to the *rapper* or *MC*—symbolizes the sole possession necessary to project the voice and amplify the lyrical ambition of the rap artist to the world, as Nas immortally proclaimed in his classic "One Mic."

The MC is the heart of hip hop, the centripetal force that draws the varied elements of the culture to its rhetorical center. The MC's story is hip hop's story, and vice versa, since they came up together in the same hoods and either floundered or prospered under the same racial and economic forces. The MC has carried the symbolic weight of hip hop in his throat from the start as the art form rode the golden throats and silver tongues of its greatest artists all the way to platinum success. That success, however, is not the greatest measure of hip hop's achievement. The honor belongs to the genre's most gifted creators who obsess over the complicated lyrical content and complex rhythmic flows of hip hop at its best.

A few of hip hop's best MCs may sport gold teeth, but the bulk of rap's most talented artists surely weren't born with a silver spoon in their mouths. Their lives often tracked the evolution of the genre itself, which matured in the 1980s as budding MCs faced the cruel consequences of Ronald Reagan's voodoo economics, the alleged benefits of which never trickled down to working and poor people as advertised. Hip hop's original MCs often grappled with the low economic growth of the seventies and a vicious recession in the early eighties, high inflation and interest rates, energy crises, unforgivably high unemployment rates for black males, and the bottoming out of the manufacturing sector in an economy that brutally transitioned to a service industry where the high end excluded poor and undereducated people of color. The public school system was equally abysmal: Talented black students were steered toward vocational tracks while their white peers were over prepped for college. To make matters worse, budgets for visual art and musical training were ruthlessly slashed, hampering the musical and artistic prospects of black and brown youth for generations to come.

It is no small wonder that black youth experimented with technology and literacy in creating an art form that has reclaimed poetry for common folk and opened the ears of the world to beautifully chaotic meters, spectacular cadences, and snaking rhythms. The argument about whether hip hop was even music raged for a spell, until the spell of hip hop became the rage of the world. The children of white snobs and black moralizers often made their parents' objections to hip hop obsolete with their discerning consumption and sophisticated analysis of rap music and the culture in which it was spawned.

The MC is the lightning rod and arbiter of hip hop's meaning in a world where lyrics matter so much that their creators are sometimes dragged before congressional committees and made to account for their menace to youth. MC's aren't alone in such ventures. Perhaps there's a fifth element, another metonym, that's gone unrecognized but which is crucial to hip hop's fortunes: Man and Mac—that is, the journalist, writer, and intellectual who uses his or her computer or notepad to critically engage a seminal art form. (Knowledge already unofficially exists as hip hop's fifth element alongside graffiti, breakdancing, DJing, and rapping, and can easily be absorbed in my proposed fifth metonym).

My own pilgrimage is an example, though my journey as a critic, scholar, journalist, and writer on hip hop surely isn't unique. My experience as a curious intellectual grappling with rap music is not unlike the struggle of many thinkers to define, defend, and deconstruct an artistic juggernaut that often barrels into the social and political arena. I began writing about rap music as a graduate student at Princeton University in the mid-eighties, publishing articles in magazines and journals that explored the history, politics, ethics, and aesthetics of rap. My first book, published in 1993, included several essays on hip hop culture, and I've returned to the subject in my subsequent work, especially my critical estimation of the life and legacy of Tupac Shakur, my interview reflections on various elements of the culture, and my edited treatment of Nas's classic debut album, *Illmatic*. I've also taught college courses on hip hop culture since the mid-nineties at the University of North Carolina at Chapel Hill, Columbia University, DePaul University, the University of Pennsylvania, and now at Georgetown University, where my course on Jay-Z drew national media interest and ire.

I've written about rap for the *New York Times*, discussed hip hop on countless television shows, including the *MacNeil/Lehrer NewsHour* on PBS and on HBO's *Real Time with Bill Maher*, and talked about rap on nearly every major radio show in the country. I've debated hip hop in lecture halls across America and, indeed, around the globe, most recently in London where I was the advocate for hip hop in an international debate on the genre's virtues and vices that was broadcast on Google. And I've appeared before Congress on three separate occasions to debate rap: Before the United States Senate in 1994 and again in 2000, and before the House of Representatives in 2007. I've done all of this because I find hip hop a viable artistic medium of expression of culture. But as a man of faith, I find hip hop teeming with religious meaning, holy signifying and transcendent truths that come most alive when artists embrace their abilities to be most human and make the needs of their fellow human beings divine.

The best of hip hop culture looks beyond bigotry to embrace the heroic use of words and beats to cast light on the dark places of the black experience and the American soul. At their noblest hip hop artists carry the weight of the black and poor in their speech and rhythms and exorcise demons as they encounter them in their own minds and in the world around them. It is in performance that rap's rhetorical royalty often massage the grief and encourage the ecstasy of their audiences and cast word spells over a transfixed constituency. To paraphrase the holy book: In the beginning was the word, and the word became flesh and spoke among us through pavement prophets.

Michael Eric Dyson, 2015
Georgetown University, USA

Introduction: Context and other considerations

Anthony B. Pinn and Monica R. Miller

"Home" in the academy

From studies of the spirituals such as that contained in W. E. B. Du Bois's *The Souls of Black Folk* (1903), John Lovett's massive treatment titled *Black Song: The Forge and the Flame* (1972), or James Cone's *Spirituals and the Blues* (1972), to more recent studies of gospel music and the blues by figures such as Jon Michael Spencer, an appreciation for the cultural language of music has given some shape to the content and form of religious studies.[1] This is highlighted in particular ways by Spencer, who developed an alternate methodology—*theomusicology*—and an accompanying journal related to the study of African American music using a religious studies/theological approach that takes seriously history and cultural developments.

If slave narratives and the spirituals and the blues served as cultural blueprints into the religious and theological imagination of people of color in the New World, then the turn to hip hop culture, as source material, is a logical, chronological, and rational one. The pressing question of "why hip hop for the study of religion?" remained a constant discursive fixture. For some, hip hop was too crass, deviant, and nihilistic—without significance and evaluative merit. However, for others, the shape-shifty and constantly emergent culture that is hip hop held within it vital clues regarding changing patterns and configurations of meaning, life, community, politics, and so on. Moral panics about the look and form of hip hop ironically created space for new and different questions to be asked—room for a new context of engagement beyond a strict institutional purview of religion and meaning.

Now a global and transnational phenomenon (i.e., no longer solely housed in urban pockets of the United States)—US-based hip hop culture has become a vital component of political, religious, educational, economic (and so on) progress, relevance, and recognition. Leave it to rapper Jay-Z to suggest that President Barack Obama would not have been elected to office (or be so popular among young people in America) had it not been for the hip hop "nation's" support generally and Jay-Z's public support in particular. In this new context of insurmountable relevance and achievement of recognition, hip hop has positioned itself as one of the most vital cultural forces to be reckoned with globally.

Over the past two decades, those who have taken up hip hop culture for its intellectual weight and contributions to the cultural life and self-understanding of the United States have come from a variety of methodological disciplines. As such, the cultural modality of hip hop culture has often been utilized as a means of exploring and analyzing the complex and ever-changing configurations of religion within and among today's current landscape. For instance, against what many refer to as a "decline" in religion and belief, scholars have queried to what extent cultural production like hip hop replaces traditional modes, varieties, and spaces of religiosity and spirituality, while others have pushed up against this replacement-like logic, and instead explore hip hop culture as a means by which to tackle identity construction and the acquisition and marketing of various forms of capital (i.e., uses vs. effects). Existing scholarship has explored what the uses, practices, rhetoric, and deployments of religiosity within hip hop culture say about altered and ever-shifting patterns of notions such as belief and irreligion. Rather than using institutional and more traditional religious participation as a means of measuring patterns of religiosity—critical attention to cultural production, such as hip hop, has assisted scholars of religion in charting and mapping more forceful and complicated perspectives of the religious among particular social and cultural economies. For example, if rhetorical uses of religion in rap music depict little about confessional claims to belief among artists, then what do such uses accomplish? What is their purpose? How might such deployments alter how traditional categories such as the sacred and profane are approached and navigated? What to make of the assemblage of seemingly conflicting uses of religious rhetoric in hip hop products (all and at the same time)? More recently, the academic study of religion has given hip hop culture closer and more critical attention—with some considering what it means disciplinarily to study hip hop and religion. Such queries have not only been responsible for the proliferation in approaches, sources, and methods, but also, the raising of larger theoretical concerns regarding the differences and similarities between theological, philosophical, and religious studies concerns.

In some ways related to postmodern postures, questions and categories, academic attention to hip hop culture was interested to expose, disrupt, and alter dominant modalities and understandings of metaphysical (e.g., epistemology and ontology) concern within the hard places of urban life.

One can see such interests and influences in early hip hop studies scholarship across academic disciplines where the constructed narrative of hip hop culture most always begins and emerges within and among a discourse of postindustrialism, struggle, urbanity, and marginality. And, what is more, it was meant to offer new, organic, ways of (re)configuring socioeconomic, political, and religious meaning(s).

This book assumes and inherits much of the historiography and narrative associated with this growing concern with hip hop and religion, and seeks to codify it in a particular way—that is, to point out the manner in which it represents a significant and new area of study with its own intellectual and organizational integrity and internal movements and shifts. *Religion In Hip Hop: The New Terrain in the US* seeks to expand beyond past contributions by building upon—yet advancing work on hip hop and religion by highlighting current contributions, thematic parallels, ongoing debates, and pressing issues and intellectual concerns.

By religion, we mean the manner in which the existential and metaphysical arrangements and rhetoric of meaning are developed, worked out, and (re) arranged. That is to say, we do not use this conceptual category as proxy or code for institutions, doctrines, beliefs and creeds defining particular religious traditions. It is not a way of signifying to readers Christianity, Islam, or another religious orientation. Rather, we simply mean to understand religion as a conceptual and taxonomical "place holder" of sorts, a way by means of which humans parse out and explore the social world, the self, and human experience in relationship to a desire for a wide variety of things from "unity" of experience, framework of meaning, or strategic acts of identification. And, by hip hop, we mean a particular cultural world marked by rap, dance, film, technology, visual arts—an aesthetic often expressed in terms of clothing, language, disposition as well as a general posture toward the world that emerges during the late 1970s.

There is a synergistic relationship between religion and hip hop culture that merits rich and sustained investigation and description. Although earlier work in religion and hip hop studies involved a lively debate about the relationship (and manufactured divide) between the sacred (e.g., religion) and profane (e.g., hip hop), the score and contest between these contested distinctions seems settled—provoking new questions beyond what of hip hop should or ought be catalogued for religious studies reflection and engagement.

Studying hip hop/hip hop studies

While the first wave of "hip hop" scholars of religion worked hard to prove the academic legitimacy and religious "merit" of hip hop culture, more specifically rap music, second and third generation scholars have built on and extended the scope of inquiry by engaging a wide range of data and employing a variety of theoretical and methodological approaches that vary in form, content, and style. As academic interest in hip hop culture steadily increases, lacking is a coherent, pedagogically sophisticated text that highlights the contemporary terrain of religion and hip hop scholarship, where it's been and where it's headed.

While the study of hip hop as a unique subfield is almost three decades old (with hip hop culture being roughly forty years old), it is only in more recent years that the study of religion and hip hop culture has gained recognition (i.e., intellectual acceptance) within the academy. That is not to say, only recently—within the past few years—have scholars wrestled with the nature and meaning of this connection. By this, we have in mind the limited systematic effort to advance a methodological and theoretical housing for the study of hip hop and religion. This scholarship for the most part was not conceived fundamentally as a field, unique in its theoretical arrangements and consequences. And, it is only recently—very recently—that such a turn to the formal structuring of this type of study has been undertaken.

What's the purpose?

The book you hold is the second of our interventions into the constitution of a field known as *Hip Hop and/in Religion Studies*. The first book involved a reader of previously published materials that spoke to various aspects of this subfield's interests, postures, and positions.[2] This book pushes beyond that type of rehearsing of the outline of this mode of study and offers original pieces constituting new insights, sources, approaches, queries, and concerns. It is meant to fill a void by bringing together contributions that consider the relationship between hip hop and religion within the context of a field of study. This volume highlights the intersections of and confrontations between hip hop and religion and the future possibilities of this vital area of thought. Not only does this book seek to engage important and timely themes related to both the academic study and public practice of hip hop and religion, but also highlights, in a productive way, the existing tensions present in this field (i.e., theory, method, approach, etc.). Moreover, this text brings together not only scholars in the field of study, but also, is a collaborative endeavor with a hip hop artist (Bernard "Bun B" Freeman) which we hope opens up and models new approaches of engagement. In this way, this book incorporates an "insider" perspective, that is seldom included in **existing texts**. In doing so, we attempt to distinguish between scholars of religion talking and theorizing about religion in/and hip hop culture and hip hop artists returning the gaze—rapping back about the who, what, where, and why of the dizzying world of religion *in* hip hop.

The main themes of this text address critical issues in the area of study— ones that are ever growing in debate such as: theory and method, the role of technology and new media, aesthetics, the role of hip hop in faith institutions, critical attention to the category of religion, and the future of the study of hip hop and religion. Moreover, attention to topics such as these consider the variety of trends that currently exist in the field by highlighting and bringing together a plethora of voices, perspectives, and thoughts. As such, we learned that not only is rap music, for instance, full of religious uses and significance, but also that this cultural modality houses and boasts a depth of religious variety—from Christianity to Humanism, rap music in particular and hip hop culture in general, is full of religious play, claims, and performativity. The objectives of this text are threefold:

1   To offer an expansive contribution to the field of hip hop and religion that highlight critical issues, formative/new questions that engage a variety of hip hop cultural products and sources.

2   To bring hip hop artists and scholars together in an equitable way— hoping that such a text will be of use not only to academicians, but also the larger public, especially hip hop cultural workers and the wider community.

3   To provide the study of hip hop and religion with a critical roadmap that not only provides a material base but one that is thematically organized according to major topics, questions, and critical trends. Our goal is to be able to provide students with both introductory and critical introductions to major topics of considerable weight and purchase.

Structuring the book

The volume, divided into three sections, is meant to provide various takes on what we reference as hip hop and religious studies—they are as follows: (1) Hip hop on religion as/for the embodied self, (2) Hip hop on religion and the "Other," and (3) Approaches to religion in hip hop on the margins.

The first section explores the reconstruction of identity and personal meaning, with attention given to issues of gender, race, and class as discourses impinging upon notions of the individual's being and meaning. The second section concerns itself with the manner in which the intersections, the synergy, between hip hop and religion is often worked out through adaptation of technology as well as through what one might be said to resemble Michel Foucault's "technologies of the self." Shadowing much of what is presented in this section is a concern with the nature and meaning of capital for "production" of the self and the self in relationship to others—both physically present and virtual. The third and final section explores the guiding theme of this book through attention to marginality—including under-explored religious systems as well as under-explored themes, and challenges to normative assumptions of "belief."

We begin, in the first section, with essays by Margarita Simon Guillory, Daniel White-Hodge, Julius D. Bailey, and Michael Eric Dyson. Framed through attention to both the lyrical content and the visual representations of ideas, Simon Guillory argues identity, the dynamical self, is marked by "creative self-expression" and fluidity, and these are represented brilliantly, she suggests, by artist Erykah Badu. Hodge explores the life and cultural output of late artist Tupac Shakur and artist Lauryn Hill, arguing for an "ethnolifehistory" methodology that takes scholars far beyond lyrical analysis toward fuller portraits of those individuals or institutions under investigation. Bailey turns to existential insights from Nietzsche and Sartre to sketch out the embodied, "terrestrial" ethos of hip hop for the ways it might speak back to contemporary concerns involving the black church and and religion more generally. Michael Eric Dyson concludes section two arguing for a rereading of Jay-Z through critical attention to linguistic and conceptual play around "god," that has continuously marked African American communicative practices—the black oral sermonic tradition in particular. Dyson explores the relationship between the creative manipulation of rhetoric and the assertion and role of religious legitimacy in the production and maintenance of social structures, authority, and legibility.

The second section begins with a piece by James Peterson, where he explores the posthumous presentation of Tupac Shakur and the existential ruptures made possible by virtual-spiritual presence of an artist long after their death. Next, Elonda Clay continues this attention to technology by offering insights for a methodological mapping of religion and hip hop expression and activity in cyberspace, such as attention to the new religion called Yeezianity. The following chapter finds Maco Faniel giving attention to Houston hip hop— its origins, key thinkers and artists, relationship between "H-Town" hip hop and other cultural, regional and ever-expanding contexts, and the meaning-making dimensions—with attention to the impact of locality and geographic particularity.

Next, James Perkinson argues that hip hop is an example of struggle against the subjugating political codings of racial identity, and challenges scholars to look to the embodied dimensions of hip hop culture for what it offers to a Western sensibility struggling to get out of its own violent past, present, and future. The final piece of this section is an interview with recording artist Bernard "Bun B" Freeman, a Center for Engaged Research and Collaborative Learning (CERCL) distinguished visiting lecturer at Rice University. While hip hop scholars have done well to crossover into the art world of hip hop, less effective have been our attempts at direct engagement with artists. We write about artists, but rarely do these artists, speak back. In this interview, Bun B discusses the role of religion in his life and childhood, providing a rare peek into his perspectives and thoughts on a robust range of topics that address the perils and possibilities of hip hop culture, religion, and identity for himself and the wider hip hop community today.

The last section begins with Greg Dimitriadis' description and analysis of southern rap and elements from Jay-Z and Kanye West as humanistic in scope and tone. Here, Dimitriadis is not seeking to categorize hip hop (per se), but to situate hip hop's transformative cultural force against fundamentalisms of thought and action, historically. Next, John L. Jackson, Jr. begins his piece by bringing us back to one of the most historically significant sites in hip hop cultural history—the Marcy Projects housing complex in New York City in order to raise questions about hip hop's current "center of gravity." Through an analytical lens and trope of conspiracy and religio-racial paranoia, Jackson tackles and probes some of the most talked about conspiracies haunting hip hop culture today—such as rapper Jay-Z's involvement in Satanism and the Illuminati, among others. Following Jackson, Joseph Winters' piece makes use of the "constellational" stylings of artist Lupe Fiasco that are marked by a penchant for troubling flat, linear, and one-dimensional accounts of history that often guide American exceptionalism by bringing into focus and methodologically reclaiming the critical cultural theory once so integral to cultural analysis before its dismissive dangers were exposed by new streams of thought. Next up, Anthony B. Pinn brings us to the theme of death and the undead, and argues that African Americans have been created (discursively constructed and physically "arranged") as zombies—the un/dead—by which they have become the housing for the larger society's fear of meaninglessness. And what's more, hip hop culture provides a creative response to this construction through a reenvisioning of death so as to naturalize it, capture it as a component of life, and deconstruct fear surrounding death. Monica R. Miller's essay, the final essay in the volume, raises theoretical and methodological questions regarding themes such as survival, authority, legibility, and illegibility by turning to the strategies of artists such as Jay-Z, one of culture's "New Black Godz." Through an analytic lens Miller calls "Aporetic Flow," she asks, "what happens for those in hip hop for whom survival is seemingly no longer at stake?" and queries the extent to which inherited artistic and aesthetic flows (e.g., calling oneself "God") and tactics (e.g., authenticity) can be redeployed to address issues of hyper-legibility (black presence) and illegibility (black absence).

The sections, and the entire volume, end with a conclusion from Miller and Pinn that outlines important features of hip hop and/in religion scholarship moving forward. Echoing some of the insights from the conclusion, entexting them as well, one last word comes from Bun B, who encourages us all to "keep it Trill!"

PART ONE

Hip hop on religion as/for the embodied self

1

Searching for self: Religion and the creative quest for self in the art of Erykah Badu

Margarita Simon Guillory

My name is Erykah Badu. Also known as Medulla Oblongata, also known as Sara Bellum. Some people know me as Analog Girl in a Digital World ... I'm Annie, I'm Manuela Maria Mexico, sometimes. She-lll. That's who I am. I'm an artist.[1]

Music is the 5th element and I'm so happy to be able to use my platform to express myself.[2]

The opening excerpts, drawn from two interviews with Erykah Badu, depict her specific understanding of how art functions in identity formation. In the first quotation, Badu acknowledges that her multiplicity of personas points to a unified artistic articulation of whom she is as a person. In the second, Badu recognizes music as an outlet, by means of which she can creatively express these various conceptions of herself. This essay explores Badu's employment of art (in the form of her songs, videos, and album cover graphics) as a creative means to express, and hold in tension, multiple notions of self, presented in this essay as the personal self, collective self, and dynamical self. This analysis of the intersectionality between art, creativity, and self-interpretation, as displayed in Badu's usage of art, is guided by two tasks. The first considers the religious life of Badu. Here, religion is to be understood as a life "orientation," or, how Badu conceives of her own significance, whether in relationship to herself or to the external world.[3] The first task of this essay, then, is to examine Badu's religious orientation, which begins with an open espousal of the Five Percenter "way of life" (beginning with her first album, *Baduizm*) and moves toward a view of religion as art.[4] It is this understanding of religion and art that allows Badu to create self-significance expressed in the form of multiple views of herself. The second task of this essay treats the work (particularly videos, album cover art, and lyrics) of Badu as a case study, to get a closer look at how this utilization of art expresses a multidimensional notion of selfhood. In particular, this deeper analysis reveals Badu's dissatisfaction with seeing herself in just one way. She not only wishes to define herself through the maintenance of social solidarity (collective self) or differentiation from others (personal self), but also seeks to articulate an interpretation of self that occurs at the intersection of collectivity and individuality (dynamical self).

The religious evolution of Erykah Badu

In a 2011 interview with Red Bull Music Academy, Badu, in a response to a question about the gutsy moves she took in the production and release of "The Healer," discusses the essentiality of evolution in taking such a risk. She states:

> It's just what I like and as my taste evolves, as I get introduced to more and more things, I understand more and more things, lyrically, musically, sonically. The whole thing. Taking more chances, evolving. I think that's the main focus of who I am as an individual person. Evolving is very important to me.[5]

Here, Badu establishes a direct relationship between individuality and evolution. For her, the ability to constantly undergo developmental progression defines who she is as a person. This openness to malleability, then, allows Badu to expand her understanding of "things," such as the lyrical and vibratory predicates of music. While her commitment to personal progression includes expanding her musical consciousness, this same evolutionary stance also characterizes her understanding of religion. This shift is important, because it shows the various ways in which Badu attempts to locate/orient herself in/ toward the external world. And, as the second part of this essay will show, it is with her present artistic understanding of religion (which results from her religious evolution) that allows her to apprehend a sense of significance, which finds expression in multiple self-interpretations. Badu's religious progression can be traced by examining both her lyrical content (dispersed across six albums) and direct interviews (captured in popular magazines and online venues). What one finds is a religious trajectory that spans from the Nation of Gods and Earths (Five Percenters) to a view of religion as a creative medium.

Between 1997 and 2000, Badu released two studio albums (*Baduizm* and *Mama's Gun*) and one live album (*Live*). Each of these albums contains nuggets of the Five Percenter way of life. For example, in "On and On" (1997) Badu references the "Divine Science of Supreme Mathematics," acknowledges the godliness of black men, and establishes an interconnection between the movement of her cipher and the apprehension of knowledge.[6] Additionally, she utilizes "Ye Yo" (1997), "... & On" (2000), and "Orange Moon" (2000) as canvasses upon which to paint a lyrical picture of the relationship between man and woman, according to the Five Percenter way of life.[7] Badu speaks of being the moon (i.e., the black woman) from which the sun (i.e., the black man) reflects back light. She captures the relationship between these embodied celestial symbols, and how they are particularly essential in creating a star, that is, a black child, who is the very embodiment of understanding.

Scholars like Felicia M. Miyakawa and Michael Muhammad Knight have briefly considered Badu's espousal of the Five Percenter way of life, in two of the songs listed above.[8] They do not, however, recognize the simultaneous presence of another aspect of her religious orientation, nor how she attempts to achieve self-significance. From the beginning of her career, Badu acknowledged the existence of what she calls "the creator." For example, she begins the live version of her song "Ye Yo" by thanking the creator: "Hey, I like to thank the creator for giving me this gift."[9] In this way, Badu recognizes the creator as the originating source of her artistic abilities. While she uses her lyrics to initially introduce this belief, Badu expanded upon this conception of the creator in an interview in 2001. She stated: "Personally, I don't choose any particular religion [in a strictly institutionalized form] or symbol or group of words or teachings to define me. That's between me and the most high. You know, my higher self. The Creator."[10] Badu publicly proclaims her non-commitment to any one institutionalized religious ideology. She goes on to maintain that whatever she chooses as a catalyst to shape her identity is between herself and the creator. She ends by establishing an interconnection between the creator and selfhood. Here, Badu offers a dual conceptualization of the creator. On the one hand, the creator is an externalized force (as expressed in "Ye Yo"), that is responsible for endowing Badu with artistic gifts. On the other hand, however, she views the creator as her higher form of self. So, while she acknowledges the role that an externalized form of the creator plays in negotiating what actually shapes her as a person, as expressed in the previous quote, she simultaneously humanizes this same creator. Badu is the creator. She represents an internal creator that possesses the ability to bring into existence external works of creativity, as displayed in her art. It is important to note that, from 2006 to 2011, Badu begins to bracket the acknowledgment of an external actualization of the creator. Instead, she turns her attention to expanding her conception of the higher self—a view of self that implicitly incorporates Badu's parallelism between self, which is equal to creator, without explicitly mentioning the "creator." For example, in a 2011 interview conducted after the release of her latest album, *New Amerykah Part Two*, Badu discusses her belief in this higher self:

> What I believe in whole-heartedly is that people want to be loved and acknowledged and needed. So however they go about getting whatever they need to connect with the higher part of themselves ... it's just what they need. I understand human beings.[11]

Badu establishes a direct correlation between evolution, selfhood, and human nature. She recognizes that accessing one's higher self involves the evolutionary progression of the individual and, furthermore, requires a medium. The selected medium is really of no concern to Badu, because, for her, connecting to the higher self is more important than how an individual chooses to get to this destination. Attainment of this higher form of self for Badu represents an apprehension of love, recognition, and belongingness. Even more importantly, Badu recognizes that the resolution of these longings by way of self is an innate human quality.

The centering on inherent qualities of humans, particularly by de-centering an externalized conceptualization of the creator, denotes yet another shift in Badu's religious orientation. In an unpublished interview conducted in 2010, Badu openly proclaims, "I'm a humanist."[12] Her comprehension of the human condition, according to Badu, makes her a humanist, for, she "understand[s] human beings." Badu's humanist orientation is additionally characterized by an intersectional relationship between human potentiality and human creativity.[13] For her, humans possess the inherent capacity to create. Specifically, Badu maintains that humans are akin to sculptors in that "they take a lump of clay and just carve away at the clay [until they find] the thing," or creative product.[14] In this way, Badu once again conceives of herself as the creator. It is this focus on human creativity that shifts her toward a more artistic approach to religion. She briefly introduces this fresh religious stance in 2004, and develops it over the next six years. This gradual progression is captured in several interviews, which Badu granted from 2004 through 2011. For example, in a 2004 *Houston Chronicle* article, Badu stated, "I don't practice any particular religion; my religion is my art."[15] Badu continued to proclaim this religious stance in a 2008 interview with *Westword* (a Denver-based blog). She proclaims, "I've been blessed with so much creativity in every area of my life. My religion is art. Functional art—my clothes. It's all about presentation. With my food. It's just something natural in me ..."[16] Two years later, Badu used the social media outlet Flickr to proclaim that if she had to chose one religion, then art would be that religion.[17] It is in a 2011 *Visions of Visionaries* interview, however, that she meticulously unpacks this artistic view of religion, which is worth quoting at length:

> I think my religion is probably art. It's in everything that I do—the way I cook a meal, hair, clothes, conversation, the way I write, the way I text. ... Everything comes out of some form of creativity for me. Art is an effortless thing for me. It's pretty much how they made me, and I embrace that part of me. I was encouraged through my life to express who I am ...[18]

Taken together, these quotations capture Badu's artistic conception of religion. She erases categorical distinctions between religion and art. Religion is art and art is religion. Badu meticulously unpacks this artistic notion of religion by establishing an interconnection between art, creativity, and selfhood. She maintains a mediumistic view of art: first, she recognizes art as a transcending medium. Badu believes that individuals can use art as a vehicle to transcend social compartmentalization. She uses her artistic forms to constantly move beyond labels and categories that are placed on her as a musician. Badu uses art, in this way, to gain freedom. The freedom of artistic transcendence, according to her, is a defining predicate for creativity. Secondly, Badu treats art as an expressive medium. Art is, in her words, "how I express my anger, pain, joy or fear, or love."[19] Badu also laces this emotive usage of art into her lyrics. For example, in *My People*, she sings about the frustration involved in mentally releasing a past love(r), while in *Telephone* (a tribute to producer Dilla)[20] she candidly shares her existential struggle with suffering and death with listeners. Beyond serving as an emotive outlet, art, for Badu, is also a direct expression of creativity. It is the very medium through which creativity is concretely manifested, in the form of creative products. For Badu, humans naturally embody creativity, so much so that each action, particularly that of the artist, is representative of a creative act aimed at producing a creative product. In this way, Badu maintains that art permeates every human action; it even saturates activities that others may deem mundane. Cooking, combing hair, and writing music are, for Badu, activities that result from the natural ability to create, which dwells within her.

While Badu acknowledges the ability of art to afford opportunities of emotive and creative expressions, art is for her, more importantly, a way to creatively express who she is as an individual. Art allows for the articulation of self, defined here as how an individual views or defines him or herself. An example of Badu's usage of art as a platform to define herself is captured in a 2013 interview, with *Stop Being Famous*. Badu is asked to close the session with a poem, and this is what she offers:

> I'm a recovering, undercover, over-lover, recovering from a love I can't get over.
>
> I'm a 20-foot-tall phoenix on the edge of a ten-foot cliff.
>
> In this world of covered wagons, I'm a UFO.
>
> I'm a bumblebee, with airplane wings with a hollow body and a million reasons to soar.
>
> I'm the master of molecules and matter—manipulator of that which is not yet manifested, whether it matters or not.
>
> I'm a warm puddle of concrete.
>
> I'm a cold front happening to your surprise.
>
> I am the deal.[21]

Here, Badu uses poetry as a creative medium to articulate various ways in which she views herself. Badu is a vulnerable human capable of being in a loving relationship with another person. She is a beautiful, mythical creature of immortality whose technological savviness distinguishes her from the other "covered wagons." Badu is creator: capable of bringing into existence that which is without form or concreteness. She simultaneously exhibits calmness and forcefulness. Badu is indefinite, for, according to her, she is "the deal." This poem exemplifies her use of art to articulate categorical and trans-categorical notions of self. On the one hand, Badu offers a view of herself that is dependent on relationality with others (e.g., her former lover). On the other hand, she professes a self-definition premised on differentiation (e.g., UFO among wagons) from others. A careful look at the above poem also reveals yet another processual mode of self: she views herself as a process occurring between competing dimensions: a cold force occurring at the interplay of cool and warm air, a gravel puddle coexisting between states of mixture and solidification, and an individual caught between emotional recovery and relapse. This mode of in-betweenness affords Badu the ability to acknowledge but, at the same time, transcend categories of relationality and individuality when defining who she is as a person. To this end, Badu uses art to creatively construct and express multiple modes of selfhood premised on collectivity, individuality and the in-between space of these two categories.

Creating selves: Case study analysis of *New Amerykah Part Two* (*The Return of the Ankh*)

In this section, a smaller sample of Badu's art is treated as case study material, to take a closer look at her artistic expression of these multiple selves. The very words of Badu dictate the material to be analyzed in this portion of the essay. She states, "If people were to ask my children about their mother, I'd hope they could give them Mama's Gun or New Amerykah and say: 'This is who she was.'"[22] Thus, audiovisual and lyrical content associated with the latter album, *New Amerykah Part Two* (2010), are considered, in this exploration of Badu's usage of art, as a creative medium to conceive of herself in multiple ways.

"Window Seat" video and the expression of the personal self

On March 13, 2010, Badu posted a tweet. "I just finished walking down the street naked, and I feel liberated," she shared with her followers. Two weeks after this posting, on March 27, 2010 at 3:33 a.m., Badu released the video for "Window Seat," the first single released from her album, *New Amerykah Part Two*. The video opens with two inscriptions, "inspired by Matt and Kim" and "a story by Erykah Badu." Then the video zooms in on Badu, as she parallel-parks a late model white car along Dealey Plaza (the site of President John F. Kennedy's assassination). She steps out of the car, and the music begins. After placing coins in the parking meter, she starts to walk down the sidewalk toward a cross street. And, it is at this crossing that Badu begins to remove layers of clothing: she sheds her coat, shoes, sweatshirt, t-shirt, pants, bra, and then lastly, her underwear. Suddenly, a single gunshot is fired and Badu's naked body hits the ground and blue liquid flows from her head, spelling out the word "groupthink," a term to be discussed later in this section. Here, it is Badu's public nakedness that garners negative media attention. In a 2010 *Vibe* interview, Badu openly discusses this privileging of only one aspect of the video. She states, "I did a poem at the end of the video that explained exactly what I did but that's not news; that you are trying to expose a philosophical, sociological norm, they don't want to talk about that, that's not interesting. What's interesting is 'Ooh, she's naked.'"[23] Thus, for Badu, the public sensationalism of her nakedness overshadows her use of multiple artistic devices in "Window Seat" to convey an overarching message. She points out how this focus on only one element of "Window Seat" marginalizes other artistic elements, like the poem with which she closes the video. In this poetic terminus, Badu discusses the public assassination of individuals like herself who attempt to deviate from societal norms. She identifies fear as the element that drives the group to kill those persons that are perceived as different, and, finally, she presents the individual as one who is powerful, fearless, self-loving, and constantly undergoing evolution.[24] Badu, then, explicitly states the overall intent of the video in this poem. She uses the words of this artistic medium to protest the detrimental effects of pack-mentality, or what social psychologist Irving L. Janis calls "groupthink."[25] Janis defines groupthink as "the psychological drive for consensus at any cost."[26] This mode of thinking leads to a privileging of group cohesiveness and homogeneity, which results in the suppression of individuality and heterogeneity. For Badu, viewers who choose to ignore this poem do so at the risk of missing her usage of art to challenge the repressive intent of groupthink, particularly in regard to the expression of individual difference. Instead, they chose to peel back only one layer (Badu's nakedness) of meaning, thus missing the opportunity to experience the multiple layers of meaning contained within the video for "Window Seat."

Badu's usage of the video to challenge groupthink is representative of one such layer. However, her employment of this same performative protest as a means to articulate a view of herself, particularly one that is oppositional to groupthink, represents yet another layer of meaning. In her quest to express this notion of self, Badu highlights interconnectivity between groupthink and individuality. Groupthink, for her, produces an atmosphere of fear that paralyzes the individual. "It's like you don't want to be who you are because you're afraid to be assassinated," she shares in an interview.[27] Groupthink, for Badu, in this way inhibits individual difference. It inhibits the desire of the person to ascertain a sense of beingness separate from the demands of the group. Badu challenges this fear "to be," in that she utilizes the "Window Seat" video as an artistic means to articulate a view of herself that is premised on individual difference, not on the obligatory demands of the group(s). Badu maintains that this form of self-expression requires collective distancing. In particular, the individual seeking to be who they are, apart from the group, must not fear operating outside the group. In the video, Badu uses her personal body as a point of departure from the collective body. Specifically, the removal of clothing becomes a mechanism of social distancing. Clothing here represents layers of group mentalities that seek to suffocate and hide a person's uniqueness. Thus, she sheds these collectively oriented mentalities by removing her clothing. For she states, "As I took a step, I shed a piece of clothing; in essence shedding a thing I learned … a thing I was forced to believe, I shed one thing with each step."[28] For Badu, this act of shedding symbolizes the power of the individual to not only separate from the group but also, more importantly, utilize this newly acquired power of personal differentiation to articulate a view of self that is premised on one's uniqueness or individuality. In a 2010 interview, Badu maintains that this move (to create a self-view premised on separating oneself from the group) is "horrifying because we are afraid of being ostracized and assassinated by the group if we have our own thoughts, our own minds, our own will, and our own direction."[29] Regardless of this fear, she walks naked among the crowd. And, it is her very nakedness that serves as a distinguishing mark that separates her from the surrounding clothed group. This same mark of uniqueness, however, leads to her assassination. For Badu though, this assassination of the physical body ironically frees her from the debilitating shackles of the collective body. The bullet sets free a personal self, one that is based on her own individual uniqueness. This personalized self-construct appears at the very end of the video in the depiction of Badu—adorned with a large smile and long braids—as she walks away from the murder scene. It is in this very act of walking away that she implicitly states how she is finally liberated to embrace and "love herself" as a person who is unique and different.

"New Amerykah Part Two" album cover and the expression of the collective self

While Badu uses the "Window Seat" video as a means to creatively express a personalized form of self, she employs the *New Amerykah Part Two* album cover as a creative medium to articulate a more collective mode of selfhood. In a 2011 interview, she discusses the importance of album art: "To me an album is not just about the music but also the liner notes, the image, the whole package. That's what I grew up seeing. No video, you just saw the album cover. If you're looking at a picture of this band Con Funk Shun, that's all you know, this picture."[30] Thus, Badu believes that in order to understand artists, one must consider their entire body of work: lyrical arrangements, instrumental beats, and album cover art. In particular, Badu focuses on the important function of the album cover in this excerpt. For her, album cover art captures a visual representation of the artist. So, for example, even if a video for "Window Seat" never existed, Badu maintains that a visual image of her will continuously exist in the form of the *New Amerykah Part Two* album cover.

What does an analysis of this specific album cover art reveal about Badu? A look at the *New Amerykah Part Two* album art (see Figure 1.1) depicts: (1) an image of Badu dressed in metal armor; (2) images of objects like handcuffs, cigarettes, foreclosed homes, nuclear war-heads, and broken chains drape across her shoulders; (3) multicolor flowers embedded with images of tiny infant faces and bodies; (4) a naked image of Badu with a turning fork in her left hand, a tattoo on her back, and a tree with sprouting leaves that spell

FIGURE 1.1 New Amerykah Part Two: The Return of the Ankh. *Album cover art. Permission granted by EMEK.net.*

out her name rising from her head; and (5) a swirling vortex hovering in the upmost most part of the cover.[31]

The visual capturing of these complex symbols here displayed, results from the collaborative teamwork of Badu and graphic artist EMEK. Badu speaks candidly about EMEK, in an interview with Red Bull Academy:

They call him the thinking-man's artist. He did the painting for *New Amerykah Part I and Part II*, "The Healer," every poster I have for every show. His work is traditionally silkscreen posters … I like that feel, because that's what

I remember seeing growing up. That goes along with the music, you've got to have a good piece of art. He's great, he finishes my sentences visually.[32]

In this excerpt, Badu not only identifies the extensive projects that EMEK worked on for her, but also discusses various reasons why she works well with him. For her, EMEK possesses the ability to visually capture a nostalgic feeling that Badu associates with album covers of her childhood. More importantly, however, EMEK's ability to provide a visual representation of the thoughts of musical artists in general, and Badu in particular, is the primary impetus driving the collaborative efforts between these two artists. EMEK possesses the keen ability of, in Badu's words, "… finish[ing] my sentences visually." Badu provides the conceptual meanings, they both think through various symbols that can be used to represent these interpretations, and, finally, EMEK provides the visual landscape for Badu's vision. In this way, Badu's album covers, like that of *New Amerykah Part Two*, is the result of a shared collaboration that "involves an intricate blending of skills, temperaments, effort … sometimes personalities to realize a shared vision of something new and useful."[33] Specifically, symbols (like those previously identified) on the cover art of this album, illustrate this collaborative form of creativity that occurs between Badu and EMEK. For example, Badu stated that she wanted the cover of the album to depict her current state. She explains, "With PART TWO, I'm hovering over me, looking at what's going on inside me."[34] Working with EMEK, this introspective state is captured on the album cover as her nude image rising from the head of her armored body, symbolizing a liberated Badu birthed from the mental womb of a woman who adorns herself in a "tough exterior [in order] to protect herself form the harsh realities of life."[35]

While this mode of collaborative creativity brings to life meanings through symbolic representations, the album cover also captures Badu's usage of art, as a creative means to articulate a view of herself, based on collective action or collectivity. Cocreating her album cover with EMEK also involved the equal distribution of creativity. Such stress on collaborative action provides Badu with a measure of satisfaction for group solidarity. Thus, the artistic piece affords her an outlet to express a perception of herself that is based on shared categorical membership—a mode of identity known as "the collective self." Badu's collaborative work with EMEK provided her with a relational "meaning-making system," which promotes group solidarity, that in turn actualizes an internal desire for the expression of a corresponding collective self.[36] When Badu acts as a collaborative part of a whole, she displays an interpretation of self that is larger than her own individuality. This type of identity construction counters her usage of performative protest of groupthink in the "Window Seat" video to express a more personalized conception of self. Badu's longing to be a part of a group collaboration, and, at the same time, wanting to be seen as an individual apart from the collective, points to her desire to express two identities: one based on collectivity (collective self) and the other on individuality (personal self). But, a deeper analytical plunge into the work of Badu, particularly as presented in the lyrics of "Window Seat," allows a third, more complex form of self-interpretation to rise to the surface.

"Window Seat" lyrics and the expression of the dynamical self

The overall structure of "Window Seat" is verse/chorus/verse/chorus/half-chorus.[37] In the first verse, Badu provides listeners with a glimpse of her everyday life experiences filled with demands from various individuals, which results in Badu imparting all of her energy into the lives of her loved ones, her children and lover, and her music. The second verse commences with Badu reflecting on the mental anguish associated with the daily grind of life. Taken together, these two verses attempt to explain why Badu longs to purchase a window seat plane ticket and to get away from the demanding matters of life. These verses provide reasons why Badu longs for separation and how she plans on achieving it. It is in the elongated chorus, however, that Badu reveals another, more implicit desire— she longs to express a more complex way of viewing herself. Accordingly, she uses the chorus of "Window Seat" as a creative medium to express this dynamical self.[38]

The first part of the chorus begins with Badu asking for a window seat. She then states her primary reason for this request: she wants the seat next to her to be empty, so that she can focus all of her attention on the aerial view. Badu wants to escape from her current geographical locale and arrive safely somewhere else. For her, this temporary escape will offer an opportunity to miss those persons who constantly compete for her attention. It is clear from the first part of the chorus that Badu desires to be alone. These lyrics express her desire to be an individual and not be connected to a partner or a group. She explicitly states, "Don't want nobody next to me." In this way, this portion of the chorus represents a creative space in which Badu constructs a view of herself premised on her individuality. Badu desires to fly, to cry, and to experience a long bye-bye. These actions are what make Badu unique at that particular moment, and she cannot express these attributes of uniqueness unless she separates from the group by getting a window seat. Like the "Window Seat" video, Badu uses art to construct an identity premised on personal distinctiveness, not groupthink or social conformity.

While Badu depicts a personal self-definition in the opening part of the chorus, it is within this same lyrical space that she offers listeners a conflicting desire. She begins the second part of the chorus with the coordin̄ conjunction, "but." With this usage, she not only conjoins the two parts the chorus together, but, furthermore, this grammatical move also signā that the words to follow are in contrast to the previous lyrical content. What follows is a string of needs. She explicitly states that she "needs" to be "missed," she needs the "attention," she needs "somebody next to her," she needs her listeners to clap for her and, really when it's all said and done, she needs to be "needed." These lyrics reveal a desire to belong. She desires interpersonal relationships. For it is within these relationships that Badu becomes satisfied with being a part coalescing with other parts in making a meaningful whole. Badu identifies with the collective in such a way that shared incentives, especially expressed in belongingness, become the lens in which she forms a collective conception of herself (i.e., the collective self). Such a view minimizes the distinguishable markers of her individuality that she so painstakingly emphasizes in the "Window Seat" video and in the first part of the song's chorus. Badu's dissolution of her own individuality in this way maximizes assimilation in that common collective—features that take precedence over personal predicates. Thus, in the second part of the chorus, she sees herself not as a unique individual or "I" but as an interchangeable group member or "we."

Overall, the "Window Seat" chorus in its entirety captures Badu's conflicting desires for unification with a social group and separation from the societal demand of this same group. The artistic movement back and forth, between collectivity and individuality, points toward Badu's desire to form a view of herself that cannot be characterized by the polar pronouns of "not-me" or "me," respectively. She desires to express a dynamical form of selfhood. The dynamical self here occurs where the edges of the personal self and collective self meet.[39] The dynamical self finds a place of expression between the individual's desire to separate from a group and this same individual's desire for unification with a group. Badu creatively constructs this dynamical self in the chorus of "Window Seat." In the first part of the chorus, she wants separation, while in the second part, she wants unification. Ultimately, she wants both/and. It is at this intersectional point of the two parts of the chorus that she expresses a dynamical mode of selfhood, in that she forms a view of herself that holds in tension her desire for both individuality and collectivity. Whether through performative art, album cover art or lyrical content, Badu employs her *New Amerykah Part Two* album as a medium with which to push toward the viewing of herself in a multidimensional way. To this end, Badu's art, which she also conceives of as her religion, serves as a creative outlet in which she expresses personal, collective, and dynamical modes of self.

2

Methods for the prophetic: Tupac Shakur, Lauryn Hill, and the case for ethnolifehistory

Daniel White-Hodge

The field of hip hop studies has developed exponentially over the last decade, into much more than a lyrical and aesthetic sensation echoed in the words of artist KRS-One, when he asserted, in 1997, that, "Hip hop is a lifestyle; something that is being lived."[1] Despite hermeneutical and interpretive, debates regarding what hip hop is, and/or what hip hop means, how might KRS-One's proclamation, heuristically, push us to consider a less engaged query—that is, "How ought hip hop be studied?" Grounded in a concern for theory and method in the growing field of religion and hip hop studies, this method presents the possibility of exploring new pathways between religion and hip hop. The essay makes use of the cultural output of late rapper Tupac Amaru Shakur, and artist Lauryn Hill, as case studies to explore and make the case for a methodology that I term as "Ethnolifehistory" as an editorial methodological possibility within the field of religion and hip hop.[2] By focusing on major life events, the artist's cultural phenomena and the role and changing impact of religiosity throughout the artist's life and work, this method holds much potential to analyze the significance of the cultural spaces created by artists in society, and, in particular, for the growing field of religion and hip hop studies. Moreover, such an approach provides a scope and framework that helps to show the deeper connection between the "why" and "how" of artists' cultural output and overall life philosophy, more generally. Here, attention is paid to how artists discuss religion in their cultural work and craft.

What is "Ethnolifehistory?"

Ethnolifehistory is a method that charts varying peaks within a person's life into periods, eras and stages, by focusing on: (1) the creation of life eras, and their development and transition from one major event to the next; (2) key moments that help to shift one era to the next (i.e., what regression may occur, and are there identifiable overlapping eras that may also affect the person or culture being studied?); (3) transitional effects on the subject, from one era to the next (i.e., are there eras or moments that create stress, joy, or mourning for the person? If so, how might such instances be interpreted over and against what is happening in society and culture?), and lastly, (4) how said eras, shifts, and effects of such changes impact the cultural products under study? I am persuaded that the multi-method of ethnolifehistory, that is, its utilization of interviews (active, structured, semi-structured), case studies, ethnographic processes, and discourse analysis, make it a promising methodology for religion and hip hop studies.[3] Ethnolifehistory not only pushes religion and hip hop studies beyond lyrical and aesthetic analysis but also includes close ethnographic attention to underutilized sources in the current terrain of religion and hip hop studies, such as interviews, for example. Attention beyond a sole focus on the lyrical and aesthetic dimensions, to consider the lived realities and geography of a seldom considered artist's life might offer a more expansive window into how and why meaning or religion is constructed and plays particular roles, taking on different shapes at certain moments in an artists' life. Might religious references and uses proliferate in an artist's cultural output at particular "highs" and "lows" of their life or craft? Might this method help to adjudicate material previously deemed "theological," "spiritual," or "religious," by other studies in religion in hip hop? Ethnolifehistory, for example, might call such prior classifications merely coincidental or a product of the religious marketplace. In light of such possibilities, ethnolifehistory takes into account and concerns itself with the following:

- Change over time in major life events and why such events emerged
- How said shifts affect and influence religion in hip hop
- The durability and length of major occurrences
- Influence on cultural context in significant periods and eras

Taken together, attention to such areas assists in creating a sense of how the events occurred and what factors contributed to shaping an artist's worldview. The artists Tupac Shakur and Lauryn Hill were selected mainly for their popularity in hip hop culture as being "prophetic"—as artists who are seen to call out social ills. In the case of Tupac in particular, his work helped create a sort of eschatological futurist vision for hip hop culture for his time and context. One could argue that religion is made much more explicit and commonly discussed among these two artists in the social conscious genre of hip hop.[4] Existing scholarship on both Hill and Shakur offers little attention to the role of religion and spirituality both in their work and life and in the manner in which significant shifts within their lives affect and mediate their engagement with such sensibilities. Much of the work on religion and/or spirituality within hip hop has largely focused on musical content.[5] A major component of ethnolifehistory is the component of, what I term, "life era function"—the frame by which one considers how significant moments in an artist's life are being considered by the researcher (e.g., myself), as well as a consideration of how such events and periods in the artist's life might have affected the culture as a whole—that is, the social significance function, an element of the life era function, which investigates a set period designated as either "important" or "relevant" in and for the hip hop generation.[6]

While it's certainly not possible to consider and do justice to the whole of an artist's life in a single chapter, I use ethnolifehistory here to focus on specific events and moments such as Tupac's life eras and Lauryn's religious contribution to the hip hop cultural continuum in her album *The Miseducation of Lauryn Hill* (1998). I end by considering the possibilities and limitations for future work with the application of ethnolifehistory as a method for the growing field of religion and hip hop studies.

Remembering life, after death: Tupac and the construction of life meaning

Chock full of primary material and data, let us begin with the artist whose palpable impact on the hip hop world and society is felt throughout and evidenced by the proliferating conspiracy theories that still cannot come to terms with his death: Tupac Shakur, the artist dubbed "Black Jesuz."[7] My data consisted of: 62 interviews, 255 pages of Pac's writings, and numerous video interviews, including interviews with former roommates, bodyguards, family members, and Pac's own writings, that were used to verify shifts (i.e., tone, style, perceived disposition, and content) within and among his own thinking.[8] Although some of the data presented in this section has already been used in previous work, here, I revisit and revise this data using ethnolifehistory as a new approach applied to a substantial body of work already surrounding this artist.[9] The importance of charting such shifts entails the cataloging and studying of data, as a historian, to find out what Tupac was "up to" in that particular setting or time and how that spoke of religion and/or spirituality.

Pac's move from Baltimore, Maryland to the Bay Area in California was quite an emotional and difficult geographic transition. As noted in journal entries, Pac was "upset" and "angry" about the move away from a "good school" (Baltimore School of Performing Arts) to Marin City, which placed him back in a public school setting. On this point, his childhood friend, "Maurice"—as he wanted to be called—described the ordeal:

> Pac was a sensitive dude. People don't know that about him. He cared a lot and felt a lot. He was like traumatized when he came to the Bay ... he saw for the first time, that Black people were living like shit all over; not just in Baltimore. That really made him see life differently at that point.

For Pac, the move demonstrated that "life" was unjust, not only on the East Coast but, also, on the West. In an earlier interview at the tender age of seventeen, Pac stated[10]:

> ... we're not being taught to deal with the world as it is. We're being taught to deal with this fairy tale land we're not even living in anymore ... then I came to California to escape that [violence], escape that violence ... come to Marin City and there's skinhead violence. There's racial violence. There's racial violence, which I deplore.

Pac began to wonder what this life meaning was—particularly for black people. The move demonstrated to him that this thing called poverty was, in reality, everywhere—in his own words, "If I hated anything, it be that ... poverty." During this time, his journal entries were filled with doubt and ambiguity toward a deity, which would allow such a thing like poverty to happen. Tupac was quoted in a telephone interview as saying, "Leaving that school [Baltimore School of Performing Arts] affected me so much, I see at this point where I got off track."[11] Pac would come to assert this frustration toward systems of inequality and hegemonic powers, best expressed in and through his music. Yet, as noted in much of his poetry and interviews post-1994, "God" and "God's goodness" remained an enduring question rooted in the continued pain he felt. Such agony reverberates in statements such as, "All my songs deal with pain. That's what makes me me, that's what makes me do what I do. Everything is based on the pain I felt in my childhood. Small pieces of it and harsh pieces of it."[12] For Pac, "the move" to Marin City was a significant

[handwritten: Asking Q's about God in a world of pain]

moment of awareness, something that was often referenced in his music.[13] At this point in life, Pac's theological imagination took shape in asking critical questions about God's role in a world of pain, as seen in one of his ideas for a film which would later lead to the song—"I Wonder if Heaven Got A Ghetto" (circa 1988). In it, Pac paints a situation in which life, death, hope, and doubt all intersect with and among each other. Papa Green, one of the main characters in the story, is an older man who is a street hustler, yet someone who looks out for the youth, Kato—whose death haunted Tupac for many years—killed over a matter of twenty dollars. The subtext is how one can figure such a place as "heaven," often the epitome of a perfected religious life, as handling someone like Kato, and, eventually, himself, Pac. In this sense, Pac was very much influenced by urban societal conditions such as violence, poverty, and ghetto living, within his context, that in turn created an urge in him, to try and reconcile such realities with a traditional image of God as an "all good" "deliverer." In Pac's case, this societal influence affected the manner in which he constructed his music and, in some sense, overall worldview.

[handwritten in margin: Trying to reconcile]

What specifically helped to shape Pac's music? How does Tupac develop his sense of religion in and through his craft? What follows are Tupac's main life eras and their constructs of meaning, with special attention paid to the religious. The names of these eras were chosen to closely match the theme of that period that follows the chapter titles of the Tupac documentary, *Tupac Vs.* (2004).

The military mind era: Opposition and the making of a spiritual mind

This era represents a time in Tupac's life, marked by a militant and oppositional stance toward the world, that was sparked by varying representations of "manhood," and witness to a violent geographic landscape, marked by violence and social disparities.[14] Once again, societal conditions affected the personhood of Pac, which, in turn, impacted how he created art and imagined aspects of religion.

Most of Pac's poetry and early to mid-life output were grounded in this era, in certain particulars that saw a strong formation of spiritual and political sensibilities. For example, one of Pac's better known poems, "Lady Liberty,"[15] was initially created in this era:

> Emancipation, proclamation? Please, Lincoln just said it to save the nation, these lies we all accepted … the war on drugs is a war on you and me, the home of the free … constitutions? It don't apply to me, Lady liberty? That stupid tramp lies to me …[16]

His early journals and poetry explore death, a sense of loss directed toward a father, and, by extension, an awkward position toward a male God, and a desire for a "heaven" within his own life. This worldview would give birth to songs such as "Ghetto Gospel," "So Many Tears," and even "Dear Mamma." This foundational era, rooted in disenfranchisement, economic disparity and violence, set a tone for Tupac's life. In an interview with Tabitha Soren, Pac noted, "If you listen to the way I talk, my language is from pimps, hustlers, and drug dealers... ." In a note he wrote thought to be dated between 1990 and 1991, in which Pac questioned the concept of freedom and the plight of the human race, his references to inequality and unjust systems resound. As this life era took on a more defined shape, Pac's emotions were perplexed as seen within his journals: "... what is our purpose here on this Earth? Why we here?." Interviewees stated that Pac was both "extremely sensitive" and a "caring dude." At times, as noted in early photographs of him, one might interpret some of this in the play Pac had with his brothers and sisters and the continual positivity he showed toward his mother Afeni, despite her addiction to crack.

This precise historical moment saw a new drug making its way into urban America called crack. Still unknown for its addictive effects, its beginnings, during what would later be dubbed "the crack era," took impoverished communities to a new low. With a rise in record unemployment for blacks, the 1980s began on a nefarious tone, and Pac internalized everything around him.

For him, this era begins to shift when he and his family moved from the Bronx to Baltimore, where he began to see the effects of widespread inequality—not only in the Bronx and Baltimore, but actually even on the bus ride to Baltimore, which Tupac took with his mother. He took notes—on the structure of the bus ride, the significance and effects of the actual physical move—all were noted by him as deeply troubling.

The criminal grind era: The construction of the street mind

A shift began with Tupac's move to Baltimore. His poetry and writings during this time, even at a young age, reflected the significant levels of crime and violence he was exposed to as a young man living in ghettoized conditions. "In Marin City you see that it wasn't just my people that were getting dogged out, it was all of us [black people] ..."[17] Moreover, anyone who lived during and in the now infamous "crack era" of the 1980s knows the realities of that context and its menacing aftershocks on black America. This move signified a change for Pac as his early roommate recalled to me, "... shoot, that move to The Bay was a lot for Pac. He always told me that, that showed him we was all fucked in essence, but, it did give him the spirit to really make his music." The word "spirit" stands out in this interview and represents similar sentiments expressed by other interviewees. That is, Pac's spirit and the almost animistic belief that other "spirits" spoke to Pac to help him in developing his music.

Mom gets addicted to cracks

Keeping with this tone, that era would see his mother, Afeni, become addicted to crack. Pac dropped out of high school to pursue a career in music while living with members of the rap group Digital Underground that afforded him fame and traction in the hip hop cultural continuum.

During this era, Tupac was seeing how indifferent and apathetic the black church was toward issues such as poverty, addiction, and the growing tensions between young black youth and law enforcement. He is noted as saying, "I don't really know if our Black pastors really give a fuck about what's going on in the 'hood. Feel me? Why they have to have big ass churches and we still living in the dirt? It don't make sense!"[18] As his former manager, Leila Steinberg—who spent a significant amount of time with Pac, allowing him to live with her while he was homeless and providing him management for his rap career notes—"Tupac was always plagued by what he thought was supposed to be the 'right way' of living, and how things actually were."[19] Building on his childhood, Tupac would later take this firsthand experience with the black church and put it into his music; both Leila and Frank (Tupac's former bodyguard) told me that this was part of the "fuel" and ethos behind his album *The Don Killuminati: The 7 Day Theory*, in which he had several tracks blasting the black church.

This blast toward the black church is important, especially given the new generation of black youths who were questioning the worth of the black church at the time. Furthermore, this generation, which some dubbed "Gen-X" or even the "hip hop generation," were nursed and raised in the womb of media culture. Having seen firsthand that there were, as Pac would say, "Two Americas," many felt that they had been shorthanded and that their voices were missing from the public sphere.[20]

Noting Tupac's subtle restlessness from interviews during late 1988, and, as expressed by his roommate as the time to "go solo," this era's shift began as he moved toward a solo career and broke away from Digital Underground. Pac's rise into stardom and fame would serve as a life period mover—a significant moment for the ethnolifehistorian to take note of. We now turn to the next era in Pac's life as he took stock of how the hood could be used as a site for social change—in other words, using his life experience for artistic and monetary gain while attempting to bring about change to the social conditions of the hood—something which I feel Tupac desired deeply.

[margin handwriting:] Felt the Black Church was indifferent to urban Black youth issues

The ghetto is destiny era: Constructing a pathway for change

This moment came when Tupac began his solo career by hosting small venue concerts around the Bay area and parts of southern California. This era is also marked by Tupac's use of music videos and his desire to transmediate the conditions of the hood to help bring about awareness of the issues and, as he had hoped, change. Tupac said during this time:

> It's like you've got the Vietnam War, and because you had reporters showing us pictures of the war at home, that's what made the war end, or that shit would have lasted longer. If no one knew what was going on we would have thought they were just dying valiantly in some beautiful way. But because we saw the horror, that's what made us stop the war. So I thought, that's what I'm going to do as an artist, as a rapper. I'm gonna show the most graphic details of what I see in my community and hopefully they'll stop it quick.[21]

[handwritten margin note: Tupac's use of music videos to show the conditions in Black neighborhoods]

One might also think of this as an existential claim by Tupac, in looking at this era and the art that he produced; Tupac continually reminded his audience of the human condition and the ideal juxtaposed to the reality—a tension seen throughout his life and eras. This also gives insight when exegeting Tupac's videos in music as to the "why" behind the images and detail within the music. Again, ethnolifehistory examines those meanings beyond a biographical event and broadens the search for those constructs of meaning.

There is, for instance, the case of his half-sister, Sekiwa Shakur, during a time of her own addiction. She exclaimed once, "I don't know why people keep calling me a bitch, I ain't nobody's bitch." Tupac, in his own artistic fashion, then created a song for his sister titled "Wonda Why They Call You Bitch" which, as he recalls in an interview with Ed Gordon in 1994, was a way to help his sister realize that the life she was living was not good for her. Sekiwa later recollected that while Pac's song about her was initially infuriating, it helped her realize that there were "better things in life for her."[22]

[handwritten margin note: Tupac's song to his sister]

This era, while not as long, created a legacy for Tupac and one that grounded him in a Gramscian mantra in relation to society. It also saw Tupac enter his film career and begin a journey with Hollywood. Almost everyone around him noted this shift from being just a rapper to now being an actor, and Tupac's numerous journals reflected this too, sitting alongside his work on developing of screenplays and concepts for films.

This era's biggest moment, for not just Tupac but the broader culture as well, was the now infamous Rodney King trial, and the ensuing Los Angeles

Rodney *King Trial - crowds in LA*

uprisings on April 29, 1992. In an interview I reviewed on VH-1's documentary entitled *Uprising: Hip Hop & The L.A. Riots* (2012), Tupac was noted as leaving the studio and joining the crowds in Los Angeles. This coincides with a later interview he gave in 1995 with, once again, Tabitha Soren. He stated that he "needed to be with his people and be out there in the mix with them." After the uprisings, Tupac helped organize in the south central community, and this gave genesis to his "Thug Life" mantra, the premise of which was to bring "organization" to street life. The uprisings in LA were a point at which Tupac saw the culmination of his childhood come to a head in one substantial moment.[23] It would give him even more "fuel" to do "good" in the community, but it would also place him in the public eye, in which he personally encountered law enforcement, who did not look favorably upon his critique on "police brutality."

In December 1992, Tupac filed a ten million dollar lawsuit against the Oakland Alameda Police Department for brutality. This event gave him a social reputation for being a "thug" and an "outlaw," because of his numerous interactions with the law at that time.

The outlaw era: The defining of a reputation

Better For 'all un Walking

The Outlaw Era (from 1992 to 1995) began at the end of 1992 and ended toward the latter end of 1994, when Tupac had over twelve known judicial interactions with the law, lawyers, lawsuits, and arrests. This era, then, begins with Tupac's trouble with law enforcement, which originated from when he was brutally beaten by an Oakland police officer, for—allegedly—jay walking. From there, a series of similar events created this "outlaw" era, for Tupac and his reputation of "being real" continued to develop from.

Law enforcement was not the only constituent to play a role in developing the "outlaw" ethos that Tupac expressed during this time. Pac's interaction with Delores C. Tucker, leaders from the National Congress of Black Women, Dan Quail and Rev. Calvin Butts, to name a few, are just some of the better known oppositional interactions with public leaders that Tupac had. His lyrics and perceived "violent music" was on trial in many regards. As one pastor, who in 1994 was a young youth pastor, once recalled to me:

How many ^ blacks church saw Tupac?

Tupac was seen as the most secular of secular. He was almost like the Devil. I was sadly among those who would agree with them at the time too. I don't think the Black Church, and others like Delores, really knew what Tupac was up to at the time. I for one am sure I missed it, and fell victim to the media's hype of how 'bad' he was … which he really wasn't.

Such sentiments were common during an era that bore witness to the OJ Simpson case, and a host of instances in which men of color were criminalized. It culminated, for Pac, with his trip to prison in 1995, which, by all accounts, affected him to the point of depression and a near complete nihilistic attitude toward life. Interestingly enough, it is in this era that Tupac's greatest body of work would develop. As Frank told me, "All he did was work; he was the hardest working man in hip hop. Tupac wrote, and wrote, and wrote. He lived in that studio." This was also a time during which Tupac gave some of his strongest interviews and critiques of religion, the black church and how he felt "called by God" to do "God's work" in the "hood." In a lively interview with Ed Gordon in late 1994, Tupac stated, in regards to "missions" and "God":

> If I can't be free, if I can't live with the same respect as the next man, then I don't wanna be here. Because God has cursed me to see what life should be like. If God had wanted me to be this person, to be happy here, he wouldn't let me feel so oppressed. He wouldn't let me feel so trampled on; you know what I'm saying? He wouldn't let me think the things I think. So, I feel like I'm doing God's work, you know what I'm saying? Just because I don't have nothing to pass around for people to put in the bucket don't mean I'm not doing God's work; I feel like I'm doing God's work. Because, these ghetto kids ain't God's children? And I don't see no missionaries coming through there. So I'm doing God's work. While Reverend Jackson do his shit up in the middle class and he go to the White house and have dinner and pray over the president, I'm up in the hood doing my work with my folks.

In this interview, Tupac is, in rare form, using varied tones and continual movements, and his approach to the interview could almost be interpreted as hostile and aggressive. Yet, this quotation seems to coincide with sentiments expressed in other interviews I have conducted, which point toward Pac as a type of "messiah" and "intercessor."[24] Body language, tone, facial expressions, eye movements, rhetoric, and even non-verbal language, can all be used to determine what is happening in an era or life period. This in turn, however, should be corroborated though interviews and the body of work from that person, to extract meaning and define how this in particular affected the era for that person. His death in September 1996 begins a *Ghetto Saint Era* in which Pac, in retrospect, became an instant global "Ghetto Saint." Tupac was more than just a fad, or an "estranged artist." As Dyson asserts, "he edified those people who were both the 'thugs' and the 'niggas,' and gave them a transcendental force... ."[25] Pac was a by-product of the postrevolutionary black spirit that was alive in the early 1970s, and a voice of the ghetto/hood, the marginalized, oppressed and downtrodden, connecting God to a people group who would never imagine gracing the pristine hallways of a church.[26] Tupac's God was the God of the hood.

Lauryn Hill: Exploring an enigmatic era

Lastly, we turn to a brief consideration of the artist Lauryn Hill—research that is still in the early stages of data collection. This section relies on interviews conducted with twenty-eight individuals, who self-identify as "hip hop" and/ or a "hip hop head" interviews with Hill on MTV, BET, and VH-1. The interviews I conducted specifically on Hill will demonstrate her effect on the hip hop cultural continuum. I focus on Hill's most popular and most discussed album, *The Miseducation of Lauryn Hill* (1998), and the time period of 1997–9 as a "primary" era, as it possessed significant material related to Hill, and the album's popularity and cultural uses of religion and spirituality.

The Miseducation of Lauryn Hill (1998) created a cultural mark on hip hop that still reverberates today. The following responses speak to the near "religious" impact and significance that Hill plays in hip hop culture, in particular, sentiments that frame her in the following ways:

- Spiritual director

- Making space for dialogue around sex, life, and death

- Inspirational figure for thinking about relationships

- Godlike, Jesus figure

- Cultural icon who is missed

- Healer

Interviews revealed common tropes related to Hill's impact upon a certain population within hip hop culture. Regaled as a "female prophet of rap," Hill created a cultural sensation when she engaged with sex, sexuality, relationships, intimate relationships, God, religion, and faith in this album. Each interviewee saw her as a type of "hip hop pastor," able to challenge the soul beyond what any ordained minister could do. With one album, she created something that reached out to the hip hop community, which has lasted for almost two decades.

Hill created a space for those struggling in relationships, love and faith, with God there to connect, meditate, cry, love, and doubt in safety. This opened up the door for some to find a deeper meaning as to who God was. As Dave, an interviewee, stated:

Lauryn was like … man … she was like a damn pastor who preached faith in a time of doubt. That album [*The Miseducation of Lauryn Hill*] was that for me. I used to listen to it when I was going through my divorce. She was my counselor and therapeutic space. Whew. God used her for sure.

What Hill created was a space for those who were hurt, disenfranchised, and disinherited, in which to find meaning, and, essentially, God. Much like Tupac, she brawled with God and the pain she had—and still has—in her life, in broken promises, failed relationships, questions regarding faith, and the reality of being a black woman in the United States. Hill was a voice within an era marked by a resurgent black intellectualism during the late 1990s, which capitulated to a hip hop consciousness that called on black women to develop a higher sense of their self-worth and realities.

What Hill did

Summary of Hill's era

Hill, in a subtext of her album, asks where God or talk of a higher power is during these times of pain and suffering. This is powerful for the hip hop community, because it does not answer fundamental existentialized questions, but rather allows listeners to grapple with the unresolved ambiguity within. She would go on to take part in that ambiguity, and mix it with divinity, in songs like "I Used to Love Him," where she begins the song by claiming her connection to God, while questioning marriage and having her identity wrapped up in "man" rather than "God." This was something she mentioned in an a 1998 interview on MTV, in which two interviewees noted the album as being "life changing," as it helped them conceptualize where their own relationship was with God. Hill is able to fade into that gray theology in which many—especially those within urban enclaves—live and reside spiritually. "I Used To Love Him" is a song that interweaves with these issues. TJ, an interviewee, notes:

How Hill impacted an interviewees relationship w/ God

> When I heard her music, I was convicted … cause that was me! I was living that lifestyle of a dude who used women. I was saying I was Christian and living a life that was jacked … ya know what I mean? Shit, Lauryn called me out through that album and helped me to live a better life for God … shoot, better than any preacher could ever do.

TJ went on to describe how Hill was instrumental in his faith formation and development. Six others also referred to Hill as being their "pastoral guidance" in a theological journey with God. All of them were under the age of twenty-five, suggesting that these interviewees were just children at the time of Hill's prime. Hill created a kind of socioreligious ethos around herself that some in hip hop culture—albeit at times with an almost conservative evangelical feel—regarded as "good."

Ethnolifehistory takes into account the impact that an artist like Hill has, and then explores the meaning of someone like Hill from the voice of the people. Analyzing Hill's album—the cover art, lyrics, videos, and its position within the hip hop cultural continuum—then cross-analyzing the interviews with Hill's work, gives a glimpse into the marks left by Hill, and the meanings that Hill constructed, as expressed among interviewees. We can then begin to extrapolate some exploratory initial meanings from Hill, and her mark upon the hip hop cultural continuum:

1   Hill's album created a trans-period connection for hip hoppers, in that hip hoppers today still reference the album as something relevant and "real."

2   Hill created space for women in hip hop to be heard, by combining sex, relationships, and faith into one concise album.

3   Hill gave voice to abuse, intimate partner violence, while also giving hope that things would "get better."

[handwritten margin note: What Hill accomplished]

Hill's recent trouble with the law, poor concert attendance, and controversial lyrics suggestive of a condemnation of the LGBTQ community demonstrate that she is not the "perfect prophet." While Hill is facing charges of tax evasion and dealing with her own psychological well-being, she released a single entitled "Neurotic Society." What is troubling is that it makes comparisons to society's ills by connecting them to being "girl men" and "drag queens," thereby suggesting that the eroding of our society can be connected to gay men, who are, in turn, "girly" and "not real men"—a cultural pathology that hip hop has, in general, wrestled with.[27] In an effort to address this complexity, the ethnolifehistorian could then process the heteronormative and hypermasculine traits couched in dogmatic and rigid Christian belief structures of sexuality to discover some of the roots of such beliefs by examining (1) religious discourse and rhetoric of that period, (2) popular religious marketplace consumption (e.g., WWJD wrist bands and purity rings) and the social significance of that, and (3) how elements of a "secular" hip hop world are in turn understood by such religious symbolism.

Implications & the future of ethnolifehistory

This chapter argues for and puts to work ethnolifehistory as a methodology that pushes beyond lyrical and aesthetic analyses by utilizing a multi-method ethnographic approach, which takes context as well as content and product into account. Moreover, I have argued, throughout, that this approach is quite useful in analyzing constructs of significance (i.e., religious, spiritual, and so forth), within the work and life of the artist. Lyrical analysis and interviews alone do not detail the scope of an artist as well as ethnolifehistory can. Moreover, the insight into religious meaning making is something this method can help uncover and engage with in more systematic ways.

Ethnolifehistory is a method of investigation that pushes beyond lyrical analysis and researcher-implied meanings, and asks for a much deeper and broader scope of the artist or artists behind the music, and what factors shaped them and their cultural products—indeed, the "mapping" of a "new terrain." Bolstering both the historian doing multiple studies on individuals and/or even record companies, as well as scholars moving beyond lyrical analysis, this method takes into account the broader and thicker consideration of the life period and era for the artist, and not just the song or lyric itself. It has the potential to investigate the meanings, narratives, societal memes and various cultural traits as they relate to the theological, spiritual, religious, and/or absence of all three within a given person or culture. The fresh approach to life eras is useful in understanding how a person's life, in general, evolves over time, and in the case of Tupac in particular, how death affects the fans, hip hop culture as a whole, and the posthumous ethos, most palpably felt in his case, to date. Allowing the research to speak for itself through investigating the eras and social significance of an artist, and by developing space for a new cultural terrain through attention to moments of significance related to an artist's breadth of work within their life scope (not just their music), is something that every hip hop studies scholar should consider of value.

3

Existentialist transvaluation and hip hop's syncretic religiosity

Julius D. Bailey

Laying the groundwork: Hip hop's altered ethic

As both social movement and cultural form, hip hop was, as Cornel West says, "a cry that openly acknowledg[ed] and confront[ed] the wave of personal cold-heartedness, criminal cruelty, and existential hopelessness in the Black ghettos of Afro-America." The emergence of gangsta rap in the late 1980s made death a ubiquitous meditation. Despite the secular character that often inhabits popular culture, Christian—and Muslim—inflected religiosity was never truly absent from hip hop's poetry (Lauricella and Kyereme 2012). Brother J, X-Clan, or the late Tupac Shakur—rap's deep thinkers, who, in their music, raised existential, ontological, and eschatological meanings—brought to the fore sensibilities that, though largely absent in hip hop's party-atmosphere lyrics of the '70s and early '80s, became increasingly relevant as the decade progressed.

It would certainly go too far were one to argue that all such artists share in the same intentionality, or have the same religious take on life. It is, however, and by the same token, unjustified to presume that their spirituality is necessarily shallow or even false—as if claiming that there is a true form of religiosity, whether Christian, Muslim, or Hindu. Therefore, I propose that exploring the spiritual character of their music by means of a philosophical analysis will provide sound and accurate insights into the character of the religious sentiment and the spiritual character present in hip hop artists. Hip hop has already been conceptualized as an art form that mixes religion, spirituality, and sacred messages, even as it makes references to criminal activity or aggression (Utley 2012). Accounts of the vacillation between the holy and the profane can be found in thorough analyses of humanism (Pinn 2003), Lil' Wayne (Lauricella and Alexander 2012), Tupac Shakur (Stephens and Wright 2000), Kanye West (Bailey and Miller 2014), and even M. C. Hammer (Sorett 2010).

The proposed analysis departs from the sociological perspective that attempts to understand and comment upon the structure and mechanism behind expressions of religiosity. Instead, I will trace the ways in which religious sentiments in hip hop gain meaning from a philosophical perspective. I understand these religious sentiments as concrete yet fluid proposals that help the bearer to both understand and navigate the moral vicissitudes of human life—especially when that human life features socioeconomic marginalization on a massive institutional scale. The way in which such sentiments arise and are expressed, impacting both individuals and institutions, is fundamental to the philosophical reading intended. The philosophical reading intended can be said to reveal a pragmatic character of sorts inasmuch as it has a materialist underpinning, which is crucial to my pedagogy as professor and phenomenology as agent within the world.

I begin this chapter by exploring ideas found in Tupac—a line of thought that has matured into a form of religiously framed radical individualism preached by contemporary artists like Kanye West and Jay-Z. Such individualism, especially in terms of its antiauthoritarian moral outlook, emphasizes the individual's autonomous quest to both find and understand the transformational horizon of Nietzsche's *will to power*.[1] Beyond the hubristic core of statements that affirm the effective power of an individual to dictate his life as he pleases, I suggest that there is an appeal to a self-regulated moral authority, based on the individual will, found in contemporary hip hop tracks like "No Church in the Wild" and "The Devil is a Lie."

This chapter's focus on existential angst in hip hop will begin to develop through Tupac and, in a way, perfect itself in Kanye West and Jay-Z. Like the main character in Jean-Paul Sartre's *Nausea*, Antoine Roquentin,[2] Tupac Shakur represents the hip hop generation's struggles with feelings of despair. The purpose here is not to show how hip hop sheds light on the work of Sartre or Nietzsche as such, but rather that hip hop is in and of itself engaged in a project that reflects and parallels the existential. As with Roquentin, reflection is framed by the abstract disinterest necessary to understand the existence of things as being determined by forces beyond the human will. That is to say, reflection entails a level of abstraction that reveals the constant and paradoxical clash between self-determination and impotence of individuals to change their lives and their world. Perhaps like the existentialists before him, this sway may have vanished due to the arrival of despair or the more joyful relativism of postmodern spirits—spirits whose father predates Sartre and are found in the Nietzsche of *Thus Spoke Zarathustra* and the *Will to Power*.[3]

If existence, as Sartre says, does indeed precede essence, then God was created in humanity's image, not vice versa.[4] That is, humans are determined by their actions, which are the result of their free will unconstrained by metaphysical forces, spiritual or celestial. Such freedom, however, radically changes as soon as the individual is placed at the center of the dispute, as soon as the individual life is highlighted over the life of the collective from which it emerged, emphasizing the antithesis between the individuals and the society they belong to. If, as Nietzsche says, man has killed God, then mankind has the moral duty to move outside of the orbit of his self-made terrors.[5] If humans' will, not God's, is sovereign, human life becomes a challenge almost exclusively directed to the creative mind, to those who dare make their lives a work of self-creation (as in the work of Foucault).

Tupac Shakur: Lyrical blasphemy, relational reimagining

In many ways, Tupac took up 1960s soul artist Sam Cooke's revolutionary statement of doubt: "It's been too hard living, but I'm afraid to die/ I don't know what's up there beyond the sky," and recreates their context so as to grasp their profound meaning; a statement that recognizes that there is no causation between hardship and reward, no contradiction between religious belief and uncertainty in what lies above or below this earthly life, making it relevant to the hip hop generations, by contextualizing both himself and his poetry within the urban landscape with which the hip hop generations are familiar.[6] Like Cooke, he is unafraid of expressing doubt, at some times affirming conventional belief models and, at other times, rejecting them. Though he frequently denounces hypocritical religious institutions and leaders, his candid moments reveal him to be a man whose doubt has brought him to a faith that is more negotiated than absent.[7] It is the product of the man's inherited beliefs filtered through a deconstructive (destructive even) philosophical mind.

Take Tupac's "Blasphemy," for instance, which appeared on his final studio album. It begins with what appears to be a sermon, delivered through a vocal modulator that gives human speech an inhuman, authoritative quality:

> God has a plan and the Bible unfolds that wonderful plan … Christ is returning someday soon to unfold the wonderful plan of eternity … as long as we're cooperating with God by accepting Jesus Christ as our personal Lord and savior.[8]

Once he has grasped our attention, we hear Tupac's voice as he shouts, "Don't start that blasphemy in here!," and as the intro makes way for the first verse, Pac can be heard in the background, "Follow me, follow me."[9] The sermon, with its intended robotic nature, deconstructs in an instant the moral authority of those who expect the faithful to accept the sermon's message uncritically, as a meaningful and relevant expression of religious belief. Is Tupac challenging institutional religion? Surely he is. Do his intentions end in such an easy disqualification of Christian belief? No, they do not, but one must go further into his lyrics to understand the core of his artistic intentions.

> It's hard enough to live now, in these times of greed
> They say Jesus is a kind man, well he should understand
> Times in this crime land, my Thug nation

With true Sartrean discontent, Tupac uncovers his deepest angst. Despair is hidden in deep thoughts about the weight of our sad state of affairs. More than a truism, it is a question directed to his listeners: how can we deal with the greed, with the disconnection between morality, selflessness, respect for the other, and the nation that seems to undermine at every step? From an intellectual point of view, Tupac contextualizes despair by confessing the lack of meaning within such a state of affairs. Such despair is not suitable for a Christian according to tradition, as faith is expected to withstand doubt.[10] Tupac is not a traditional Christian—not a traditional anything perhaps—yet he abstains from being truly blasphemous, that is, from the verbal offense of religion or spirituality, and its chief component, faith. Just as Tupac reaffirms his faith at the end of a *Vibe* interview, asserting, "I believe in God," he includes in "Blasphemy" an un-ironic recitation of the Lord's Prayer at the end of the song, reaffirming not only his quasi-Christian faith, but also his respect for a humble and honest Christian religiosity—a faith that is no less deeply felt for being antiauthoritarian and antichurch.[11]

"Hell," says Sartre, "is other people." People, he thought, cannot live together in peace; war and sorrow are the inevitable byproducts of social life. Despite such evident pessimism, Sartre held out hope: *things could be otherwise.*

Despite the persistent pessimism that inhabits existential reflection, there is always at the end a hope for a better future, one where equality and justice prevail. It is this call for hope that explains Tupac's similar claims for divine justice in his (1997) *I Wonder if Heaven Got a Ghetto*: "Heaven will be divided between the haves and have-nots when he bemoans / 'I wonder if heaven got a ghetto?'" (Stephens and Wright 2000, p. 31).

Tupac tacitly identifies with those in the ghetto, an identification that cannot simply be reduced to weak sympathy with black communities—Sartre identified with the Algerian struggle for reasons beyond shallow sympathy: he saw them as a people—a national community—and, as such, as having the inalienable right to self-determination, and in the process, he became the victim of two bomb attempts on his life. In the case of Tupac, in his own friendships, his own lived experience of "ghettoes" partly rationalizes why he identifies with their own struggle. Yet, as an artist, this identification breaks all geographical boundaries and thus becomes an existentialist tool of self-determination, which is heard by ghettoes far and beyond the ones he knows. Existentialism should, in turn, not be taken as a rationalist approach to human existence, for in its rejection of essentialism it also rejects the distinction between the objective and the subjective, emotions and reasons. The existentialist, thus, despite the doubts about absolute claims, is still committed to a sense of morality and spirituality, which differs in kind and substance from tradition—and it is that tradition that wants to condemn it as amoral. Is Shakur not talking as much about the ghettoes in America as of those that existed in Poland?

In *The Devil and the Good Lord*, Sartre writes, "When the rich wage war it's the poor who die." In an equally existentialist fashion, Tupac adds, "Cops don't give a damn about a ne-gro/ Pull a trigger, kill a nigga, he's a hero." Both Sartre and Tupac see themselves as part of a community—even if hell is the other—yet traditional political categories are useless to understand the coordinates of such political commitment. They know well that it is the strong man, the one that takes the initiative, who comes closer to justice. They call over and over again for their followers to accept these painful truths, but nowhere do they ask them to become reactive to them. The purpose of the existential reflection is for awareness to awaken their spirit, to provide them with a pathway to travel and a strategy to succeed. The work begins after the fact: after one accepts the violent, the absurd, and the unjust, as essential components of human life.

There is nothing easy in such acceptance; resignation and despair are always looming in the corner. According to Sartre (1946), there is neither hell nor heaven, thus no justice for those that suffer or for those responsible for the suffering. When Tupac wakes up, he asks himself: "Is life worth living should I blast myself?" Both Sartre and Tupac must struggle with the weight of their own reflections and of their own success. The purpose of their artwork is never explicit. Beyond its expression of anguish and suffering, their followers are most likely to disagree on how to move on: if in Sartre's time the question may have been "Shall I join the guerrillas in Algeria or Cuba to make my life meaningful?" In Tupac's world, a follower would ask himself, "Shall I find meaning if I join a gang of Outlaws and thus resist the authorities that oppress my community, or resist anyone, even within the community, real or imagined?" What is clear is that people must find their own pathway as they muddle through the hell that life is.

However, neither Sartre nor Tupac are nihilists, and Tupac's lyrics reveal a hunger for justice, an interest in the sociopolitical realities that affect the poor. Perhaps he is a moralist in the tradition of Camus and the marginalized? Still, his words are not those of a preacher or those of a politician. He criticizes religion as much as he sees hypocrisy and disinterest in those who claim to be shepherds. Tupac's God, therefore, is difficult to pinpoint, for his belief is cloaked by his uncertainties and his doubts. His denunciatory tone, in this regard, is more akin to Luther than to Feuerbach. It is in truth the corruption in organized religion that seems to ignite his incendiary claims in "Blasphemy": "The preacher want me buried, why?" he asks, "Cause I know he a liar."

Jay-Hova and yeezus: The new breed of Hip Hop prophets

While Tupac maintained a constant sway between social critique and existentialist angst, postmodern sensibilities of rappers in the new century depart from the ambivalence between the weight of the collective and the effectiveness of the individual will, rejecting any possible dialectics, which would reconcile the heavenly (Apollonian) and the terrestrial (Dionysian). Identities were still meaningful, in the set of oppositions that appeared in Sartre and Tupac (rich/poor; haves/have-nots; cops/negro), attempted deconstruction in postmodern thought, which sees harmony (synthesis) as a myth that can only perpetuate divisions and marginalization. Take, for instance, the words of Hardt and Negri in *Empire*:

> The White and the Black, the European and the Oriental, the colonizer and the colonized are all representations that function only in relation to each other and (despite appearances) have no real necessary basis in nature, biology, or rationality. Colonialism is an abstract machine that produces alterity and identity. And yet in the colonial situation these differences and

identities are made to function as if they were absolute, essential, and natural. (Hardt and Negri 2000, p. 129)

Accordingly, the postmodern (seemingly) erases the edificial and artificial boundaries between black and white, colonizer and colonized, poor and wealthy, and the sacred and the secular.

Jay-Z and Kanye West are exemplars of just such a postmodern turn. Their spiritual reflections seek, and utilize, fluid definitions for terms like "spirituality," "God," and "religion."[12] Their brand of twenty-first-century individualism frequently engages with religious themes in ways that, like Tupac's thought, carry a strong sense of irony, sarcasm and, at times, virulent denunciation. Jay-Z's and West's challenges to traditional or established values are Nietzschean gestures, critiques of Christian values and exercises of the will to power that Nietzsche explored throughout his works. Relativism in Nietzsche is neither desirable nor inevitable but the consequence of having oppositional thought at the base of all metaphysics (Derrida 1998; Heidegger 2007).

The oppositions have an important place here, because the bridge toward West and Jay-Z appears as one pays attention to the Dionysian which is, in turn, likened by Nietzsche to a narcotic, to a feeling of intoxication, consisting in a lack of boundaries of restraint to the imagination—man goes from being an artist to a work of art himself (Nietzsche 1886, sec. 1). Tupac wanted to make his message meaningful, to sound the right spiritual chords in people's minds. Jay-Z and West deconstruct the presumed separation between artist and artwork, putting creation at the core of what it means to be an artist. As such, creation is primarily taken as a Dionysian force of transformation.

The transformation we see in the track "No Church in the Wild" in many ways imitates Nietzsche's refutation of Christianity in favor of a radical transvaluation of values.[13] As Nietzsche suggests in *The Antichrist*, Christianity, for centuries the moral foundation of the West, is inherently "hostile to life"—hostile to the Dionysian. It inverts natural human inclinations.[14] By Nietzsche's account, Christianity's oppression denies and denigrates the instincts and inclinations—sexual and otherwise—that are most natural to humans. The consequence of such oppression is the limitation of human potentiality: those most truly human, for Nietzsche, are adventurers, creators, and courageous; they are human if—and only if—they embrace their Dionysian destiny, their natural lust for life. Just as Kanye's radical upheaval in "No Church in the Wild" declares that there are "no sins as long as there's permission"—allowing him a sexual freedom that conventional religion precludes—Nietzsche disavows the very idea of conventional sin, sanctioning the kinds of euphoric and life-affirming experiences that the Christian faith denies. Kanye's declaration against the moral weight of sins is in line with this appeal to the Dionysian nature of the self. The rejection of sin is not the automatic embrace of hedonism, but the rejection of an abstract morality that purposefully dismisses the concrete and embraces emotions, circumstances, accidents, struggles, etc.

Nietzsche's proposal is that of *the will to power,* which entails the Dionysian passion for life that does not exist in the Christian worldview (Nietzsche 2004). By the same token, one must note the stark differences between a vision of Christian institutional force as hostile and one that sees it as deviated from its true calling—as fundamentally hypocritical. If one were to say that Kanye does not completely reject the religiosity of the Church—in "No Church in the Wild," he "form[s] a new religion"—it remains true that he appeals for one grounded in the freedom of the individual and in a recognition of the other, in mutuality (which is as close as one gets to the Christian "love thy neighbor" commandment). If Kanye is a prophet, the church he establishes is not a lawless one. West's new god is created in (super) man's image, where Sartre—working in Nietzsche's godless legacy—might suggest that this is the only kind of god that can be.

Like Kanye—the two frequent collaborators share so much in this regard—Jay-Z is no stranger to ideas of divine judgment and heavenly reward (in recent work he references himself as god—"you're in the presence of a king ... no you're in the presence of a god."), but even as he does so, he wants to assure his listeners that "the devil is a lie" and, as he says, "I'm the truth."[15] The spirit of Nietzsche's will to power takes over any resemblance of traditional religiosity that may have been left: as "King Hova," "Jay-Hova" Carter is representing himself as all-powerful, a familiar trope in hip hop lyrics, in any case,[16] but makes it a point to draw some sort of line: "I'm far from being God, but I work God damn hard."[17] Like Kanye, he is preaching a philosophy of self-empowerment and entitlement that refuses the idea of mediation between the self and whatever higher power one may feel close to. Echoing Tupac's sentiment, Jay-Z is sure that "only God [can] judge us" and that "religion creates division."[18] In this sense, like West, a certain nostalgia for Christianity comes forward in Jay-Z. Still, one should abstain from taking his nostalgia too seriously, for his lyrics, for example, the "devil is a lie," or Kanye's "I am a God," do not pass Christian appropriation, without sounding blasphemous and megalomaniacal.

The spirit of the Dionysian triumphs over any understanding of religiosity that may seem paradoxical. The understanding of the human spirit that these two artists maintain stays far from the Apollonian nature that underlies Christian morality, yet it goes much further than a rejection of a long lost tradition. They also reject with as much vehemence the spirit of modernity, which may still be present in Tupac's or Sartre's politics. This is best seen in their rejection of Victorian and, by implication, modern-day scientific approaches to human sexuality.

"We formed a new religion," says Kanye in "No Church in the Wild." "No sins as long as there's permission/And deception is the only felony/So never f- nobody without telling me."[19] "Nobody shall be f-cked without letting you know Kanye"—it's almost impossible to keep a straight face while going over some of West's darkly humored statements. His mockery of confession as a gesture of emancipatory truth is illustrative of his postmodern inclination and is precisely what Foucault criticizes from modernity's hypocritical attitude toward sex; one must bear in mind that what is rejected is primarily the idea of there being a binarity in sexuality: a truth and a falsehood (Foucault 1990).

In the context of human natural instincts, religion is too often seen as a barrier to the absolute, Sade-reminiscent sexual freedom. To understand the coordinates of human sexuality at stake with West and Jay-Z, is it important to understand the tradition against which they rebel: Victorian sexuality. I say Victorian rather than Christian alone, because it is in Victorian times that sexuality becomes a subject of open discussion, albeit following a codification of sexual behavior according to a language akin to the clinical, the psychiatric, and the physiological (Foucault 1990).[20] Victorian sexuality entails, hence, a reintegration of the taboo, by means of a process that recodifies and innocuously normalizes it to traditional morality (Foucault 1990). Once sexuality has been "tamed" an "institutional incitement to speak about it, and to do so more and more, through endlessly accumulated detail" becomes possible and, in fact, is the case (Foucault 1990, p. 18).

Sexual behavior is normalized when it becomes a regime of truth, when individuals are forced to choose for the truth in sex, where adjectives such as health and sanity are commonplace, while accepting the consequences of its falsehood (being sick and an outcast) (Foucault 1990). Repression, thus, is by no means the hidden secret behind human sexual behavior, which characterizes the air of victimization in contemporary society. It is instead the prejudice that makes liberation possible: we are asked to liberate ourselves from such repression, to express freedom by means of an unbounded sexual conduct (Foucault 1990).

West and Jay-Z find themselves in this disjunctive: accept the repression hypothesis and join the (modern) voices of sexual liberation, or reject it and propose an understanding of sexuality that differs and exposes the vacuity of its regime of truth. The type of fulfillment that Kanye speaks of is at odds with Judeo-Christian sexual morality, yet it is not hedonistic—it does not join the voices against sexual repression.[21] West rejects the idea of sex as a physiological function or an unconscious libido: the love of the other is, for Kanye, the absolute foundation upon which all else is built. As long as he has his lover's continued love and approval, as long as everything is all right in her eyes, he can be assured that he is a good man, a moral man, even a holy man.

When well-meaning yet intellectually unsophisticated critics and commentators spill rivers of ink claiming that Kanye West and Jay-Z are megalomaniacs, chiefly for upholding a godlike status, they not only ignore the history of the term multi-variance in hip hop, but also remain trapped in a Christian—or perhaps monotheistic—frame of reference.[22] When artists self-identify with religious figures, and claim to possess powerful ontological and eschatological truths, these, as it has been argued, are not intended to present them as enlightened figures.[23] On the contrary, they shock only the faithful, while resulting in a guide and a form of spirituality for those who are yet to find their will to power: it is directed at those who eschew submission. It is a doctrine of personal responsibility and divine personhood that sanctifies the life you want to live—no matter what shape that life takes. Is it any wonder that hip hop should be fertile ground for the spreading of such ideas?

[handwritten margin note: About JayZ & Kanye God Complexe]

Of course, we must ever remember that, whether we are talking about the hip hop generation(s), hip hop as a culture, or the black church in America, monolithic understandings of each leaves one holding a bag brimming with contradictions and inconsistencies—mainly because they are not intended to be self-contained silos of particular truths or dogmas. Hip hop and the Church are diverse and ever-changing social and communal bodies, which can and deserve to be studied in the analytical isolation of scientific discourse; they are no doubt phenomena of sociological, anthropological, and cultural importance. There are, to be sure, crossings and recurring themes that justify a close examination of the way they contaminate each other; hip hop's role in shaping the religious understanding(s) of hip hop and the divine within the cultural phenomenon that is hip hop—perhaps in a pattern not unlike the return of the repressed.[24]

"Take 'em to Church": A rejoinder between tradition and hip hop

It is impossible to accurately assess how much impact (if any) Tupac's religiosity had on the religious beliefs of the hip hop generation, but there is, at least, anecdotal evidence that suggests that the impact was far from negligible. Rahiel Tesfamariam, in an article on Tupac and the black church, notes, "Seeing the 'Makaveli' cover art—which depicted Pac hanging from a wooden cross—may have been the first time that I saw a crucifixion portrayal that I could relate to."[25] It is Tesfamariam's hip hop generation (those born into a post-segregation America who remember the deaths of Tupac and Biggie the way the previous generation did those of MLK and JFK), more than any other, that is so clearly aware that black churches (especially those in inner-city America) are struggling to remain relevant institutions in the communities they serve (Glaude 2010).[26] Young African Americans are, in ever-increasing numbers, absenting themselves from church-centered worship.[27] In his 2009 study of black politics in America, Manning Marable sounded the alarm: "We are in the midst of a major ideological realignment within black America with the demarcation of potentially antagonistic and confrontational formations and groups that will battle for the future of our people."[28] Martin Luther King Jr., in his prophetic way, warned black church leaders in *Where Do We Go From Here* (1968) about the status quo path that church leaders were walking, and in many ways, the declining fortunes of the black church in the twenty-first century are the result of the failure of church leaders to address King's concerns.

Though black churchgoers overwhelmingly vote for Democratic political candidates, there is a strong streak of conservatism that, preached from the pulpit, is widespread in black communities (Glaude 2010).[29] They lean right on a variety of social issues—most notably, but not only, same sex marriage.[30] And one can only presume that this conservative streak has contributed to pushing the hip hop generation toward searching for spiritual guidance in places other than those traditionally sanctioned or sanctified though the albatross of homophobia is pervasive in hip hop too.[31] During a Columbia University round table, Anthea Butler savaged the church for its inability to welcome or inspire young black men and women in any palatable way: "I'm sick of this crap," she said, criticizing the aforementioned conservative streak which tells black men and women who are sexually active that their "sexuality and personhood [are] not worthy."[32] This echoes Tupac's question posed to the church in "Blasphemy": "Why you got those kids' minds, thinkin' that they evil?"[33]

Given this widespread institutional critique and the seeming agreement that the church is now—and has long been—at odds with the realities of life in the communities in which they are situated, rappers and hip hop artists no doubt play an important role in filling the gap of discontent between an ever more alienating tradition and an ever more unconstrained social and romantic life. Rappers are denunciatory and critical voices, but they are also putting forth positive proposals for a new understanding of community. The message of rappers like Tupac places the need to survive (a photo finish with the need to thrive) above all others; the G's only judge is God himself, and any earth-bound authorities who attempt to assume His mantle and judge His children and burden them with guilt and self-loathing are, Tupac surely felt, sorely misguided and misguiding. How prescient King's conditional:

If today's church does not recapture the sacrificial spirit of the early church, it will lose its authenticity, forfeit the loyalty of millions, and be dismissed as an irrelevant social club with no meaning for the twentieth century. Every day I meet young people whose disappointment with the church has turned into outright disgust.[34]

The idea that hip hop artists are shaping the religious sensibilities of the hip hop generation in significant ways may seem, at a first glance, far-fetched, but from the moment that hip hop began to address its acolytes with consciousness-expanding lyrics, the moment they began to preach a message of self-reliance and non-conformity, they were setting the table for just such a communion—their bodies and their blood are not figurative; they are very literal, and they pulse with the same rhythms and bear the same scars as the blood and bodies of those who find spiritual guidance in their words. Their words fill the spiritual and educational vacuum of the ghetto, whose denizens so often feel the street and its prophets to be better educators and shepherds than any found behind brick and mortar resembling the existentialist commitment and Sartre's committed intellectual fighting for the enlightened ideas of his time. Hip hop's emergence and popularization may also be likened to the role that existentialist thought played in postwar Europe, in particular, through the works of Sartre, whose novels inhabited popular culture at the time. After the calamities of the war, the loss of faith (not only in religion, but also in the legitimacy of political ideology and in the old European elites) became a breeding ground for existentialist discontent. Hip hop's emergence comes not as a result of war, yet it still channels discontent and the unfulfilled expectations of the civil rights movement. For the younger generation, their relation to hip hop is filled with an existential jostling that reifies economic success and the party atmosphere as symbolic of ostentation, while at the same time being suffused with messages of community and collective struggle, meditations on violence, death, and the individual's movement through the concrete social realities which surpass abstractions and circumvent traditional morals. Hip hop's will to power appears, hence, primarily as a rival ethics to the individualistic and egoistic ethics of capitalism. Part of the social change that has accompanied the decline of the black church has to do with the demands that such utilitarian capitalism places on black Americans in their daily lives. Pluralism, despite its smack of liberal political agenda, must be taken instead as a sociological fact about the porosity of identities and of the different moralities that must coexist side by side. From a philosophical standpoint, hip hop is an existential route that enables individuals to construct a viable community, even as they understand their way of life as individualistic at its core. Another way to put it is that hip hop's existential perspective acknowledges the enigma of what is the Other; the face of the other appears as an enigma, as both a provocation and an invitation (Waldenfels 2002).

The existentialist understanding of otherness as fundamental to the individual experience (see Levinas) allows for hip hop followers to relate to one another, while maintaining and highlighting their individuality. What is at stake, therefore: an ethics of the face, of the Other, that must be understood in contradistinction with Totality—with rational appropriation of a phenomenon—with the aim of reducing it to something familiar (Waldenfels 2002). This ethics of the face in Emmanuel Levinas stands primarily against an ethics of neutrality: of tolerance as an attitude characterized for its neuter connotation. The liberal topic of tolerance has no place in the ideas of Levinas. The existentialist approach in Levinas functions, however, as a phenomenological study of the face, where the face is deconstructed as a totality, and its presence is put into brackets. The purpose is to discover the Other in its existential struggle, which is not the same as feeling empathy for another person. The recognition of an existential struggle is not the recognition of emotions, but the recognition of a way of life, and of a will that has as much interest as anyone else in creating his own life, in being recognized in his rights for self-creation.

This is precisely why morality remains relevant when discussing the irruption of hip hop artists within any axiological framework, despite the decline of traditional identities and communities—ethics, rather than a set of rules or norms. Hip hop lyrics are characterized by constant changes and gradations, by proximity and distance between friends and enemies. There is an infinite character to the face of the other, an incommensurable aspect to their choices and struggles. A spatial metaphor best illustrates Levinas' intentions: relationships are configured and reconfigured as changes in proximity and distance take place. That is to say, I come closer to the Other, but can never fully occupy the space of the other. This use of the spatial metaphor is illustrative of the reality of inner-city life, where one is constantly clashing with others and, thus, constantly in need of either recognizing her or denying her, by means of indifference, moral judgment, and marginalization. This is why, in other words, an ethics of the face is, thus, an explicit recognition of the other's choices—morally and politically—that cannot be reconciled with the stringent moral standards of Christian tradition.

When Rev. Ralph C. Watkins was collecting data for one of his many projects that seek to bridge the gap between the hip hop generation and the church, he interviewed hundreds of young black Americans in Pittsburg: "The names of certain rappers continually surfaced. As we would talk about God, religion, and theology, someone was bound to say, 'Well, you know Tupac says… .'"[35] As much as those who, like Watkins, attempt outreach programs aimed at the hip hop generation (with varying degrees of success) imagine a movement from street and corner into safe and morally constructive arenas, the appropriation of religious themes by rappers is, in tangible ways, effectuating an opposite movement whereby the church is pulled off its pilings and into the street. Strictly speaking, the church is not being replaced by hip hop *in toto*, but hip hop is, in effect, quite comfortable in the tunics of the church.

When the church, on the contrary, attempts the opposite movement, trying, as Monica Miller says, "to [take] on the 'tastes' and 'values' of the subaltern (hip hop) group in the name of membership expansion and institutional participation," the results are more often comic than they are effective.[36] There has been a concerted effort on the part of some black preachers to appeal to black youth by emulating, verbally or sartorially, hip hop's style, but, unless organically linked to the culture, this comes off as transparently insincere. Unless such initiatives are grounded in the same recognition of the Other, in the same ethics of intrusion and disruption, they will remain ineffective and utterly shallow. Though across this nation we see many of the current generation of church leadership influenced by hip hop energies, it is the strategic appropriation of religious iconography and broad interpretations of the will of the divine that is transmitted—by lay-rappers, not priests—that seems to be more effective. While retaining a semblance of its situated power, religious iconography and language have largely been emptied of meaning and translated into the language of the streets and the corners. Self-representations of rappers in the guise of Jesus—crowned with thorns and nailed to the cross—became something of an industry commonplace.[37] Utley notes in her study of religion and hip hop, "When gangstas represent themselves as Jesus, they are usually not healing the sick, feeding the multitudes, teaching in the temple, or loving women and children. Gangstas represent themselves as a crucified Jesus who is resisting authority."[38] What is important here are not Jesus' words, but his power—in particular, that will to power that is exemplified in his rise from the nadir to ultimate.

Hip hop's horizon for the future: Community against cultural capitalism

The rampant materialism and capitalism that characterizes hip hop's imagery of success are commonplace today; they clash not only with Christian tradition (Protestant ethics in particular), but also with the history of destitution of African Americans. According to Bakari Kitwana, for the hip hop generation, "achieving wealth, by any means necessary, is more important than most anything else, hence our obsession with materialistic and consumer trappings of financial success."[39] The same, however, could be said, for example, of the black church, which has increasingly come under the sway of televangelists and mega-church leaders who preach the prosperity gospel. Michael Eric

[handwritten margin note: Prosperity Gospel]

Dyson notes that these new church models are providing blinkered readings of holy writ that allow followers to "justify [their] upward mobility and middle-class existence without feeling guilty."[40] Hip hop first appealed to a population already permeated with corporate messages and dreams of material success; with its particular songs, locations, and hierarchies, hip hop, albeit pluralistic and diverse, is not unlike a church adopting the prosperity gospel when it harmonizes its own material aspirations with God in a bid to reconcile the zeitgeist with sacred doctrine.

[handwritten margin note: Tupac: why God need ceilings to talk to me?]

With evident frustration, in his famous *Vibe* interview, Tupac spits rhetorical questions at the interviewer: "Why God need gold ceilings to talk to me? Why do God need colored windows to talk to me? That makes ghetto kids not believe in God."[41] The wealth of the church and the hustle of the faithful (perceived or otherwise) make it harder and harder for the religiously unaffiliated to see organized religion as anything other than a common business. Clearly, the stained-glass and gold accouterments predate "the African-American Church," but ostentatious wealth juxtaposed with and utterly immersed in impoverishment sets the rapper's teeth on edge. This attitude opens the door for hip hop artists to formulate their own perspectives and critiques of the established spiritual order.

Hip hop musicians offer bespoke religious perspectives fitted to the material conditions of many of their listeners in a way not dissimilar to Sartre's appeal to his listeners: those individuals who unapologetically express their doubts, including their doubts on the capitalist promise of success and the end of political conflict. Their understandings of spirituality are, for the most part, syncretic and organic, an after-the-fact set of counterinstitutional beliefs that allows spirituality to function in their lives without any significant changes to the way the participant navigates through "amoral" landscapes.[42] This may be symptomatic of a much more generalized phenomena: the decline of Christianity in the West. It may also be a much more strategic approach on behalf of hip hop musicians, who are aware of such decline and use it, in order to propose different alternatives to their moral tradition, as well as to the values that they want to advocate. Such a strategic approach is certainly playful in nature, for otherwise it would simply repeat the initiatives of what it rejects (Christian and Victorian morality). Therefore, both hip hop and existentialist thought fight against the constrained freedom experienced by man, for specifically Sartre's idea of freedom that rejects the doctrine that God's freedom is sovereign and human freedom is limited by God's will.

The cultural form, in all its facets, is the vehicle by which black America moved through and overcame the problems that faced the community in the years following the civil rights movement, and hip hop's very existence proves to the artist that God's interests "are clearly in harmony with [his] own."[43] There are, of course, other factors that influence the religious beliefs of the hip hop generation, but in an age of celebrity worship and emulation, hip hop stars like Tupac and KRS-One in the '90s and Jay-Z and Kanye West in the last decade have undoubtedly contributed to the ongoing dialogue with the community that attempts to define what it means, in the twenty-first century, to be religious, spiritual, or, in extreme cases, godlike. Christian tradition in all its facets has, no doubt, loosened its grip on the social fabric, but such a grip still exists and is still an important force with which to reconcile within many communities, including many of which are hip hop artists and followers. While much emphasis is still discursively and publicly placed on the role and dominance/privileging of the black church to provide meaning and the housing for black communities, here, I want to suggest that we take a cue from the work of religious studies scholar Anthony B. Pinn, when he suggests that "rap music is a continuation of the creative manner in which meaning is made out of an absurd world" (Pinn 2003, p. 1).

What has emerged is a community that, while eschewing dogmatic directives and communal worship, defines itself as spiritual. The amoral city, which seems an inhospitable terrain for faith, is maintained in hip hop and expressed and interpreted in new ways.[44] The sacred may intrude upon the secular in paradoxical and, at times, laughable ways, but where contradictions are perceived is often the result of the prejudices of the critical eye itself and its assumptions about what words like "God" and "religion" mean or ought to mean.

4

God complex, complex gods, or God's complex: Jay-Z, poor black youth, and making "The Struggle" divine[1]

Michael Eric Dyson

Handwritten annotations in the margins:

(top left): Better written version of the questions not google doc

(left margin):
P1) Can we do a lyrical analysis of the two sets of lyrics on Page 63 as a class?

P2) More information on the history of Humant talk in the Black community? (topic is touched on on Pg. 60)

Introduction: Jay-Z and the manipulation of the black rhetorical tradition

This chapter pays attention to a powerful argument that has been the topic of much academic and public discussion, that is the nature of the "popular," and critical analyses about the popular in all manner and form. In this sense, I understand the "popular" as: (1) a demographically driven domain, (2) a racial or class construct, and (3) a folk element or a product of, or against, modernity. With this in mind, this chapter considers such complexities over and against the work of rapper Jay-Z who, I argue, brings into sharp and luminous focus our thinking about popular religion, religion of the popular, and religion in a popular vein while complicating static and rigid conceptions of both terms. Here, I introduce a kind of symbiotic syntax of—and grammar within—both domains to raise critical questions of inquiry around ever-changing concepts that circulate around the boundaries, and constitute the borders, of notions of religion and the popular in American culture more generally.

I titled this lecture "God complex, complex gods, or God's complex" with the many, and sometimes controversial, self-anointed and publically given names surrounding Jay-Z—Jehovah, J-Hova, Hova, Hov, and a host of other permutations of this neologism—in mind. Such creatively generated terms and names work to signify his Godlike status emblematized in both "God of the microphone" and "small g" spelling of god that, together, point toward and corroborate his commanding presence as an MC. Such divine-like signifiers establish and highlight a direct link between the manipulation of rhetoric and the assertion of religious legitimacy, especially in hip hop culture. Such configurations within black popular religion point toward one of the mainstays of, and defining characteristics within, it: the role of the rhetorical. More specifically, across and among black popular religions, whether you are reading Kenneth Burke or Ralph Ellison, closer attention must be given to how rhetoric operates and is constituted. Here, I have in mind the manner in which rhetoric becomes a means of articulation of religious identities as they are deeply entrenched within oratorical performances with a profound lineage in American culture, and, in particular, within histories of the oppressed.

Consider for example, Albert Raboteau's brilliant essay on the chanted sermon[2] and the history of what is commonly known within African American culture as the "hoop."[3] Is not the hoop itself almost like an act of onomatopoeia so that the very articulation of the term itself conjures the phenomenon it aims to explore and to illuminate? And so, the sermon, the performance of the oratory, links a figure like Jay-Z to critical black preaching traditions within the history itself. I have been quite interested in and curious about the conversation regarding the relationship between prosperity gospel preachers and other traditions of black rhetoric. Consider the point that varieties of black sacred rhetorical performance are still relatively invisible to dominant culture and are obscured en masse today. Figures such as Jesse Jackson, William Gray, Martin Luther King, Jr. among others have all contributed to and personify extraordinary exponents of black rhetoric, but that barely begins to touch the tip of the iceberg and certainly does not reveal it. For every Martin Luther King, Jr. and Jesse Jackson and Al Sharpton, there is a Caesar Clark, in terms of the rhetorical ingenuity of the chanted sermon, or a Gardner Calvin Taylor, who is one of the magisterial prophets of the American pulpit, a colossus of black American rhetorical performance. This reality is complexly paired with varied kinds and types of rhetorical performances, even within that tremendously fecund and fertile history and reality we have come to call the black rhetorical tradition. Gardner Taylor was deeply steeped in the traditional and highly nuanced European canonical texts within the so-called mainstream white and European pulpit. You would hear him quoting something like, "God saves us not by flattering us, but by opposing us."[4] And then you have an individual like Caesar Clark who so beautifully demonstrated a certain sort of internalized expression—so that the chanted sermon and the sermon that is highly disciplined by allusion to European canonical texts, constitutes a legitimate diversity, among other things, within black oratorical and rhetorical performances.

With this in mind, someone like rap artist Jay-Z is fundamentally linked, whether consciously or unconsciously, to this tradition of black preaching and rhetorical performativity. In this regard, he is certainly not alone. The performative differences and synergies shared among and between various figures within contemporary black culture today are quite palpable. For example, there is a "difference" between an artist like Nas, whose voice perhaps resonates in his throat, and someone like deceased rap artist Tupac Shakur, who spoke from his gut, or a hip hop icon like Biggie Smalls, who, lyrically, swings like a jazz musician in a different fashion. Beyond hip hop, consider the difference between someone like Ella Fitzgerald, articulating a nasal tonality, and an artist like Sarah Vaughan, who amplified sound, nearly through her neck. Think now of the divergences between Cannonball Adderley, and John Coltrane on the saxophone—such differences literally register and signify, both phonically and sonically. Black preaching traditions have legitimately been compared to those oratorical performances or, at least, those registers of aesthetic appreciation and aspiration in different fields of pursuit. What do we make of this when considering hip hop culture today? What do we imagine when we think about the complex tapestry of black rhetorical tradition—a Nas versus Jay-Z versus Tupac versus Lauryn Hill, or Gardener Taylor versus Caesar Clark versus Dr. Frederick D. Haynes, III versus Lance Watson versus Caroline Knight versus Prathia Hall—all names that we should be familiar with, to be sure? The very notion of Jehovah, Jay-Z—the oratorical performer, the rhetor, the Burkean signifier within the complicated configuration of identities— becomes mediated through text, textuality, intertextuality, and post-textuality in a certain sort of way. That is, his identity challenges the construction of a solidified stable set of signifiers that go underneath and are subsumed within the rubric of the very text to begin with. They are breaking out even as they are constituted and are constituting. When I think about Jay-Z, Jehovah, Hova, God MC, the self-conscious manipulation of a rhetorical tradition of identifying with God— transcendence indeed comes to mind. This is where someone like Jay-Z begins to shatter the boundaries of this identification, because for ministers who claim to have divine authority by their identification with God, Jay-Z ups the ante and says, "I'ma raise you one. I am God," both rhetorically and metaphorically.

In the following section, I turn my attention to why people think he's sacrilegious. When I think about the name itself, the names themselves that simultaneously signify a transcendence to which Jay-Z alludes, and the mediation of that divine experience, one then begins to witness what Jay-Z says in one song, or what he talks and thinks about in a hip hop culture without the God MC, and, most presciently, he argues that he is the savior of hip hop.

God on the mic: Jay-Z and lyrical styling

Jay-Z consciously manipulates divine-like rhetoric. He constantly talks about God, in the relentless association of himself with God, thus deriving some benefit from, and legitimacy within, this context of divine grammars. But it also suggests something powerful and unique that he begins to both assert—and to shatter—tradition. And so, the association of Jay-Z with black rhetorical forms most closely and intimately linked to black preaching also begins to encourage us to think more deeply about the nature of the divine in transcendence and in the ways in which it is mediated through mundane and extraordinary moments of speech. What is or what might Jay-Z be trying to accomplish with his divine-like lyrical acrobatics and play?

Such rhetorical stylings put forth an intellectual argument which was the bulwark against the oppressions that people were the very subject of, and subjected to. Such lyrical play becomes the very substitute for both God—in terms of the ministerial office—and the masses, the people, literally the vox populi, a different take, indeed, on what constitutes the popular. Vox popular, vox populi, that is the articulation of a consistent creative community that is mediated through rhetorical acts and gestures. So then, the rhetorical performance signifies a divine moment of interaction with human vulnerability—one that transposes that vulnerability and puts it back on the very "God" being seen. That is the space of theodicy, no?—asking the question *if* God intends good stuff then why does bad stuff happen? The rhetorical force and form are merged, fused, mingled, creatively conflicted, and, at the end of the day, operate within a tradition out of which ministers and MCs have given enlivened expression.

The name Jehovah, Jay-Hova, God MC, Hova, is a self-conscious manipulation of that tradition. These signifiers can be juxtaposed: Jay-Z says (if you read his book, *Decoded* [2011]) in some songs, and I'm paraphrasing: "I'm not a Christian, but I listen to the people who deal with different religions, and I derive the wisdom from them." In *Decoded*, one encounters him reciting his lyric, "I'm not God, but I work Goddamn hard." A close listen to some of his earlier material, such as "D'Evils," reveals that he is dealing with the presence of dark forces, lyrically taking us all the way back to his first album,

Reasonable Doubt (1996), and then back up to his first retirement album, *The Black Album* (2004), in which he discusses the figure of Lucifer, and praying for this person because he has got those dark forces in him, too.

Constantly dealing with religion, Jay-Z is conscious of religion, and, in some cases, spirituality, but he also refuses to hunker down in any one of these seemingly singular domains. Methodologically, then, it is not the smorgasbord approach, nor the cafeteria approach. Perhaps, as I discuss in more depth below, what we witness is a more eclectic approach. When we juxtapose *Decoded*—where we see his openness to different religions and varieties of thinking—versus what he points to in some of his lyrics—where he is engaging with a notion of God as different from, yet identified with vulnerable people— what some see are notions of incarnation and transcendence being hijacked for earthly purposes. But, for Jay-Z, when we consider his lyrical content and outpouring, looking at the way in which the very notion of the divine has to be relentlessly deconstructed, we begin to witness the complicated ways in which he signifies on religious tradition.

[handwritten margin note: Not so simple as hijacking these notions for earthly purposes]

Religion and the popular: Jay-Z and god complexes

Combining *ligare* (to bind together) and religion, *religio*, with the concept of the popular, a host of fascinating queries begin to emerge. How do we constitute it? What might it mean to talk about "popular," as associated with certain folk traditions? As remnants of an engagement with identity and the way in which such imagination are mediated? What role do class and race play? Is something popular because it appeals to the masses? Is it popular in the sense that it has folk elements or is the product of a genealogy of modernity, and contests the forces of destabilization that came in modernity? And, if that is true of modernity, is it also true of postmodernity?

Indeed, considering the domain of "what's popular," it is, no doubt, a difficult undertaking, for in doing so, "whose" version gets popularized needs interrogating. Are we talking about the Kim Kardashian West's fleeting version of popular that lasts a few days and then moves into different realities like marriage, or is it like how media are deployed for purposes of engaging identity, or at least reestablishing the protocols of narcissism? Popular in the sense of the concretization of a belief about how that which is ineffable and impenetrable can be brought to bear in a very clear fashion? Is something popular because it is consumable by more people, and not just by a few of the esoteric? Or, are we talking about popular in terms of the class-based stuff, where folk religion signifies in a particular way? Certainly, all this has racial, and certainly class, and perhaps even gender, consequences to which we should all pay attention. Consider an abbreviated genealogy of the notion of religion as binding something together, the institutionalization of inspiration, the desire for spirituality to have some grounding, and then, on the other hand, for the popular to have its multiple significations.

I argue that Jay-Z is trying to—or at least we can use him to, whether he is trying to or not, which is up to us to think through—challenge a very narrow conception of what might be "authentically" religious. Additionally, I think he is also raising questions about the function of a certain branch of theology—theodicy in particular—and the way in which it functions in both African American and, more broadly, American life. And lastly, the radical identification with a transcendent deity, God, becoming human, is the very reassertion of an incarnational ethic that Jay-Z dares appropriate for communities which have been rendered economically, politically, and racially vulnerable.

And so, what is the offense? The great theologian Paul Tillich talked about shattering the *logos aposiges*, the divine silence of God—in Jesus. I believe that an artist like Jay-Z wants to continue to shatter that silence, which is typified in one of his songs where he says:

> I'm from the place where the church is the flakiest/And niggas is praying to God so long that they atheist.[5]

It's as if he's saying: "I can't hear, can't feel a connection to the divine, and I don't know where the voice of God is located, so I'll locate it in my voice.

Here, the *locus classicus* of divinity becomes the very voice that is seeking the divine inspiration that ultimately will be supplied by one's own work. That is why Jay-Z's work ethic is a profound meditation on something like a Weberian conception of the Protestant ethic and the spirit of capitalism.[6] One might ask, how does Weber become any more materialized than in an artist like Hova?

Let's consider the ways that Jay-Z operates here through the trope of "The God complex." A lot of young people now think that Jay-Z thinks he is God. I was recently discussing this with some colleagues as we gave thought to some interesting responses of young people who think that Jay-Z and Kanye West are devil worshippers. They are tripping out, while I am thinking, "Wow, that is just pretty fascinating. Who knew that a guy from Marcy was in the Illuminati. That might be a divine trick, right?" Here I am thinking of when Jay-Z says, "I'm not a businessman, I'm a business, man!/Let me handle my business, damn." So to these hyped up and exaggerated conspiratorial claims, Jay-Z might retort, "I'm not Illuminati, I'm illuminating." Thus, something like a "God complex" as animated by the obsession with identification with the transcendent is more than simply a "God complex." Such an obsession is not the desire to—or a hankering for—the divine to become human. Is such not the original sin—believing that the human is the divine? And so this is the charge that has been leveled against Jay-Z and others, but from whence do such claims emerge? I suggest it is not from a profoundly Derridean misreading, if you will, that can have powerful consequences that are edifying. Rather, I think it is a profoundly flat reading of the landscape of black American culture. In one sense, as my younger colleague, Salamishah Tillet, has suggested, Illuminati stuff among black people is not a new charge. What is new, however, are the objects of such a claim—in fact, black folks have been talking about the Illuminati for a long time. Now, though, it's not about white folk—those with the ends—that is, the money, the dope, the bread, the capital. Here, the tables begin to turn with black success, as black folk begin to emerge on top. Remember, Jay-Z in *Watch the Throne* reminds us "… domino/Only spot a few blacks the higher I go," articulating something to the effect that the more success he enjoys, the fewer people who share it are black: "What's up, Will? Shout out to O! That ain't enough, we gon' need a million more." Here, Hova knows that the fewer black people climb, the higher he gets. Such a sentiment raises the suspicion of arrival, the very "suspicion of success," the suspicion of creative outlets granted to people who had heretofore been circumscribed in a vicious fashion. Taken together, the skepticism and suspicion gets concentrated on how the conspiracy theory is turned against other black people.

Here we find the conflation of paranoia and conspiracy within the new narrative of black exceptionalism. Is this not why Obama too is considered part of the Illuminati, along with artists like Jay-Z and countless other rap artists? Not any 'ole black person can be a part of this group—you have got to have a certain kind of income to be Illuminati. It's not for poor people, right? Literally, in this sense, the poor need not apply. In such a narrative, people without money become figured as weird, whereas people with money begin to be depicted as eccentric. The Illuminati charge, then, is a political and sociological judgment about the forces of capital and the ways in which such capital has converged with politics to create unhappy alliances between powers, powers over which the masses feel they have little control. The resistance to Jay-Z (as an Illuminati) is a sort of grassroots theodicy, an "on the ground" attempt to try to figure out the gap, especially when one considers theodicy as the disjuncture between destiny and merit in the Weberian sense. To press the metaphor further, such interstices are characterized by what one thinks they deserve, what one ends up with, and the gap between that measures such a theodical reality. Partly, the Illuminati discourse is rhetoric of criticism dressed up as a religiously identified assertion that also has profound sociological consequences. So the "God complex," thinking that you are God, becomes the sense of the deification of the temporary.

Jay-Z is often read by those who are very critical of him as trying to be God in the most inappropriate fashion possible, and, to these instances and thin claims, I think he is actually doing more than simply claiming a God Complex—Jay-Z is asserting "Complex gods." By "Complex gods," I mean that Jay-Z wants the public to know that there is no question that human beings who are vulnerable have the potential to rise above their circumstances. Such greatness is, in many ways, recognized in lyrics themselves. They call us to recognize the greatness of who we are, the greatness of what we do, the value and worth and significance of the struggles in which we engage, so that we, you, are complex gods, complex human beings who are centers of moral gravity around which meaning and significance orbits, that, in one sense, we can control, or, at the least, generate, meaning and significance. Above all, Jay-Z and artists like him generate a lyrical way of arguing against the dehumanizing impulses of the broader culture and society.

So, between the God complex and the complex gods is this next domain—God's complex. This, to me, is the socio-spiritual, the urban geopolitics of the black oppressed and the popular, which gets fundamentally associated with poor black people. These are, for sure, legacies and lineages of authenticity when we begin to consider, "who is real," "what is black," and "what is real" within hip hop? Black, poor and authentic are animated by the hoods of America and its inhabitants—the urban merchant, the urban urchin, the citizen of the destabilized postindustrial or urban cultures where enclaves of civic terror like slums and ghettoes continuously proliferate. The geopolitics of such urban misery begin to constitute a ground for urban theodicy, and so, by "God's complex," I am signifying on the "complex" as in "the compound," "the projects," "the hood." The geopolitics of urban theodicy is God's complex.

These are the bounded realities that human beings acknowledge and reinforce in the face of tremendous devastation. Jay-Z works hard to make the needs of the people divine. Not all people, just specific people, in particular: poor, mostly black or brown people whose backs are economically against the wall, people who have been devastated by the permanent trend of the economic downturn that hemorrhage jobs and people from core economic processes in our cities.

Jay-Z and making the struggle of the people divine

In what follows, I briefly discuss how Jay-Z speaks about these ideas, in trying to make the struggle of the people divine: how he twists it to shape and reverse it, and how he ultimately embodies the great mantra that "the last shall be first, the first shall be last." In one sense, he has got what C. H. Dodd would call a "realized eschatology" but for Jay, it is not only the end stuff that is of importance; it is also about being realized in his, or ones' own success.[7] Jay's own achievements are, in fact, a realized eschatology. Here, the *telos*—the goal and purpose of history—has been redefined—some would say reified—in the very means of his success, which is why even *Watch the Throne* (all that luxury rap as Kanye calls it) is aspirational.

Now, calling it "aspirational" is not to say it does not have deep and profound indices and traces of the most mortifying materialism, or that it is not in the grip of the vicious economic processes which have damaged communities that are the site of this urban theodicy. Rather, it is a down payment against the meaningfulness that can be extracted from that very devastation. When I think about Jay-Z putting forth his most important religious concept, to me, it is not about a narcissistic preoccupation with the divine or a legitimate understanding that the divine intersects with the human—there is much more going on here. Consider the fact that William R. Jones said that he believed in humanocentric theism—that we have to posit the legitimacy of the human as the site of the divine.[8] In this way, we take away divine responsibility, by asking the question of theodicy as opposed to anthropodicy—the question of what are *we* doing? For instance, an anthropodicy would not ask "why is the plane broke, God, you messed up and slipped up and didn't watch over us?" Rather, an anthropodicy asks "why did the plane makers not do their job right?" With such a humanocentric endeavor, the historically contingent conceptions of responsibility and accountability are refracted through the prism of our own making and, therefore, our own control.

For me, Jay-Z's religious thinking is embedded and material rather than terrestrial. It is deeply inscribed in the flora and fauna of local sites and spaces. What do we point to when we talk about the production of local knowledge of a place like Marcy Projects, of the projects more generally, the slum—God's complex? Is God's complex not the specific site for the emergence of religious narratives that deify the folk who have been devastated? It is not merely compensatory, though it is certainly that, too. Such a scenario is not merely a kind of revenge against those who have been the vicious mediators of that dislocation and displacement, though partly that, certainly. Rather, it is the assertion of the positive value of the lives that have been shaped in the midst of those circumstances.

This sort of religious thought is embedded rather than terrestrial also in the sense that the philosophical origin and the theological intent is not simply to locate God in a heaven or hell beyond where we are, but instead to talk about

Poor Black Youth are the object of his adoration

the deeply entrenched and embedded conceptions of God in heaven, on earth, and the realities that we confront right here where we are. It's deeply and profoundly embedded—perhaps even incarnated—in the sense that it comes from the earth and the terrain of the geopolitical struggles waged in slums and ghettoes across America today and in history. I would also argue that it is implicit rather than explicit—ain't no great theological "system" going on here; rather, it is poor black youth who are the object of his adoration, his hymn to the universe, if we can borrow Teilhard de Chardin, in making their struggle divine.

Jay-Z's (and, perhaps by extension, these hip hop generations') religious thought is more implicit than explicit, because they are deeply embedded and inscribed in the narratives which Jay-Z puts forth that value the lives of poor black people that talk about their suffering, that narrate it in Jay-Z's "December 4":

> Now all the teachers couldn't reach me/ And my momma couldn't beat me /Hard enough to match the pain of my pops not seeing me, so/With that disdain in my membrane /Got on my pimp game /Fuck the world, my defense came.

Or on "What More Can I Say?"

> God forgive me for my brash delivery/But I remember vividly what these streets did to me/ So picture me letting these clowns nitpick at me/Paint me like a pickaninny.

Lyrics

There is a lot of interesting imagery at work in these lyrics—the pickaninny, the absent father. Such thinking embedded in these lyrics puts forth an argument about the relationship between an absent father and a subsequent surrender of the authority of traditional institutions in the lives of these young people, and a surrender of the concomitant meaningfulness that is derived from an identification with institutions which served others, but which continue to fail young black people in particular. And so, these institutions are thus mediated through the space of the home—"mama couldn't beat me," or the school—"teachers couldn't reach me."[9] Consider the stark reality that Jay-Z does not graduate from high school and that Nas drops out in eighth grade. Who is at fault? These kids or the institutions? It is undeniable that they Jay-Z and Nas turned out to be geniuses, and if they turned out to be that smart without formal education, then who failed them? The argument here is that there are enough of these young geniuses (Jay-Z and Nas are merely representative of them) who are embodied priests of an order that has been marginalized. Perhaps there is something to be said for the difference between "schooling" and "education," and maybe these discourses also have something to say about that. The point that I am trying to make is simply that inherent and implicit in the music of an artist like Jay-Z are varieties of thinking, logics, and rhetorics that are mobilized within the context of that community that allow us at least to determine and detect and discern some serious and significant political thinking at work.

I am reminded of a Jay-Z concert that I attended at the Verizon Center, and during this *Made in America* tour, you have got the image of Martin Luther King, Jr. on stage, and it's not the "I Have a Dream" Martin Luther King, Jr. rather, it is Martin Luther King's last speech, "I May Not Get There with You." That's a different sort of scene and scenario altogether. And if you've ever read that whole speech, that's certainly a hip hop performance, perhaps even King's greatest hip hop performance, historically. Think about it: King's at the crib and he doesn't want to go to the meeting that night. People try to paint it as if King was depressed, and for sure, he was. It was raining cats and dogs, and he didn't like small audiences either. That's the human part. He didn't want five people looking at him—"If I'm going to speak, let me at least have a thousand." Now, he didn't say it that way, and we know that King is a humble man, but, well, if King did not want to show up because there ain't enough people there, then that's his prerogative. We are always going to figure it out; we are going to finesse it. King was deeply and profoundly depressed. Look at the uncomfortable parallels between the sacred King and that so-called degraded hip hop generation. Dependence upon certain drugs to make it through in the hip hop generation has been a palpable reality, but King too, by order of his doctor in New York, Dr. Logan, increasingly relied upon both antidepressants and alcohol, and it wasn't working. And on that fateful night, King goes to the hotel under the threat of death. He's tired, and Ralph Abernathy gets to the Mason Temple [and] says, "Doc, this is your audience. They showing up. There's a couple thousand people out here." So, King gets up and dressed, with that rough-skinned after depilatory look, takes a cab, and delivers arguably the greatest speech of his life, hands down. He takes his crowd on a tour of history in a brilliant thought-scenario as he discusses the great moments in history—Abraham Lincoln, Aristophanes, and so on. And he said, "If God allows me to live a few years in the 20th century, I will be satisfied."[10] And he said, "America, all I'm asking is that you be true to what you said on paper."

In this historic speech, he talked about young people digging the wells deep of democracy, and then he goes on to say that he had been written a letter by a young white girl, "It shouldn't make a difference, but she was a young white girl from White Plains, New York. When I got stabbed," he said, "in Harlem." A whole book has been written about the day Harlem almost killed Dr. King—and Izola Ware Curry, to quote, a "demented black woman," almost ended King's career before it got started. I mean it's like the story of Isaac and Abraham, becoming the inadvertent victim, an unwitting object of death at the hands of one's fathers. King said that he got the letter, and he didn't remember the letter from the governor, or the mayor, or the president, but he remembered this little white girl who had written to him and said, "Dear, Dr. King, I read in the paper that had you sneezed, that you would have drowned in your own blood and died. I'm just here to tell you I'm so glad you didn't sneeze."[11]

King played this off of like any brilliant preacher would. He said, "I don't believe you all hear me." Black people know how to beg against silence as a down payment on an affirmation. So, King uses this story like any great storyteller, any great artist, any great orator, any great rhetorician, any great rapper, and weaves it into his own story, then ends by saying:

> I don't know what will happen now, But I'm not concerned about that now. I just want to do God's will, and he's allowed me to go up to the mountain, and I've looked over, and I've seen the promised land. I may not get there with you, but I want you to know tonight that we as a people will get to the promised land ... I'm not worried about anything. I'm not fearing any man. 'Mine eyes have seen the glory.'

He then turns on his heel and falls into the arms of Jesse Jackson and Ralph Abernathy. Passing the baton, without really understanding it.

Such a rhetorical performance not only signifies the improvisational element of jazz and certain elements of the blues, but also anticipates particular rhetorical gestures that have been greatly amplified within hip hop culture. Implicit in what happens, that last speech, facing death, the consequences of one's own mortality, the parallels between what King is doing here and what happens in other communities where young people like Jay-Z, Nas, Scarface, were deeply depressed—even depressive, in the case of Tupac—are stark and undeniable. This speaks to my argument about the sociological analysis that is implicit even if it may not be as explicit as what we expected, desired, and received from Dr. King. Are not such figures, historic and contemporary, the representatives of religious value within black America to begin with?

Implicit versus explicit is one aspect for further consideration, but undeniable, powerful politics are at work here. Robin Kelley makes an argument for the infrapolitics of James Scott, as every day forms of resistance.[12] To state it more bluntly, people began to assert the legitimacy of their struggle as the means of warehousing something more significant, more divine. Not only that, we must also consider how it's *situational versus apodictic*—it is more than just speaking *ex cathedra* from authority. There is constant and relentless adjustment, revision, hermeneutical play, and interpretive warfare going on, and Jay-Z and hip hop more broadly embody this. It's also situational, in the sense that authority hinges upon arguments to be made within the context of the suffering that exists.

Now, that is a lesson that a lot of other religious people might want to pay attention to. I know it seems all about this big argument between relativism, on the one hand—stuff going all out of control—versus the kind of stability of tradition and truth that are mediated. But what is interesting here is that the situational character of the knowledge that is produced and the suffering that is alluded to is important because you have got to make arguments that make sense within the context of the suffering you are enduring. I see the evidence for this in Jay-Z and his artistic output. So, I would suggest, it is situational in the sense of not just situational ethics, right? But it is also situational in the sense that it pays attention to what the biblical scholars called the *sitz im leben*, the life circumstances and situation that people have to confront, and that these rhetors and these orators, these rappers, these MCs allude to. You have got to make arguments based upon the circumstances and situations of your own given finite context so that the Kantian *a priori*, is acknowledged as the boundary of knowledge, not the critique of pure reason, where you are seeking transcendent norms—transcendental norms that instantiate knowledge and that bind epistemic authority because they limit it in terms of abstract conditions. No, it is within the context of history and contingency itself.

Is this not what we see today when people critique New Age spirituality? Such thinking is a gesture that something like new age religion is not rooted, grounded, or empirical. They assume it is not rich, since there are no means for testing it. They are anxious that something like new age philosophy and practice are coming up with other ways of thinking and being, trying to avoid some of the rules and discipline in the liturgy and the ritual of religion—like a floating signifier that cannot be nailed down, that is simply isolated.

Spiritual or religious?: Jay-Z, and "Nailing Down" the cosmic consciousness of rhetoric

What is interesting about some of these elements of *spiritual versus religious* is that the taxonomical war is waged over an institutional expression of certain impulses versus a kind of impulse that would suggest criticism—not an Archimedean point of objectivity outside of the flow of history, but again, one that comes from within it. In this case, spirituality might make religion behave correctly, as a form of cosmic consciousness—the awareness that, as Martin Luther King, Jr. put it, we are cosmic citizens. My religion, my institution might tell me, "hate gay people" or that "they're problematic and wrong." Women might also be subjugated in such thinking, especially through the prism of patriarchal authority, whether conscious or not. Spirituality may want to challenge that by replying, "Dang, didn't Jesus say within a certain Christian hierarchy that it all came down to loving the Lord God with all my heart, my soul, love thy neighbor as thyself? Wasn't that it? No asterisks? No conditions?" So, what is institutionalized, at the least, has to be challenged by new, fresh developments that are unregulated by extant liturgy and ritual. So, in that sense, we might think about Jay-Z's own refusal to be nailed down to one religion, and to say, "Hey, I want to use religious insight to say a couple things," while also reminding us, in *Decoded*, that religion has been primarily used to separate and control. That is Jay-Z the rapper saying that, not Jay-Z the preacher. It would be hard to argue against the reality that religion has been used toward separation and control, divide and conquer. So, Jay-Z speaks back to this history and reality.

The spiritual versus the religious is not the only interesting dichotomy at work here, but also *eclectic versus dogmatic*, most aptly seen when people say, "See, that's the damn problem with religion," referring to the people who pick and choose what they want and leave the other stuff behind. But don't we all do it this way? This can be seen not only in the war of interpretation waged over the Christian *Bible*, but also, in the *Qur'an*, the *Tao Te Ching*, the *Bhagavad Gita*, and so on. We might even speak about *The Art of Motorcycle Maintenance*. Or Superman. Or Batman. Those are religious texts signifying in interesting ways—especially within the dominant drama of patriotism.

Conclusion: Jay-Z, America, and the precarity of "Contradiction"

In a post-9/11 world, nostalgia for anachronisms, which in turn become forced, interspersed, and interpolated into contemporary narratives, are alive and well. This kind of eclecticism that we war against is no different than those of us who pick and choose this stuff over here, and leave that stuff over there. For instance, I was once at a conference speaking on the topic of the church and popular culture, especially around hip hop, and a young minister got up, and said, "You know,"—referring to some things I said about gays and lesbians in my talk—"Sir, you're talking about that gay stuff, and do we all have to accept gay marriage?" And I replied, "Hey, I get it. It doesn't mean that you're not Christian, I'm Christian, or I'm not Christian, and you are Christian. Although the evidence usually goes that the people against gay marriage think that people who advocate it 'ain't Christian, just 'ain't right." At the end of the day, I think about Obery Hendricks's conception of making the needs of the people sacred, which does not mean you make every desire sacred. It means that you begin to understand the ways in which the fundamental issues of justice have to do with the expressed needs of people, not their desires to contaminate, control, or distort, but their desires to eat, breathe, and think. So, I responded, "No, I'm not saying that—but for me, if I can do some extra biblical analysis—black people need to be the last people in the world trying to talk against anybody getting married in a gay relationship." I continued, "We need our numbers up. So if we got roaches and rats that are somehow related to black people, we should count them, too, in the numbers. In the narrow, patriarchal, nuclear family kind of way." Because that is the logic if we spin it out. I went on to state, "Now that would be problematic for many people, and I agree with that, but what is interesting is if we're going to be serious about interpreting all of reality through a narrow biblical lens, then let's admit ain't no Jheri curls or fried chicken in the Bible either, or Cadillacs or Mercedes. I mean, really? And if Jesus was so obsessed with gay identity, why he ain't never mentioned it?"

So, my point here is that dogmatism has been the enemy of the kerygma, of the teaching, the holy, sacred dimensions of interpreting peoples' lives. So, "eclectic," in that sense, does not have to mean the kind of cafeteria smorgasbord of choosing what I want, and leaving the other stuff behind. It is just that the line through is not about a theological expression of a dogmatic tradition. It is about the assertion of the primacy of love as the organizing logic and principle. Jay-Z certainly talks about the organizing principle of love, not without contradiction, because killing is up in there, too. As Walter McDougall, the University of Pennsylvania professor, suggested in his Pulitzer Prize-winning work *Freedom Just Around the Corner*, hustling is the central motif of American history. There is a relationship between Harlem's founding of money, just as Alexander Hamilton in Harlem founded American money.

When we think about eclectic versus dogmatic, we think about the assertion of the fundamental principles that organize the logic of one's existence. Jay-Z, as a topic, opens up both the contradictions and the conflicts—making the suffering of the poor sacred, focusing on the geopolitics of urban culture, and stressing a powerful urban theodicy. These creative complexities are worthy of serious acknowledgment and a fundamental scholarly and public appreciation. This is not to advise uncritical, total agreement but rather an acknowledgment of and attention to the possibility that hip hop, represented in this case in Jay-Z, is fueled by a deep compassion to make arguments about the vulnerable in an intelligible and publically compelling way.

PART TWO

Hip hop on religion and the "Other"

5

A PARTICULAR PAC:
Ontological ruptures and the posthumous presence of Tupac Shakur

James Braxton Peterson

The response to the 2012 onstage projection of the late hip hop artist Tupac Shakur (Pac), a "hologram" that virtually performs alongside Snoop Dogg, with whom Pac performed while he was alive, has been equal parts technological amazement and profound dis-ease at the eerie reconstruction of Pac's visage.[1] No artist in hip hop culture has been more formative in the hip hop generation's understanding of the concept of an artistic afterlife than Tupac Shakur.[2] Pac's virtual-spiritual presence and posthumous impact on the hip hop generation is both unparalleled and hitherto under-explored. This connection, between the virtual and the spiritual presence of Pac in one sense, and the ways in which that symbiotic presence has a particular impact on hip hop from its most prolific posthumous artist in another, underscores certain ontological realities with respect to how audiences engage Tupac's music in the twenty-first century. This particular phraseology supports claims that I will outline in the following chapter, regarding the posthumous impact of Pac on the hip hop generation and certain "ontological ruptures" that suggest particular ways of engaging with Tupac posthumously. The tension between the virtual and spiritual is taut with critical interpretations of materiality and embodiment, as well as complex approaches to prophecy, posthumous artistic production, and certain religious interfaces with life and death. That is, in the posthumous engagement with Tupac exists a virtual ordering of Pac's "ontological" resurrection, that is representative of both an ontological rupture (of what is commonly and more traditionally understood as ontological) and also expressive of a new ordering of what it means to be human, posthumously, vis-à-vis the virtual.

In this chapter, I define ontological ruptures as those events, texts, lyrics, films, or moments when the ordering of Tupac's existence is called into question. At issue here is how these ruptures inform audience experiences with Tupac's music, particularly the sense of his existence, where these ruptures appear and how they intervene in the processes of experiencing Pac in the twenty-first century. This chapter constructs several close readings of Tupac's posthumous presence in an attempt to explore certain ontological ruptures and explicate the virtual-spiritual nature of his afterlife narratives in the public discourse. Afterlife narratives and public discourse serve as data that demonstrate and draw attention to Tupac's dominance in hip hop lore/culture as a posthumous presence. The virtual-spiritual divide may be viewed as irreconcilable, but it has already been closed in our interactions with Tupac after his death. Thinking of Tupac's posthumous presence in this manner, that is, as functioning across a virtual-spiritual divide, serves several purposes for the claims made in this chapter.

1   While one could argue that Pac is perhaps one of the most cited hip hop artists in hip hop studies and religion, and hip hop in particular, most work places much of its emphasis on Pac's artistic output (while alive), performing textual analyses to the extent that his ontological/embodied dimensions are sometimes ignored, (particularly posthumous analyses).

2   What is more often than not treated as "ontological" in Pac analyses focuses on life events and practices when he was "alive." Thus, talk of "ontology" is regularly understood as that which is "real" and "material" versus that which is not (that is, "virtual")—so, the over-focus on the "material" component usually considers something like holographic projections of artists to exist outside the discourse on Tupac's life and works.

3   The "virtual-spiritual" connection is arguably new and one less considered in the discourse as it troubles flat approaches to what is/is not ontological, material, and "proper" subject matter for the study of religious, theological, and spiritual ideas often caught between a secular/sacred binary and divide.

The bevy of posthumous Tupac productions and the discourses that attend to them suggest that there is a fluid range of ways in which audiences might read Pac, in certain technologically informed, ontological moments. For example, the response to the "Tupac hologram" was in many ways distinct from how audiences consume his posthumously released music or how they experienced the film, *Tupac Resurrection*. Tupac's life, music, and death project a certain "biotech immortality," and his posthumous public persona might be interpreted as a driving force in the processes directed away from traditional notions of death toward a certain set of "bionic interventions," including his recorded prophetic lyricism, televised comedic and conspiratorial narratives regarding his death, and most recently, through what most believe to be holographic imagery on display at the 2012 Coachella Valley Music and Arts Festival. According to James Perkinson (2003), "various strategies of bionic intervention" relegate death to ossified forms of human existence. He goes on to conclude that "in the very turn away from age and mortality, youthfulness has now been fashioned as the new fetish, marketed as the ultimate image of humanity on the rise toward a biotech immortality"[3] Beyond the technological/holographic, lyrics and images such as those found in the song and music video for "Thugz Mansion"; the illegally circulated post-autopsy photo and ensuing discussion over its validity or "realness"; and the now infamous Tupac "hologram," all speak to the ways in which the virtual and the spiritual intersect in the life and afterlife of Tupac Shakur. Focus on the (under-explored) audio and visual narrativity of this set of images, particularly how philosophical notions of ontology inform our understanding of them, presents the visual-spiritual sense of Tupac's exceptional impact on hip hop culture in full view. Taken together, these ontological ruptures and their attendant discourses articulate a complex of virtual-spiritual practices of engagement within hip hop culture in a twenty-first century marked by various technological, "biotechnical," and/or "bionic" interventions.

A virtually illicit autopsy photograph

At a 2007 meeting with representatives from the Tupac Amaru Shakur Foundation (TASF), while reviewing notes and strategic approaches to a collection of works related to Tupac's reading list, we came across an alleged post-autopsy photo of Tupac Shakur.[4] A representative from the foundation responded immediately to the photograph. He was visibly disgusted by it, and he used the opportunity to express how disrespectful the photograph was, both to Tupac's legacy and to the Shakur family. Several issues became clear through the words in his emotionally charged response: (1) The TASF had obviously come across the photo previously, and had more than likely made attempts to have the photograph removed from the internet. (2) The photograph was both unnerving and disturbing to those close to Tupac, and to those most responsible for continuing and developing his legacy through the foundation. (3) The photograph, the alleged imagery of Tupac's lifeless body—post-autopsy—was a direct affront to the ways in which Tupac's posthumous presence in the public sphere had been constructed (and protected) by the TASF. There has always seemingly been an esoteric dimension or quality to Pac's life and afterlife. And this photo, as well as the TASF's response to it, in many ways reflects the gravitas (or mortal seriousness) with which Tupac Shakur's body, the body of his work, and the posthumous release of any imagery or artistry are authenticated and strictly managed.

In "Dead Men Printed ..." an astute analysis of the media/newspaper eulogies of Tupac Shakur and Biggie Smalls, Lindon Barrett argues the following: "The dead body is one thing; the dead black body another. For death is a site obdurately outside all desire and, opposingly, racial blackness a site so fully defined by and within desire it demands regulation. In effect, the dead black body may be an ultimate figure of regulation"[5] Certainly, Tupac Shakur's "dead black body" has always been an "ultimate figure of regulation." Much of this regulation followed Tupac throughout his entire life: as a child of the Black Power Movement/Black Panther Party; as a young black man growing up in various urban American environs; as a rap artist who had continuous run-ins with the criminal justice system; all of which contributed to and is situated in the context of the still unsolved crime that caused his demise. Tupac was murdered as a result of a drive-by shooting on a Las Vegas strip (at the intersection of Flamingo Road and Koval Lane), following a Mike Tyson fight at the MGM Grand Hotel. Imagining a more public murder is nearly implausible, but the conflation of desire (for all things Tupac) with the regulatory forces of his record label, the media, and a law enforcement unit ultimately incapable of (re)solving the crime, presents an unusual conundrum with respect to Pac's posthumous presence in the public sphere. The unsolved status of his murder only serves to mystify the already mysterious circumstances of his death. Consider the comments sections of any of the postings of the alleged post-autopsy photo, and it is apparent that fans and followers of Tupac's life and lyrics take almost any opportunity to engage in conspiracy theory discourses. The approach to the unauthorized post-autopsy photo is to closely analyze barely legible tattoos on his body, and to then argue its inauthenticity based upon an absence or obscuring of Tupac's tattoos. According to Religion Studies scholar (and coeditor of this volume) Monica Miller: "Pac's inked body is figured as expressing the many-ness of his social complications and *existential* angst [my emphasis]."[6] While the validity of the post-autopsy photograph will remain in dispute, the TASF's position on it is absolute. That said, Miller's sense that

Tupac's body and the contestations over and within it reflect an existential angst thematically sutured into his body of music, is an important point in this discussion. For example, in the lyrics to "Trapped," Tupac details the sense of containment that he and many other inner-city black men feel.[7] His existence is delimited by the violence of urban living, including poverty, armed confrontations, and continuous run-ins with the police and the criminal justice system. He is trapped within his socioeconomic environment, and as he tries to navigate that contained environment, he is dogged by police bullying and brutality. Ultimately, he is contained in and trapped by a prison cell. While these forms of external and environmental containment are central to the thesis of "Trapped," one important underlying theme is that he is actually also trapped within his own body. He is a young black man in America, and this existential fact is one that Tupac captures and projects throughout his entire career—both while he was alive and in his artistically unique posthumous presence.

Through all of this confusion and conflation, the question of who or what regulates Tupac's posthumous body remains unsolved and unsettled. The fact that his family decided to cremate his remains—the ultimate act of regulation, especially in the context of such a public murder—again only adds to the discursive possibilities for Tupac's posthumous legacy. But what emerges from these regulated-black-body issues is the TASF itself, and Afeni Shakur's legal triumph over the most valuable aspect of Tupac's legacy—his recorded, unreleased music. In the absence of any possibility for the family (or the foundation) to actually regulate Tupac's physical body, the TASF's work began to focus on controlling and managing all other aspects of Tupac's image, his unreleased recorded material, and any additional film projects—his posthumous body of work, if you will. What the TASF has done exceedingly well since 1996 is that it has regulated the release of Tupac's unrecorded music. One by-product of this posthumous regulation has been some semblance of conventional acceptance and agreement about how the public interfaces with Tupac Shakur's posthumous public presence. Because Tupac was so committed to mortal discourses in and through his music, and because he was so artistically aware of his limited time (in existence) on this earth, channeling spiritual themes through his lyrical content, and through the potent forms of his recorded voice, the sound and sense of his voice became a staple of the public interface with Tupac Shakur, posthumously.

Pac's God consciousness

Tupac articulates a sense of God through his lyrical artistry across several songs and texts, released both when he was alive and after his death. In *Holler if You Hear Me: Searching for Tupac Shakur*, Michael Eric Dyson argues that "Tupac was obsessed with God. His lyrics drip with a sense of the divine. ... he asks God to intervene in his suffering ..., [he] seeks an answer for his existence ..., questions the divine presence ..., pleads for salvation ..., wonders if God's forgiveness is forthcoming ..., [asks] for divine favor and retribution ..., evokes prayer tradition ..., [and] questions the afterlife"[8] In a poem entitled "God," Tupac's poetic narrator claims the following: "When all I saw was sadness/ and I needed answers no one/heard me except ... GOD."[9] Through traditional poetry, Tupac's voice sincerely resonates with his own internal, existential, and ontological questions. Here, his panoramic perspective of black pain and suffering finds some resolution in his personal interface with God. In light of a bevy of lyrics such as "Blasphemy," "Black Jesuz," and "Hail Mary," one could conclude that Tupac's sense of "God" finds its most powerful mooring in the literal and metaphorical connections to the streets, and in the lived urban realities and experiences of young black folks in modern America. Several of the poems collected by Leila Steinberg in *The Rose that Grew from Concrete* have accompanying images sketched by Tupac, and republished to offer a visual complement to Pac's poetic reflections. For his poem "God," the accompanying images are of a sunrise and possibly a sun setting. The landscape of these images is not the urban environs in which Tupac personally witnessed the poverty, pain, and destruction of black life. The image of the sunrise and the sunset, particularly within the context of Tupac's existential and ontological reflections again, suggests his embrace of eschatological themes in his artistic work. These accompanying images also suggest that Pac was looking toward a landscape that signified God from his perspective. This turn to the sun should not be mistaken for some idyllic conceptualization of God's presence in the sun or in pastoral landscapes. Instead, it suggests the conflation of Tupac's existential ruminations with his abiding sense of the confines and containment inherent in the urban environments with which he was so familiar.

Dyson's hearing/reading of Tupac's interface with the divine spiritual nature of God reflects this possibility, but is also suggestive of the divine ways in which Tupac's audience consumed his artistic persona. It makes sense that the body of music recorded and released while he was alive reflects the spiritual thematics through which so many would continue to engage Tupac Shakur after his passing. Dyson references a full catalog of songs/song lyrics that underwrite the spiritual ethos in Tupac's music. It should be noted that there are many songs from Pac's ouevre that might exemplify the spiritual (and prophetic) nature of his work. One song and video also captures some of the rationale behind the consistently popular mythologies about Tupac's post-humous existence—the song and video for 1996s "I Ain't Mad Cha." Reverend Ralph C. Watkins (2003) argues that Tupac was the originator of God-Conscious rap, and that "I Ain't Mad at Cha" was a seminal subject in his discussions with youth in the immediate aftermath of Tupac's passing in 1996.

Watkins (2003) argues that God-conscious rappers, "create a dialogue among the faithful who listen to, and repeat, the rhymes in their daily lives, allowing the lyrics to influence their religious worldview and how they under-stand God."[10] The "faithful" here refers less to those who are observing faith in the Judeo-Christian tradition, and more to those who follow popular artisans, in this case, larger than life hip hop figures—especially Tupac—whose eschato-logical lyrical reflections invite a dogmatic dedication to his existential creeds. Watkins may be too quick in his correlation between religious faith and faithful followers of a rap artist. Yet in the case of Pac, his music, and his posthumous presence, these distinct forms of faithfulness do in some ways collapse into and conflict with each other. This is in part, as Miller (2003) intimates, the theology of an audience's engagement with posthumous Tupac. In *Being and Time*, Heidegger defines theology as confined within faith.[11] For Heidegger, faith obscures the primordial interface with God, and, in some senses, the use of the concept of faith to try and capture the interface between Tupac fans and his posthumous artistic existence is similarly limited. The idea that Pac knew he would die, or that his fans knew that he would die, is less about faith or theology and much more about the tragically mundane knowledge about the all too regular hyper-mortality rates of young black men in Amer-ica. Thus, a more primordial interpretation of Tupac's death would involve an acknowledgment of the social structures implicated in the deaths of too many black men, the unchecked mass incarceration of black and brown youth, the planned underdevelopment and gentrification of certain inner-city/urban com-munities, and the proliferation of drugs and guns in those same communities. When Rev. Watkins' respondents speak of Tupac's "knowing," (quoted below), it is to these structural realities that they are referring, even if only through the conceptualization of the tragedy of Tupac's (at the time) recent death.

That said, the notion of dialogue here is important as well, because the discourse of Tupac's fans—consider the Tupac Shakur archive at Clark Atlanta University that includes letters written to him after his death—establishes certain expectations, epistemologies, and rules that govern and inform the posthumous discourses related to his life (and death). Rev. Watkins' sermon, "A Tribute to a Soldier," delivered September 15, 1996, two days after Tupac's death, elicited a series of discursive interactions between him and members of his congregation. His recounting of these interactions is instructive for understanding how Tupac's audience reflected on the prophetic inclinations of his work:

As we discussed Tupac's music video, I Ain't Mad at Cha, some concluded that Tupac had prophesied his death. 'Tupac,' I was told, 'understood us, he knew what it was like, he knew what was going down, he knew what was coming, he knew they was go' kill him'. In the video, Tupac is shown being shot to death during a drive-by. The video tells the story of Tupac and his friend, to whom he returns, as a type of angel, to help. Among other things, this video asserts that one does not have to be connected to a formal, institutionalized religion to get into heaven. (Watkins, 190).

The video for "I Ain't Mad at Cha" was the last to be made during Tupac's lifetime. And while I agree with Watkins (2003) that the video makes an important assertion about the afterlife, in particular, about the construction of a heaven that is ontologically consistent with Tupac's body of work, my sense is that the song and video accomplish something more than the visual projection of a revised, hip hop vernacular version of heaven. The song and video work together to establish part of the foundational set of practices that informs Tupac's audiences about the ways in which they will interact with and engage his posthumous artistic presence. In his life after death, fans learn from the song and video that Tupac still cares, and that his voice will be audible, both in terms of explicating his own demise and in terms of comforting those who most go on beyond his passing. Although this is the last video that Tupac was able to be a "living" part of, it is not the last music video featuring his music. The timing of its release—essentially in the midst of the shooting and hospitalization that would conclude with his death—created an aura around the eschatological understandings of his work, and particularly his posthumously released work. He speaks to several audiences in the song and video for "I Ain't Mad at Cha," including his homies (read male), his love interest, his mother, and to God. These audiences, both mundane and celestial, cut across the spectrum of Tupac's audience, but also leave the impression that Pac was deliberately trying to address his audience on the particular issues regarding his death, the afterlife, and his posthumous capacity to live in his artistry and comfort listeners through his words. The solemn and compassionate undertones of "I Ain't Mad at Cha," as well as the sense of affective forecasting in the lyrics, depict the song and the video as an audiovisual archetype for Pac's last words—audible and visible—but also arrive at what can only be described as the perfect time, in terms of his ontological transition from life to afterlife, and from superstar rap artist in life to the most popular posthumous artist since Elvis Presley.

Tupac's last words

Tupac rhymed about the last words that he would speak before he actually spoke his last words. In "Last Wordz," a track from his second album, *Strictly 4 My N.I.G.G.A.Z.*, Pac's existential angst takes on a more radical sociopolitical tone. "Last Wordz" is a collaboration with Ice Cube and Ice-T, artists who were both more prominent than Tupac at the time and whose previous work—Ice Cube's verse (and writing) on NWA's classic "Fuck tha Police," and Ice-T's punk rock inflected "Cop Killa"—uniquely positioned them as coauthors of a song that endorses violent self-defense against menacing police forces. Although these antipolice themes are buried in a conflation of hypermasculine, homophobic, and misogynistic lyrics, Pac's last words in the last verse of the song are telling. He calls for peace between black youth and chicano youth, so that there might be peace in California neighborhoods plagued by gang violence. He suggests that peace among black and brown youth would make racists unhappy, and then he poetically makes the case for paying that sentiment forward by teaching other young people the value of unity over internecine violence. But his very last words in "Last Wordz" are about black and brown youth blasting back at the police as a united front.

Ironically, at least to those who live/exist outside of the Tupac-ian universe, a recently retired Las Vegas police officer, Chris Caroll, spoke publicly about Tupac's actual last words at the scene of the drive-by shooting that ultimately ended his life. Here is how Carroll recounted Tupac's last minutes of consciousness:

> He was making eye contact with me here and there, but he's trying to yell at Suge [Knight]. And I kept asking over and over, "Who did this? Who shot you?" And he basically kept ignoring me. And then I saw in his face, in his movements, all of a sudden in the snap of a finger, he changed. And he went from struggling to speak, being noncooperative, to an "I'm at peace" type of thing. Just like that. He went from fighting, to "I can't do it." And when he made that transition, he looked at me, and he's looking right in my eyes. And that's when I looked at him and said one more time, "Who shot you?" "He looked at me and he took a breath to get the words out, and he opened his mouth, and I thought I was actually going to get some cooperation. And then the words came out: 'Fuck you.'" (Jonathan Elderfield 2014).[12]

Tupac's alleged "Fuck you" to one of the officers at the scene of his shooting is a classic/vintage moment from the perspective of his fans. Put this exchange in the context of the song "Last Wordz," the antipolice sentiments of the song, many other lyrics in Tupac's oeuvre and the spiritual idiomatic meanings of the phrase in popular discourse. Then we can begin to understand the kind of existential angst that Tupac's work produced, and the ontological questions that his life, death, and posthumous presence in the public sphere continue to raise, especially among his most ardent fans.

For many, this kind of connection—between Pac's "Last Wordz," and Pac's alleged last words—only contributes to the already healthy discourse around the ontological complexities of Tupac's existence before and after death. There are many other instances of these kinds of canny connections and a full range of artistic moves both before and after his death that contribute to the ontological thickness of Tupac's persona. In "How Long Will They Mourn Me?" Tupac poses a posthumously oriented question based upon his recent experience in mourning the death of a friend/associate in Detroit by the name of Kato. According to Warren G, the coproducer of this record, Kato was murdered over a $2,500 set of Dayton rims.[13] Tupac recorded the song as a member of one of his early rap groups, Thug Life.[14] In his verse, he initially raps about retaliation but resolves the verse by wishing that he had been shot at birth—his response to being "trapped" in the ongoing back and forth violence among young black men, a back and forth which arguably contributed to his own demise. For Pac, violence between young black men threatens the existential order of the black experience. Hence, the acronym for Thug Life—The Hate You Gave Little Infants Fucks Everybody—serves as a rejoinder to the social, political, and economic forces that contribute to inner-city angst, materialism, and absent economic opportunity, all of which (in turn) serve to exacerbate tensions among young black men, who are subject to these forces.

The question of how long we will mourn Tupac remains open, but if the last twenty years are any indication, then we will continue to mourn him ad infinitum. Surely, the efforts of the TASF are to be commended for honoring his legacy at key times perennially and for the promise of new projects, including the long-awaited biopic film and recent stage play, "Holler if You Hear."[15] Both these efforts and the new Tupac texts work to provide opportunities for old and new fans of Tupac's body of work to engage him posthumously and to celebrate his life. This phenomenon, because it emerges in certain spiritually and religiously lyrical contexts, presents several philosophical complications such as oversimplification and the intentional fallacy.[16] As Miller (2013) argues, simple theological approaches "risk flattening the messier uses, functions, and negotiations of Pac's religious troping while overdetermining the intentionality of Pac's quest as religiously and politically transgressive."[17] My claim here is that certain musical texts recorded by Tupac before his death, and some released just after, establish certain ways in which audiences were expected to engage Tupac posthumously. These audio versions of Pac's "bionic interventions" are for the most part plausible and eagerly embraced by Pac fans throughout the long posthumous moment of his artistic presence.

Tupac is still alive

Within the scholarly discourses of philosophy, ontology is a theory of being that "attempts to impose a fundamental order upon everything that is real or existent. It does this by distinguishing between the most general categories of reality that there are."[18] Some of these distinctions include the following: entities or beings, universals—which are features or qualities of things and particulars that include objects and events.[19] Within the rubric of particulars are abstract and concrete objects, the distinction here being between things that exist in time or space versus things that do not.[20] The question of Tupac's ontological status among his audience of fans and dedicated followers emerged poignantly, for me, in 2003, when I was teaching a composition course on writing about Tupac Shakur. The course featured several album reviews, longer journalistic essays on Tupac, texts such as Michael Eric Dyson's *Holler If You Hear Me: Searching for Tupac Shakur*, and several films, including *Thug Angel* and the recently released *Tupac Resurrection: In His Own Words*. Students were engaged with the course materials and excited about taking a composition course that they felt so directly engaged a literary and artistic figure whom they deemed to be relevant to their experiences; Tupac reflected their zeitgeist. They often wrote about other popular figures gone before their time, including Jim Morrison, Kurt Cobain, and others.

When *Tupac Resurrection* debuted nationally, students were assigned to see it. In the class meeting following their viewing of the film, I began to understand the ways in which ontological ruptures—the range of Tupac's lyrical and visual texts that situated his ontological presence as an issue of existential complexity—formulated the substance of our posthumous engagement with him. Students were powerfully moved by the film. We spoke about it in nearly every class meeting that followed our viewing of it in theaters. My sense is that viewing it in public among Tupac's fanbase in the Philadelphia region enhanced our sense of the impact that Tupac had had upon his audience. In our initial discussions of the film, several students were moved to tears. They also spoke about audible emotive expressions of audiences at the film. This affective response to the film filtered into our class discussions, mostly as a result of one particularly ontological phenomenon present throughout the film: the fact that the film is astutely narrated by Tupac himself. It is "in his own words." Students wondered about how the narration was possible. How could Tupac narrate a film that did not exist until after his death? How could he portend the sense and sensibility of his autobiographical narrative, either from the grave or in some ongoing prescient sense of his life and death when he was alive?

Tupac's assumption of the rap moniker, "Makaveli," signifying on the historical political tactician, Niccolo Machiavelli, helped to cultivate rumors and other discourses centered on the possibilities that Tupac had faked his own death, and that he was still alive and living an undercover hidden existence in Cuba.[21] The first appearance of Tupac as Makaveli is on his first posthumously released album, *The Don Killuminati: The 7 Day Theory*. The album was released just two months after his death. The album's title, and especially its cover art, featuring an image of a crucified Tupac/Makaveli, immediately raised a slate of eschatological questions with respect to the artist's death and afterlife. Fans and spectators quickly devised "alive theories," and the discourse surrounding the album centered on spiritually inflected songs such as "Hail Mary," and "Blasphemy." "Tupac lived death," according to Ebony Utley, who goes onto argue that: "Life after death is psychologically empowering because resurrection communicates invincibility. Audiences need to believe that Tupac conquered death in order to accept their own potential for greatness."[22] Although I am not convinced that eschatological debates about Tupac's afterlife or the ontological questions about his posthumous presence translate into self-esteem or "psychological empowerment," even for his most ardent fans, the complex nature of Tupac's life and death, the confusion and the conflation of his artistic body of work with his actual body both (when he was alive and after his death), all speak to the philosophical issues ingrained in Tupac's existence in this world and beyond it.

There was no greater cinematic argument for what Utley refers to as "alive theories" then this particular film, released in 2003. *Tupac Resurrection* is arguably the most profound "bionic intervention" made by the posthumous artistic productions of Tupac Shakur that contributes directly to Pac's "biotech immortality." Even if we account for the editorial wizardry involved in the production of the film, and the countless interviews that Tupac gave to the media in the midst of his meteoric rise to superstardom, the film is an ontological feat that contributes directly to the ethos that informs Tupac's posthumous mythos. Still, it is but one text among so many others, a few of which are referenced in this chapter, that work to articulate the complex set of ways in which we engage Pac's posthumous presence/existence.

These ontological ruptures, or these textured narratives that rupture the ontological order of Tupac's existence in life and in death, take many shapes and forms and have continued to proliferate beyond the lyrics recorded during his life that initiated these processes. In a skit entitled "Tupac is Still Alive," from the first episode of season three of *The Chappelle Show*, comedian Dave Chappelle captures the humorous aspects of the ontological questions raised by the life and artistic works of Tupac Shakur.[23] In the skit, Chappelle plays himself, dancing in a nightclub. The DJ, played by Questlove of The Roots, announces that a new Tupac song is being played. The song, written and recorded by Dave Chappelle, "I Wrote this Song a Long Time Ago," gives his audiences another example of his fantastic skill as an impressionist. Yet his impression of Tupac rests more on the lyrical content of the song and certain stock tonal forms that mimic Tupac's delivery. He sounds like Tupac in some ways, and does not sound like Tupac in others. But the joke of the skit hinges on the unfolding prophetic nature of the lyrics. In the opening verse,

Tupac (or rather Chappelle rapping as Tupac) mentions Skytel and Blackberry pagers, global technology brands that existed before Tupac's demise, but particularly in the case of Blackberry, did not come into popular tech vogue until the late 1990s. But in the very next lines he references a videogame character, CJ, from the *Grand Theft Auto* series created and released by Rockstar Games in 2004. The people on the dance floor do not really notice the chronological anomaly, but Chappelle does. He initially looks confused, but then he is comforted by the refrain following the first verse, reassuring him that Tupac wrote the song a long time ago.

In the second verse, Tupac (again, Chapelle rapping as Pac) alludes to people voting for George W., and he refers to him as a snitch. Clearly, Tupac was not alive when George W. Bush was elected President of the United States. This anachronistic reference raises questions for most of the people on the dance floor, but the lyrics of the song shift just as the crowd's suspicions reach disbelief. Chappelle-as-Tupac then claims that he is referring to a George W. Smith, who ran for the Oakland City Council in 1993. The refrain following this verse begins by reassuring the audience again, but then quickly moves to referencing Eminem, an artist deeply influenced by Tupac, but who only emerged onto the popular music scene in 1996 with his first album. The Eminem reference is questionable, as he was not really well-known until the release of his second album, *The Slim Shady LP*, in 1999. If listeners within the comedic story world of *The Chappelle Show* or audience viewers of the episode are confused, Chappelle-as-Tupac confounds the situation further by referencing the war in Afghanistan. In this verse-refrain combination, the lyrics to "I wrote this Song a Long Time Ago" do not provide a response or rejoinder to the anachronisms. In fact, unlike the first iteration of the refrain, the second iteration features yet another anachronistic reference.

The final verse of "I Wrote this Song a Long Time Ago" operates from the focal point of the dance floor of the nightclub itself. First, Chappelle-as-Tupac jokingly lashes out at random people on the dance floor, commenting on the clothing and the movements of various people in the club. But eventually, the lyrics turn to Chappelle himself, naming him and marking his interactions in real time. In this last verse, Chappelle-as-Tupac calls out Dave Chappelle as he is on the dance floor dancing with someone who is not his wife. When Chappelle moves and tries, essentially, to switch partners, Chappelle-as-Tupac calls him out again. The skit ends as Chappelle leaves the club and the DJ gives a shout-out to Tupac. "Tupac is Still Alive" contributes to the same set of ritualistic cultural practices initiated by the song and video for "I Ain't Mad at Cha," in the sense that it constructs a microcosmic audiovisual text, inflected by the ethos of the audience's interface with posthumous Tupac, and reflective of the "biotech immortality" that results from the ongoing series of ontological ruptures produced through Tupac's life and artistry.

The lyrics of "I Wrote this Song a Long Time Ago" and the comedic trajectory of the "Tupac is Still Alive" skit move from the global to the national, to the local, to the individual level, ultimately pointing a posthumous finger at Dave Chappelle himself. This funneling effect codifies interactive experiences with Tupac's artistry in the long moment of his audience's posthumous interface with him. His prophetic and prescient sensibility about the national trajectory of the United States are on full display in too many of his lyrics to list here, but consider, as an example, his lyrics about America's unreadiness for a Black president that have been sampled by Nas and others, in their own tributes to President Barack Obama. His impression of the prison system, his experiences with police brutality and harassment, and the fact that he talked about these issues in nearly all of the music that he recorded produce a sense of timeless connection to the experiences of young black men in America. Sadly, that timelessness reflects the structural permanence of state-sanctioned regulation of black male bodies in public spaces as much as it does Tupac's experiences with physical surveillance, regulation, and incarceration. But the sense that Tupac is talking to YOU—the idea that, somehow, he is connecting to your specific set of experiences, that he is aware of the affective possibilities related to your particular experiences, generates the discursive terrain upon which the public's posthumous engagement with Tupac Shakur can be determined and rule-governed.

Virtual-spiritual immortality

Tupac's "biotech immortality" has, in the brief time since his death, been constructed mostly through his body of work as a rapper and actor. His appearances in film, music videos, and his recorded lyrics, released during and after his death, have, in various ways and means, contributed to the public's sense of his prescient embrace of his own artistic destiny. And to the extent that his lyrics or visual forays expand the narratives regarding his ability to effectively forecast the collective moods of the hip hop generational youth, certain rules and expectations have been established, in terms of how audiences interface with Tupac posthumously.[24] The form of this interface—the texts that contribute to the construction of Tupac's "biotech immortality"—have, for the most part, been mediated by certain types of multimedia platforms: music, film, television, and/or music video. In short, there are formal expectations for how audiences think about interacting with Tupac's posthumous artistic presence.

Given the range of ways in which Tupac's posthumous artistic presence has been available for engagement—haunting music and music videos, prescient lyrics that foreshadow his own death, posthumous films and documentaries featuring his voice speaking in the moment, and comedic treatments of these phenomena—the emergence of the Tupac hologram at the Coachella festival in 2012 should have been yet another "bionic intervention" in the ontological process of establishing Pac's "biotech immortality." But it was not. As many have reported, the audiences at Coachella felt more dis-ease than surprise or elation.[25] One possible explanation for the audiences discomfort in seeing and experiencing the Tupac "hologram" was that it did not fit the mold of the established ways that audiences interfaced with Tupac's artistry posthumously. The immediacy of the Coachella experience presents a radically distinct form of engagement with Tupac's posthumous artistic presence and, as such, some members of that audience were ill prepared to consume his posthumous presence in a manner so divergent from earlier engagements.

Note also that the Tupac "hologram" was not a hologram. According to David Thier: "Tupac walked the stage with a technique called Pepper's Ghost, which dates back to the sixteenth century. Basically, the trick requires two rooms, a main room (in this case, a stage) and an adjacent hidden room. In the main room, there's an angled piece of glass that reflects an image from the hidden room so that it appears like it's actually there. A professor named John Pepper used the technique on stage in the mid-nineteenth century, and it's now known by his name."[26] Much of the media attention was directed at correcting the public's misnaming of the technology used to construct Tupac's visage at Coachella in 2012, and opts not to mention the irony inherent in the naming of the technology in use for the conference. The Tupac "hologram" may be more aptly named Tupac's "Ghost" given the scientific context within which the technology was originally described, defined, and named. And, in fact, given the reported responses of those in attendance, and of many who watched video footage of the performance, Tupac's "Ghost" might be a more meaningful moniker for the technology with respect to how folks responded to it.

From Tupac's "Last Wordz" to Tupac's "Ghost" at Coachella, the ontological order of Pac's existence from the perspective of his fans has almost always been in flux. The boundaries between/among the philosophical particulars of Pac's existence have been muddled by the series of ontological ruptures and "bionic interventions" that continue to construct and reconstruct his "biotech immortality." For example, Tupac is a particular person, a philosophical "object" that can and should be distinguished from certain philosophical "events," for example, the day that Tupac died. Objects and events are different types of philosophical particulars, but in the case of Tupac's "Ghost" at Coachella, these philosophical distinctions are subject to collapse. Consider the distinctions between abstract and concrete objects—the ontological debates on Tupac's death and the deliberate construction of his "biotech immortality" work against these distinctions, subjecting them to a particular way, a virtual-spiritual way of engaging Tupac posthumously. Some of the established ways that audiences have engaged Tupac's postmortem have revealed certain practices for these posthumous interfaces. Only a few have been glossed and detailed here, but they all suggest that the ontological rupture in engagements with Tupac's artistry in the afterlife of his career may not actually be rupturing anything at all. In fact, ontological ruptures are the normative mode of engagement with Tupac's artistry both in his life and in the broad swath of his posthumous artistic presence in the public sphere.

6

#NOWTHATSRELIGIONAND HIPHOP: Mapping the terrain of religion and hip hop in cyberspace

Elonda Clay

Although much research has been conducted on the early adoption of information communication technologies by hip hop practitioners, music producers, and artists, the discussion of religion and hip hop in cyberspace has been understudied in both the academic study of religion as well as internet/hip hop studies.[1] This chapter sets out to bring current trends in studies on religion and the Internet to bear on relationships between hip hop cultural productions, new media practices, and in particular, the category of religion. Specifically, I argue for the need and present inchoate points of attention toward the development of a critical approach to studies on religion and/in hip hop online.

I begin by offering several screenshots of how religion and hip hop are appropriated and represented online and identify four representative types of digital content creators for religion and hip hop. I then move to introduce what it means to methodologically take a "critical" approach to the category of religion, drawing insights from Monica R. Miller's book, *Religion and Hip Hop* (2012/13), as a helpful lens to explore a rubric for analyzing religion in/and hip hop online. The last section of this chapter analyzes three case studies: (1) "hip hop as religion" debates on YouTube, (2) shifts and renegotiations of authority as expressed in such religion and hip hop data online, and (3) the role of news media in the construction of a popular hip hop religion referred to as "Yeezianity." Throughout, I suggest that themes of virtual authority, authenticity, and identity formation have potential significance for a critical approach to the study of religion in/and hip hop online.

Religion in hip hop on the internet: Stakeholders and sources

As creators and producers of digital religious content, hip hop enthusiasts or "heads" engage in a variety of activities across different website types and genres. These activities include: imaging religious practices as part of their strategies of self (re)presentation on personal homepages, YouTube, and social media, writing religious apologetics within the comments section of online hip hop articles, participating in online discussion forums (both faith-related and fan-based), downloading religious hip hop music, creating online memorials for deceased rap artists, maintaining blogs, as well as the more common practices of posting user-generated music videos under a particular screen-name.

Hip hop practitioners are not alone in producing online content that highlights the dizzy world of religion in/and hip hop. For example, large record labels such as Universal Music, Def Jam, and Sony BMG, media conglomerates such as Viacom and Turner Broadcasting, and even Christian movie producers (remember the 2013 movie, *I'm In Love with a Church Girl*, with Jeff "Ja Rule" Atkins) are powerful stakeholders in crafting how religion in hip hop is presented online. My research suggests four representative distinct producers of digital content: (1) user-generated content (UGC) which represents content internet users create; (2) entertainment conglomerates (music, film, cable television) as represented by spaces such as Sony Music, Viacom, etc.; (3) mainstream or commercial media, such as ABC, NBC, Huffington Post, New York Times, MSNBC; and lastly (4) alternative media, such as Mother Jones, The Final Call (NOI), and Racialicious. These four sources of digital content, in all of their similarities and differences, are together vital to understand in order to assess what strategies, social effects, and frames of reference are highlighted or repressed by different social actors and groups in the construction and maintenance of religion in hip hop in various online constituencies. But, before content can undergo any serious analyses, we must first have in place, a methodological framework and approach. Here, I argue for the application of the emerging paradigm of "critical approaches to the study of religion" for religion in hip hop studies.

A new approach: Getting "Critical" with religion in/and hip hop scholarship

Critical approaches to the academic study of religion are quickly becoming a new paradigm among scholars of religion, who, through their use of methodological and theoretical approaches, have come to interrogate the category of religion as it comes to bear on popular cultural data. The "critical" challenge posed to the study of religion in hip hop studies concerns the complexities in defining religion more generally. Some critical scholars of religion have argued that there is no such thing as "religion" outside of scholarly constructions.[2] The approach advocated for in this chapter builds on the work of Miller, who uses critical approaches to examine the knowledge and cultural productions of religion in hip hop culture.[3] Grounding her argument within a representative typology of academic trends within religion and hip hop scholarship, Miller proposes three approaches to investigating hip hop culture: (1) the black church and the Spirit of Market Maintenance, (2) the Rapper as (Christian) prophet, and (3) hip hop as a quest for meaning.

The "market maintenance," model (which I suggest is quite evidenced in much of current trends in religion in hip hop online today) considers how the institutional appropriation (or co-opting) of hip hop into faith-based practices and ecclesiological confines works to reproduce religiously informed othering processes, which often deploys discourses of cultural depravity and social pathology about hip hop culture in order to emphasize distinctions between "the church" and "the streets." The "prophet" type engages religious—mostly Christian, and sometimes Islamic—rhetoric and religious visual culture to animate humanity's transgressive and/or transformative social and political potential. Lastly, the "quest for meaning" variety of hip hop scholarship is characterized by the interiorization of religion as inner feeling.

The value of Miller's method for the development of a critical approach to religion and hip hop online is in its dual action of challenging *sui generis* perspectives on religion that search for the essence or presence of religion in hip hop while at the same time expanding scholars' toolkits for "engaging in theoretical and materialist interventions of cultural products."[4] This opens up opportunities to "rethink" religion and hip hop in cyberspace in three ways: (1) It encourages scholars to pay more attention to how religious language is taken up by various and contesting hip hop-identified Internet users: maintenance and/or contestation processes.[5] (2) It allows researchers to interrogate the multiple ways discursive, information, and representation practices and processes coalesce with uses of religious rhetorics in and through online hip hop communities and media. (3) And lastly, it allows for the participation in ongoing critical conversation in studies of digital religion and in internet studies.

Authority, authenticity, and religion in hip hop on YouTube

YouTube is a video-sharing website that is viewed by an estimated two billion individuals daily. Among user-generated content on YouTube, four oscillating portrayals of religion and hip hop were discovered: (1) institutionalized religion as rival to hip hop, (2) hip hop as a new religion/authentic alternative to religion, (3) rapper as real prophet, and (4) rapper as false prophet.

For example, YouTube user TDGvideos (True Disciple of God)[6] describes himself as "an international artist who has been a light shining in the darkness of the music industry."[7] TDG has created a series of eight videos under the title "HIP HOP IS A RELIGION SERIES" that feature interview clips from rap artists, such as Lil' Wayne, Jay-Z, and others. The "HIP HOP IS A RELIGION SERIES" claims not only that hip hop culture is a religion but also that it is a religion that leads youth, artists, and members of traditional religions to be unknowingly associated with the devil, evil, and bad/false religion. Hip hop culture is 'exposed' in the "HIP HOP IS A RELIGION SERIES" as a powerful vehicle to reintroduce the Faustian bargain, as artists are encouraged to sell their soul to the devil for fame and profit, while hip hop listeners inadvertently receive lessons from the occult through hip hop music. The teachings of the Five-Percent Nation,[8] particularly the teaching of "knowledge of Self as Gods," are labeled by YouTube user TDGvideos as satanic, although TDG does not claim that popular hip hop music artists themselves are satanic.[9]

In relation to Miller's typology, the "Hip Hop is a Religion" debate being played out on TDGvideos often conflates hip hop with religion, even as some representations reverse the rapper as (Christian) prophet, to re-represent rappers as false prophets. This is particularly the case when the content creators themselves are Christianity-affiliated males. Representations of females and white males are starkly absent from the TDG Video series, which focuses its attention on creating or reiterating negative stereotypes of popular black male rappers. Examining such uses of and on the internet as a tool in the self-fashioning of religious or spiritual identities and shifting conceptions of authority in online contexts calls for additional methodologies in examining the rising production of user-generated content present on YouTube today.[10]

In the next section, the hip hop is a religion debate is taken up on a different scale with another set of religious stakeholders when we turn to examine what has been called a new hip hop online religion: Yeezianity.

"Yeezianity": Media market maintenance or online humanism?

The establishment of the Yeezianity.com website and the flurry of media attention directed at Yeezianity presents an intriguing final case study for a critical approach to religion and hip hop in cyberspace.[11] Here, my focus is on the maintenance and/or contestation processes surrounding Yeezianity in online media and the presentation of "self" online by Brian Liebman and Ye'ciples or initiated members themselves.

In mid-January 2014, news of Yeezianity or The Church of Yeezus, flooded mainstream and religious media news outlets.[12] Kanye West, and his critically acclaimed 2013 album, *Yeezus*, sparked its own controversial responses, and received substantial backlash.[13] West's song "I am a God" could certainly also have served as a spark of inspiration for Yeezianity.[14] In a 2013 interview with BBC Radio 1, West explained:

> When someone comes up and says something like, "I am a god," everybody says, "Who does he think he is?" I just told you who I thought I was. A god. I just told you, that's what I think I am. Would it have been better if I had a song called "I am a n*gga?"[15]

While Yeezianity makes use of all things Kanye—his image, rap lyrics, interviews, and public statements—it is not a group founded by rapper Kanye West himself. Instead, Yeezianity, much like the creation of The Source magazine, was founded by a twenty-three-year-old white male college student from the suburbs of upstate New York.[16]

Yeezianity in online news media

Yeezianity was immediately labeled a new Kanye West religion among many online media outlets, as news coverage of Yeezianity and its briefly anonymous founder, Liebman, was featured in Time.com,[17] huffingtonpost.com,[18] and bet. com.[19] The news articles generated labels for Yeezianity, ranging from budding celebrity cult, to outlandish hoax. Religious-oriented news sources, such as

Christian Post refueled fears and moral panics concerning both new religious movements and hip hop culture.

By examining both the initial wave of news stories covering Yeezianity, familiar patterns of journalists' use of religious language and bias are uncovered. One popular portrayal of Yeezianity in the media is the religious rival/competitor frame. The *Christian Post* quickly manufactured a 'Yeezianity versus Christianity' conflict by highlighting Liebman's comment that Kanye West is a "stepping stone" to Jesus.[20] ChristianPost.com ran three stories on Yeezianity in the month of January 2014. Yeezianity went from being described as a "new religion" and "movement and website,"[21] to being called a "cult movement" that began on social media.[22] In the final article on this site, Liebman was asked to "clarify" misunderstandings about Yeezianity, and "justify" his motives for starting a new religion after a celebrity.

Another portrayal of Yeezianity in online media connected Yeezianity to hubris oriented humanist philosophy (some, vis-à-vis self-deification) more than to any substantive effort to create a religion centered on Kanye West or his music. Journalist Peter Weber from *The Week* concluded that, "Yeezianity still isn't about the worship of Kanye West, or even really a religion. It's a form of humanism."[23] It is this integration of religion and humanism that will be of interest as we analyze Yeezianity's own online presentation and digital performance.

Presentation of the virtual self—Yeezianity and Ye'ciples online identity construction

The construction and performance of online identity has been an ongoing topic for researchers.[24] Sociologist Ervin Goffman's work on self-presentation as "impression management"[25] and feminist theorist Judith Butler's definition of performative identity[26] provide useful theoretical frameworks for studying how individuals and organizations intentionally reinvent, reveal, negotiate, and manipulate information about their identities in virtual spaces. Goffman has described performance as "all the activity of a given participant on a given occasion which serves to influence in any way any of the other participants."[27] Performative identity, on the other hand, is based on the claim that identities are discursively constructed and that people act both consciously and unconsciously in the social roles they have learned over time; actions which often conform to hegemonic discourses and reproduce unequal power relations.[28] With both performance and performative identity, identities are continually reimagined and (re) presented in relation to their various audiences and embedded contexts.

The self-representation of Yeezianity differs considerably from media portrayals of the group and its statements. Unlike mainstream media outlets, the Yeezianity.com website does not state that its goal is to compete with Christianity, instead, Yeezianity encourages multiple belonging:

> We are called Ye'ciples. Our membership is entirely open and non-exclusive. We allow a Ye'ciple to be a member of Yeezianity as well as any other spiritual practice of their choosing including some of the best ones: Christianity, Buddhism, Islam and Taosim. In fact, we encourage Ye'ciples to explore and consider the tenets of any other spiritual ideas they feel attracted to.[29]

Yeezianity's dogma and declaration of faith are more aligned with humanist ideals of the human right to creativity, critical thinking, controlling one's own destiny, and ending oppression than with any specific religious tradition or practice.[30] Joining the group is simple: initiates must take a photo of themselves with the phrase "I Believe in Yeezus" and post it to their social media accounts.[31]

The playful consumption of Christianity demonstrated in the subversive reversal of norms that shift recognizable Christian ideas and symbols from the divine figure of Jesus to a messianic human rapper named Yeezus suggests that play is an important performative strategy for Yeezianity.[32] Performance theorist Richard Schechner proposes that there are two kinds of play: "make believe" and "make belief."[33] The degree to which Liebman or Ye'ciples actually believe their online performances is not my concern here, however, members' external displays of pretend or enacted belief in Yeezus did have the real social effect of being subjected to the interpretive frames of "cult movement" and "religious competitor" by journalists and certain religious media audiences.

So, what is Yeezianity, then?

The dissonance of representations between self-presentations and online news media portrayals of Yeezianity makes categorizing this phenomenon a difficult task. While debates regarding what is/isn't religious or authentic about such cultural constructions continue to proliferate, I want to suggest that play (both "make believe" and "make belief") and humanism are viable lenses for rethinking the uses of religious imagery, language, & dogma within Yeezianity. As Miller and I have argued separately,[34] play can be a serious activity within hip hop culture, and it provides clues to the complex flexibility at work in religion in hip hop culture. I have also suggested elsewhere that enthusiasts of hip hop culture, "in addition to being interpretive consumers, users, and appropriators of new technologies, 'play around with' or 'play along with' the religious through digital performance and emergent authorship."[35] As a group, Ye'ciples have found a place in digital space, what Hoover and Echchaibi describe as a "third space," and achieved online community.[36] They represent internet users who are willing to discuss and explore Yeezianity as well as demonstrate creative ways that Kanye West's cultural products can be materially interpreted, practiced, and applied.

The humanist dimensions of religion in hip hop have and continue to be understudied. Pinn's essay, "Handlin' My Business: Exploring Rap's Humanist Sensibilities in Noise and Spirit," is among the first scholarly contributions to identify the humanist sensibilities and assertions found within the lyrics of rap music. In this essay, Pinn examined the lyrical content of three rappers Speech (Arrested Development), Scarface, and 2Pac, and proposed four themes within hip hop's humanist sensibilities: (1) expresses a critical view toward religion, (2) raises existential questions, (3) proposes solutions to human struggles without reliance on a doctrine of God and, lastly (4) communicates an appreciation for "human-centered accountability, responsibility, and opportunity."[37] These four themes are helpful in examining Yeezianity, which employs multimedia in addition to rap lyrics in order to convey humanist principles. The selection of Kanye West's alter ego Yeezus as a discursive funnel or jump-off point to discuss a variety of other topics is also telling, as Yeezianity's human-centered black Jesus replaces the traditional transcendent and racially white depictions of Jesus and God.[38]

The self-presentation strategies of Yeezianity focus on multiple belonging, humanist principles valuing creativity, religious and racial/ethnic diversity, and play. These strategies, when combined with the modes of participation, online platforms, and forms of digital literacies, demonstrated in Ye'ciples digital media performances (including blogging, texting, Facebook, Twitter, YouTube, music, websites, and online community) come together to encourage shifting between humanist and religious rhetorical domains; resulting in a type of sampling from both humanist and religious performances for the purposes of constructing online identities.[39] One thing is for sure—they are technological social experiments that have caught our attention in insurmountable ways.

Studying religion in hip hop in cyberspace: New times, new methods

Critical approaches to religion and hip hop in cyberspace would benefit from engaging the large body of work that has already been done on studies of religion on the Internet, as well as Internet studies and game studies. In bringing critical approaches to "Religion and Hip Hop" in conversation with themes from digital religion and internet studies, several realities about the Internet and the category of religion come to the fore.

First, the category of religion, in studies of religion and cyberspace, is often left un-interrogated or under-explored through a hyper-focus on the places and spaces that house topics of religion. Another future direction for critical approaches to religion and hip hop in cyberspace is a more detailed exploration of virtual communities and online humanism. Finally, difference (for example, race, class, sex and gender, nationality, disability, sexual orientation, religious affiliation) makes a difference in religion and cyberspace. Yet studies of religion and cyberspace have rarely addressed racial/ethnic biases in their own research choices or in online/offline religious community interactions. Interrogating racial and other impacts of identity is an important component to developing any critical approach for analyzing religion and hip hop on the internet.

This chapter aimed to initiate a fruitful conversation between trends in studies in religion and cyberspace and critical approaches to the study of hip hop and religion. Using typologies from Miller (2013), this chapter examined how "the religious" within and about hip hop culture is strategically utilized by various digital content creators (internet users, traditional media, alternative media, and media conglomerates) in order to enhance their authority, authenticity, or to perform and maintain identities on the Internet. It is my hope that such a conclusion will not be the end, but a beginning, to a critical approach to the study of religion and hip hop online.

7

Mapping space and place in the analysis of hip hop and religion: Houston as an example

Maco L. Faniel

Historically and currently, hip hop culture is just as local as it is global, just as regional as it is national, just as "Houston" as it is "New York City." Despite the widespread global appeal that hip hop, in all of its variations, enjoys today, the larger purview often overshadows its local roots. Hip hop is too complex to be relegated to static either/or (i.e., local vs. global) binaries; methodologically, then, mapping hip hop's local contexts provides a glimpse into its global appeal and says something about how hip hoppers construct meaning from local spaces and places during particular historical moments. This approach asserts that geographic and historical location partially shapes individuation (personal and professional) and the living and performance of hip hop culture. I will use Anthony Pinn's theory of religion—in particular, his notion of *complex subjectivity*:

> Basic structure, embedded in history, is a general quest for complex subjectivity, in the face of terror and dread associated with life within a historical context marked by dehumanization, objectification, abuse, intolerance, and captured most forcefully in the sign/symbol of the ghetto.[1]

I argue that questions about the role of religion in hip hop must also interrogate the intersection of space, place, and time as significant domains of hip hop cultural practices.

To be clear, my analysis is suggestive rather than assertive. I approach this work as a historian interested in how those who lived, performed, and embraced hip hop culture in Houston, Texas, during the late twentieth and early twenty-first centuries (roughly 1983–2008) strived to become complex subjects. To accomplish this mapping of how Houston hip hoppers constructed meaning from their local realities, I begin by charting spatial realities of Houston between 1983 and 2008 that helped to shape its particular brand of hip hop culture.

Hip hoppers, space, place, and time

By the term "hip hopper," I am referring to those responsible for creating the cultural artifacts—beat makers, rappers, singers, DJs, taggers, dancers, and even custom car designers—a participant of the culture/generation, or even a consumer. Beyond the obvious artwork, namely the music, that comes out of hip hop other artifacts and activities, "are significant with respect to the study of religion in that they express 'some aspects of that which concerns us ultimately, in and through their aesthetic form.'"[2] More narrowly though, my use of the term hip hopper refers to material bodies that are at the same time socially constructed—named, defined, racialized, spatialized, politicized, gendered, criminalized, and arranged.[3] Because these bodies navigate the power dynamics of where they are located, this essay explicitly insists that investigations of hip hop must be grounded "in appropriate geographic contexts "—space and place.[4] By space, I mean abstract geographic locations that become real through human conception, perception, experience, arrangement, and occupation. Places are particular forms of space; more pointedly though, places fill up space.[5] Places are "distinctive and *bounded*" locations that are constructed by or perceived of by humans.[6] Places take on material forms like landforms, nations, states, cities, regions, neighborhoods, streets, buildings, home, etc. that are interpreted, narrated, perceived, felt, understood, and imagined.[7] Lastly, by time, I am referring to chronological sequences—past, present, future.

My analysis is specifically focused on black male hip hoppers, not only because they dominated the performance of Houston's hip hop culture but also because the culture, as Rashad Shabazz advances, "was built on an 'uneven' gendered geography," virtually excluding women.[8] The performance of hip hop by these bodies in this space, place, and time strived to, at times, move away from or to alternately become what it meant to be black and male in Houston.

The local of hip hop and spatial differentiation

My analysis continues the work of scholars and journalists like Murray Forman, who, in recent years, theorized hip hop's geocentric contexts.[9] I submit that hip hop, particularly rap music, is local in at least four distinct ways: (1) Rappers often talk about the experiences of their local space, informing outsiders of what life is like for them and their comrades. (2) The music production teams, particularly in hip hop's first thirty or so years as a consumable art form, is typically comprised of a close-knit group of local instrumentalists, engineers, and producers, who craft sounds germane to local tastes and local music history. (3) Rappers often earn their stripes in their local spaces before gaining national/international acclaim, because local legitimacy confirms one's right to represent and speak on black cultural practices vis-à-vis the hood. (4) Lastly, hip hopper's form their identities and represent their identities based on local realities.[10]

Analyzing the spatial and identity dynamics in Houston rapper Scarface's classic song "On My Block,"[11] Forman suggests that space and place play a weighty role in identity formation.[12] Forman estimates that the confluence of space (and place) and identity is somewhat cyclical, because as space (and place) helps to shape identity, hip hoppers shape their spaces and places. Rap frequently talks about the dark realities or ways of maintaining and navigating life in American ghettoes, but much of the content is a narrativization of everyday local experiences: how local bodies navigate systems of power. To be clear, although all ghettoes are characterized by stigma, constraint, territorial confinement, and institutional encasement, the codes of each ghetto are different, the built environment of each ghetto is different, the language in each ghetto is different, and the history of each ghetto is different. Thus, the black life in one hood is experienced differently than black life in other hoods, due, in part, to "the closed contours that the 'hood represents ... [whose] inward-turning spatial perspectives inhibit[s] dialogue across divided social territories and cultural zones."[13]

In 2008's "You're Everything," a song expressing topophilia for "the south," Bun B insists that his place of birth and location for living and working "made [him] the G ..., the hustler ..., the grinder, the baller, the gangster [he is] today."[14] Detailing a few distinctive features of Houston's hip hop culture—car culture, style of clothing, and drugging habits—Bun's love of place seems to derive from this distinctiveness. As another example, Houston rapper Lil Keke, who came of age in the early 1990s in one of Houston's south side ghettoes, comments: "What we was doin', whether you believe it or not, wasn't about Houston, it wasn't about the north side, it wasn't about the east, it was really about these six or seven neighborhoods."[15]

"Find Texas and See Where Houston At, Its On The Borderline Of Hard Times": Mapping Houston's spatial realities

[handwritten margin note: Geto Boys]

The Geto Boys' 1996 song "The World Is A Ghetto" is an appropriate discursive to understand how black bodies in Houston's ghettoes mapped their city.[16] "The World is a Ghetto" is a remake of a song originally recorded in 1972 by the soul/funk band War.[17] The rap version expressed the dispositions of a generation feeling the pain of deferred dreams and abandonment. *[handwritten margin note: a Remake of a funk bands song]*

The opening chorus of "The World Is A Ghetto"—"What we see everyday / Livin' in the ghetto this is where I stay/what we do to get by/Live or die, the world is a ghetto"—illuminates the sentiments and observations of bodies in Houston's ghettoes—spaces of stigma, constraint, territorial confinement, and institutional encasement—who do what it takes to make it in the face of everything that threatens nonexistence.[18] The chorus insists that the entire world, or the world as ghetto citizens perceive it, is structured like the ghetto. "Each rapper [then] offers his take on the ... injustice[s] pervading city life, [with a specific focus on Houston] circa 1996." Music journalist Pete T. reasoned that "for those removed [the ghetto], this song might serve as a painful eye-opener." But the song was also "a long-overdue cry for help," from those who were familiar with the realities. Their lyrical analysis points to systems of power in which "the destitute are hopelessly oppressed by poverty and the powerful are apathetic."[19] The chorus and verses by Scarface, Bushwick Bill, and Willie D hint at the sentiments of those in Houston's ghettoes. They knew that things in other parts of the world were bad, but as Scarface submitted, people from Houston ghettoes, like him, were used to difficulties because Houston was "on the borderline of hard times."

Scarface's use of the word "borderline" points to the negotiation of power at the intersection of spaces, in one of the most geographically expansive, populous, and economically prosperous cities in the United States. People who lived in Houston ghettoes knew about the good oil and gas jobs that afforded some Houstonians high-class living. In the ghetto, you saw the promises of a good life on your television. Yet, on the ghetto side of this intersection, life seemed to be marked by violence and unyielding personal, social, political, and economic terror. In response, Scarface insists that at this borderline of hard times you "seldom ... hear niggas prayin' and givin' God time." But he seeks prayers from his mother because he knows that death is ever present and imminent, particularly as many of his friends had already fallen victim to early deaths as a result of the hard times of ghetto life in Houston.

Bushwick Bill's verse paints a picture of what the hard times in Houston look like. But first he indicates that the dispassion toward the hard times faced by people in spaces like Houston's Fifth Ward is analogous to the indifference toward the death and terror that happens in third world countries. To back up his claims, he insists that in Fifth Ward there is illegal sex work, excessive drug use, "hard times," and a consistently high murder rate. According to Bill, you will also find hungry and neglected babies. Bill reasons that society considers Fifth Ward and its people lawless and unruly, in the same way in which the world viewed Rwandan genocide. Closing out his verse, Bill indicates that those who flee their countries seeking "milk and honey" in the United States will get there but will want to go back home, because they may find out that life is similar to where they left and that "the world is a ghetto." Bringing the focus back to Houston, Willie D, the group's rabble rouser, focuses his verse on letting listeners—ostensibly those who questioned Houston's street cred—know that Houston's hard times engendered hard people willing to "recompense evil for evil."[20] According to Willie, Fifth Ward is not like the depictions of Texas as full of horse-riding cowboys, but, rather, in its ghettoes, like other ghettoes, people are willing and able to kill, and people hustle to get by. Willie D's caustic pronouncement not only speaks to the authenticity ethic that is important to hip hop culture but also speaks in tandem with the other verses and points to Houston as a significant center of hip hop, where "situated at the 'crossroads of lack and desire,' ... [hip hoppers] negotiate the[ir] [identities with] experiences of marginalization, brutally truncated opportunity, and oppression."[21]

To understand the Geto Boys' sentiments, and to better grasp the space, place, and time that Houston hip hop embodied, one needs to understand the socio-geographic contexts of Houston.

Houston, a city that embodies capitalism, is about growth and prosperity. Houston is large and spacious; it does not like to be disrespected. Since its establishment in 1836, Houston has been a city focused on growth and prosperity. For much of the twentieth century, Houston was a "residential [and industrial] construction site ... whetted [with] an appetite for profit."[22]

Prospects of wealth led to substantial growth. To accommodate this continuous growth, Houston built outwards instead of upwards like other metropolises, such as New York City, Chicago, and Philadelphia. From the original four wards (First, Second, Third, and Fourth) covering 9 square miles (in 1850), Houston expanded to cover approximately 600 square miles, with eleven management districts, eighty-eight super neighborhoods, over one-hundred fifty neighborhoods, nine counties (Houston-Galveston-Brazoria Consolidated Metropolitan Statistical Area (Houston CMSA), and seventeen school districts. Houston's constant growth outwards makes it a massive city, one that requires its citizens to have a car to move around. Because of these spatial realities, mobility via automobile is very important to one's identity. As such, Houstonians are addicted to cars.

→ Black communities made invisible/
Segregated and not invested in

While Houston was growing out, it forgot about its black citizens, to the point of relegating them to invisibility in their segregated communities/areas—Third Ward, Fourth Ward, Fifth Ward, Acres Homes, Sunnyside, South Park, North Forest/Settegast, Studewood/Independent Heights. This forgetting meant that Houston systematically and historically practiced divestment toward black communities by failing to provide adequate public services. For a time, Houston was home to the South's largest African American community. This allowed for multiple communal black ghettoes spaced in and around the city, not in elevated projects but in row houses or spacious public housing apartment complexes. In these segregated and spaced out ghettoes were self-sufficient institutions supported by neighborhood residents. Each community had its own culture and carried its own pride, particularly when it came to sports and leisure activities.[23] All of this, especially when one considers that there were multiple high schools that students attended, allowed for competition among the wretched of Houston. Ghettoes on the north side were separated from the ghettoes on the south side. These ghettoes had different settlement patterns and different types of settlers—with the south side historically settling the black professional, artist, and working classes, and the north side settling a more rural and country class of black folk. Instead of fighting over colors, Houston's black ghetto residents rivaled each other because of allegiance to a side of town and a community/neighborhood on that side of town—they embodied their narrow spaces to the point of feeling threatened by those in other spaces.

Houston experienced a major boom in the 1970s. But the city's black spaces seemed to implode because economic and residential opportunities for blacks were disproportionately different than those for white Houstonians. As Houston began to suburbanize, a few blacks were able to escape communal ghettoes for greener pastures, though situated close to or adjacent to the communal ghettoes.[24] "This flight, coupled with high unemployment, low-wage jobs and deteriorating public schools" transformed these spaces into what Loic Wacquant calls hyper-ghettoes characterized by ethno-racial homogeneity; class segregation; a loss of positive economic function due to the effects of deindustrialization and black businesses shutting down, selling out, or moving out of once ethno-racial communities; state institutions of social control replacing community institutions; and everyday life, for many of those left behind, became marked by a sense of nihilism.[25] By the time that crack hit these ghetto streets in the mid-1980s, conditions were already "depression-like," prompting thoughts of insanity—"my mind is playing tricks on me"—because life in the ghetto did not look like what life was supposed to be and did not resemble the life that the rest of Houstonians lived.[26]

This was the Houston that hip hop found when it arrived in the early 1980s, and the Houston that Houston hip hoppers strived to make meaning of for almost twenty-five years. These Houston hip hoppers seemed to make meaning from their lives in this location mostly through fierce independence, material possessions, topophilia and collective identity, or drugging to mollify the pains of everyday life.

"Already Made, Before Da Major Deal": Embodying complex humans[27]

Once hip hop arrived in Houston in the early 1980s it quickly spread, as young people began to appropriate it, primarily through rap, to fit their local realities. By 1986, a few Houston entrepreneurs decided to professionalize the budding hip hop culture. James Prince (then James Smith) was one of those entrepreneurs. He created Rap-A-Lot Records, known throughout hip hop culture as the first independent record label from "the South." Prince recruited the best artists and groups, like Royal Flush, the Ghetto Boys, and Raheem, and gained local and regional fame, but found it difficult to gain the respect of the hip hop industry, or fans in the major media markets like New York City, where hip hop had its initial public offering. Houston rapper K-Rino "remember[s] when there wasn't a scene, when people laughed at [Houston rappers]." In an interview with Lance Scott Walker, K-Rino lamented, "People thought we was country. People said all we did down here was ride horses, rope cows and that, nobody down here had no rap skills ... I had to battle cats on the East Coast just to prove that Houston had rap skills."[28] In response to this disrespect, Willie D, as a member of the Ghetto Boys, expressed his angst, rapping "East Coast ain't playin' our songs/I wanna know what the hell's goin on/Gimme my card, radio sucker/I'll kick your ass and take the motherfucker/Everybody know New York is where it began/So let the ego shit end."[29] But soon, Prince, his artists, and other label owners began to strike out on their own, creating an independent business model that brought them much financial success and garnered imitation.

During the late 1980s and early 1990s, the city represented one of largest consumer markets for hip hop music. Not only did Houstonians purchase large numbers of hip hop albums and cassettes, but people across Texas and the Gulf Coast were also traveling to Houston to purchase hip hop at stores like Soundwaves (close to the old Houston Astrodome).[30] For Houston's independent labels—like Rap-A-Lot, Suave House, Big Tyme Records, Wreckshop Records, Swishahouse Records, the Screwed Up Click, the South Park Coalition, and a few others who employed many of Houston's hip hop artists—their independent status really paid off when, in the early 1990s, Southwest Wholesale Records and Tapes opened its doors. Located in northwest Houston, this music distributor allowed for independent labels and artists to become rich really fast.[31]

Slim Thug, from two of Houston's north side ghettoes—Homestead and Acreage Homes (better known as Acres Homes or Da 44), whose consistent thesis, "I'm already platinum," on his major label debut album, is one example of how Houston's independent business models worked to legitimize its rappers as humans, artists, and professionals. The album's introductory song not only spoke of the confidence that independent success had engendered in the third generation of rappers like Slim Thug, but also the feelings of "making it" in a free market society. "Regardless if I sell a hundred thousand, or [if] I sell a mill, I'm already platinum, already paid, with eight cars a big house, that's already laid," boasted Slim of his new level of success. But he then reminds listeners that he was "already made, before the major deal," able to "pull a Bentley off the lot, and [know] how that feel" and "turn corners through the 'hood, behind [his] Phantom wheel." Unlike his prophytes in Houston's hip hop game, like the Geto Boys, who years before had to fight for respect from industry execs and fans outside their region, Slim and his generation of rappers had benefited from years of independent maneuvering and regional prowess.

Houston rappers' independent successes in the face of delegitimizing forces underscore their strivings to become and live off of their creativity. It is not only that the spatial arrangements of Houston, where ghettoes existed as social prisons, attempted to confine, control, and limit the life outcomes of these hip hoppers, but, because of their geographic location within the United States, and the disregard attributed to their space/place, the institution which they sought refuge and salvation from also worked to confine, control, and limit their outcomes. They therefore did it for themselves.

"The World Gon' Drip Candy and Be All Screwed Up": Becoming Screwston, Texas[32]

Houston is probably most notably known as home of the "chopped and screw" or "Screwston, Texas." Screw music and the culture helped to facilitate a "collective sense of identity and feeling of community among [Houston's] dispersed diasporic populations"—blacks and brown folk.[33]

"Robert Earl Davis, Jr., [famously known as] DJ Screw [or Screw], was one of the most influential musical figures [in hip hop] to come out of Texas" in the late twentieth century. DJ Screw was not "a musician or even a rapper; he was a guy behind the turntables mixing other people's music and raps together."

In the early 1990s he began "slow[ing] down the music, [by] taking a 45 record and playing it at 33 rpm." A consummate hip hop disc jockey, Screw incorporated standard hip hop mixing techniques and technology "vinyl records, turntables, a mixer and multiple cassette decks—to create cassette mixes of strangely slow, murky versions of existing songs punctuated with repeated words and phrases."[34] At first, the tapes were made as "personals" for Screw's friends and neighborhood cats, who "shouted out" people and places important to them—drug dealers, streets, high schools, friends, neighborhoods—on the tapes. Screw then began to sell these tapes. From the personal mixtapes that Screw began making in the early 1990s, there emerged a cadre of freestyle rappers who became known as the Screwed Up Click (SUC), who made screw music "an underground sensation, so popular that people would drive [from out of Texas and from cities and towns in Texas] … to his Houston home to buy them."[35]

By 1995, screw music had become professionalized—distributed and sold on the white market (in stores).[36] The freestyle rappers associated with the SUC—Lil Keke, Big Moe, Big HAWK, Fat Pat, Big Pokey, ESG, etc.—became household names in much of the Gulf Coast (Texas, Louisiana, Mississippi) and soon began to pursue their own careers as rappers. "In the late '90s," according to Julie Grob of the University of Houston, "fans on the north side of [Houston]—… Acres Homes, Greenspoint, Homestead and Studewood began demanding "chopped and screwed" style sounds." Not that people in these north side ghettoes did not have access to Screw tapes, but the neighborhoods, ghetto superstars, schools, and ways of life "shouted out" and talked about on Screw tapes did represent for them. Also, there was a long history of sectional beef, partially fueled by high school rivalries. Hence, "established mixtape and radio DJ Michael '5000' Watts" along with fellow DJ Ronald Coleman (OG Ron C) began to further commodify the chopped and screwed sound and rapping style by curating and selling mixtapes featuring young unknown freestyle rappers from the north side. By 1999, Watts and Ron C had "founded the Swishahouse label … [and] released their first aboveground album, *The Day Hell Broke Loose*, which featured early Swishahouse artists such as Archie Lee, Big Pic, Big Tiger, Larry Jones (J-Dawg), Lil' Mario and Lester Roy plus … newcomers—Stayve Thomas (Slim Thug), Hakeem Seriki (Chamillionaire, then going by Camilean), Roderick Brown (50/50 Twin) and Paul Slayton (Paul Wall)."[37]

In screw music, we hear about allegiances to streets, neighborhoods, sections of town, Houston, and "the south." The raps were not necessarily about the vicissitudes of ghetto life in Houston, but more about living fly—material possessions that one owned or wanted which represent hood success and garnered one hood success. The everyday happenings in their hoods became a culture that others around the world began to adopt, which exalted nobodies to somebodies. In hip hop worldwide, many rappers can be heard rapping about sippin' syrup or "drank," riding slabs, coming down, and poppin' trunk, all content that originated with the screw culture in Houston.

Screw culture also brought neighborhoods together and, later, the city. Screw, along with DJ Michael "5000" Watts, promulgated screw music in such a fashion that its local representation actually removed much of the geographic schism in the Houston black body politic. Not only because Screw tapes and Swishahouse tapes featured artists from these different communities, albeit from the same side of town but also because listeners wanted to experience the life that the rappers talked about regarding their hoods. These once segregated and competing hoods became Screwston, Texas.

"Draped Up and Dripped Out": Slab culture as a symbol of self, prosperity, and community[38]

Houston's car obsession is a standard motif in its hip hop music. It is largely from screw culture that the rap world came to associate Houston with customized cars. It just seemed to fit, because screw music goes comfortably with the car culture of Houston that requires drivers to spend large amounts of time in a car, slowing the pace of life. There are exceptions, but most raps that mainstreamed out of Houston in the mid-1990s into the 2000s referenced Houston's car culture, specifically slabs.

Slabs come in all body shapes and colors, but typically they are customized full size luxury sedans—Cadillac, Oldsmobile, Buick, Impala, Lincolns. Customization includes lowered frames, candy paint (high-gloss paint jobs), swangas (vintage '83s® and '84s® 30 spoke wire rims.), vogue tires, fifth wheels mounted atop trunks, reupholstered interiors, multiple TV screens, modified trunks with electric trunk release (sometimes decorated with personalized murals and neon lights), and sophisticated sound systems that make the cars "beat down the block knocking pictures off the wall."[39]

In general this type of car customization is really about enhancing one's identity, gaining credibility, prosperity, and being part of a community. It's also about making something out of nothing, because one can purchase a car for no more than two thousand dollars and make it a one-of-a-kind treasure by adding 20,000 dollars of customizations (slab it out).[40] It is easy to dismiss material consumption, in this case car customization, as trivial, juvenile, or wasteful, but owning a slab is a sign of prosperity, and it makes one feel like a somebody in a world and a city that renders working class and poor black and brown bodies invisible. It says "Look at me. Don't forget."[41] The spatial realities of Houston made cars important to one's identity and the medium by which leisure and economic resources could be accessed. To construct meaning from their spatial realities, Houston hip hoppers therefore reconstructed cars with which to reimagine their lives.

"Drank Up In My Cup": Mimicking and coping in the City of Syrup[42]

On the cover of his 2000 debut album, SUC rapper Big Moe (Kenneth Moore) stands over the cityscape of Houston with a white Styrofoam cup in hand, pouring a purple substance over it, deluging the city. At the bottom of the front cover the album's title reads *City of Syrup*. With this image and title, Big Moe constituted Houston as the official home of syrup or "sizzurp"—a popular recreational street drug which contains codeine and promethazine hydrochloride cough syrup, typically mixed with "soda (Sprite [Mountain Dew] or Big Red) and/or fruit candy, such as Skittles or Jolly Ranchers brand candies."[43] The concoction goes by many names—"drank," "purple drank," "lean," "barre," or "mud"—but what remains static is its association to Houston hip hop culture.[44] "Just like hip hop music started in the Bronx and then diffused throughout the world," contends Dr. Ronald Peters, "codeine promethazine started here in Houston" and spread to places known and unknown.[45] At the bottom of this drug culture, we find an attachment to a unique spatial identity, and also we learn about how a generation of young people assuaged the pains associated with life on the borderline of hard times, when total salvation seemed elusive.

Dating as far back as the 1960s, sippin' syrup was something that working class black folk did in their hoods and, due to the success of rappers from Houston narrating their personal experiences and observations, sippin' syrup became an opiate for the hip hop masses. As with car culture, screw music promulgated syrup's popularity. Hence, when the screw trajectory of Houston hip hop culture was commodified by the music industry, talking about syrup and sippin' syrup became a standard—giving Houston hip hoppers another collective spatial identity.

Syrup would end up taking its toll on some of Houston's rap pioneers, such as DJ Screw (2000), Big Moe (2007), and Pimp C (2007), who met untimely deaths "attributed to cough syrup abuse."[46] Despite these highly publicized deaths, sippin' syrup remained the drug of choice for many Houstonians. This speaks to how some folk chose to make meaning of life, in the face of inadequate mental health resources, for those confined in Houston's ghettoes. This is not to say that syrup had healing or salvific powers, but it does say something about how some folk in Houston's ghettoes coped when life did not make sense or when one found it impossible to become a complex subject. Here, the construction of or quest for meaning came through the escaping of the requirements or darkness of everyday living.

Conclusion

Black southern writer Kiese Laymon says, "Henry James didn't have to tell us that geography was fate."[47] In the context of Pinn's complex subjectivity, geographic and historical location operate as "oppressive and essentializing forces," which hip hoppers negotiate to construct meaning of life. Houston hip hoppers, however, transcended these forces by amalgamating them with the best of hip hop to become "complex conveyer[s] of cultural meaning with ... detailed and creative identit[ies]." Instead of succumbing to doomed fates, these hip hoppers used the culture to speak to self, and to construct a life beyond everything that threatened life.

That is why I suggest that in order to answer the question "what does Houston hip hop say (and do) regarding the fundamental questions of human existence," investigators must fully map the geographic, historical, and social realities of the city. This is not only a suggestion for understanding the religious nature of Houston hip hop, but also for work that needs to be done on other local and regional scenes. Doing so recognizes that bodies are situated in and makes sense of the world from very local contexts.

8

Imperial whiteness meets hip hop blackness: A spiritual phenomenology of the hegemonic body in twenty-first century USA

James W. Perkinson

The other of our society is in that sense no longer nature at all, as it was in precapitalist societies, but something else which we must now identify. I am anxious that this other thing not overhastily be grasped as technology per se, since I will want to show that technology is here itself a figure for something else.
—FREDRIC JAMESON

The invisible hand of capital

Adam Smith, surveying the raft of cottage industries churning out exchange values for the English bourgeoisie in 1776, likened the realization of the common good of that scene to a great invisible hand on high infallibility, guiding the rationalized pursuit of self-interest on the part of individual producers toward an orchestrated social benefit, blessing all.[1] His vision of a "divine digitation" of the economy has taken up business school residence, ever since, in as unassailable a creed of infallibility as any historic Baptist embrace of the Bible. Never mind that fifty years after Smith, Karl Marx reconnected that dismembered hand to its actual provenance in the great "underworld" quagmire of the colonial mine and industrial factory, as a hypertrophied and "monstrous" appendage of an otherwise atrophied working class body, making the same motions a thousand times a day to yield benefits, very pointedly accruing only where the laws leveraged ownership, where race reinforced exclusion, and where police baton or military bullet beat back any attempt to unlock the stockpiled gold by revolt.[2] More than two centuries after Smith, Marxist anthropologist Michael Taussig, commenting on Smith's comment from his fieldwork site of indigenous shamanisms in the Andes mountains of the 1970s, underscored such a belief as the greatest animism history has yet seen, and hunkered down to mythic combat against its explanatory magic by trying to reconstruct academic "rationality" as itself mythic.[3] I wish to embellish on this modern misprision of the animist enchantments of capitalism and the magical conjurations of its academic acolytes as a key to some of our modes of misperceived conflict. I will do so by attending especially to hip hop creativity as a site where animisms—economic and cultural, racial, and patriarchal—lock into a peculiarly potent profile of contestation, haunting the public imaginary, and at once significant of—and signifying on—political struggle in our time. I want to flesh out a spiritual phenomenology of hip hop creativity as a postmodern animation that yet awaits its political-economy pedagogy and organization.

This chapter hopes to challenge contemporary academic pedagogies to grapple with the spirited undercurrents of human struggles to make life meaningful that more instrumentalized canonizations of rationality cannot adequately address. The political datum of prime import leveraging this line of thinking is the obdurate evidence of the power of rap ribaldry, turntable dexterity, break beat virtuosity and guerilla graffiti to command a global hearing.[4] That the cultural creativity of imperial USA's most marginalized community should find traction on a planetary scale in digitalized youth cultures demands resolute accounting. At the heart of that accounting lies a complex transvaluation of racial oppression into aesthetic signification and economic wherewithal that simultaneously "capitalizes" on black difference and mobilizes that difference as more than merely "black."[5] Whether such a racialized motility can also animate political forms of contestation that make a difference remains an open question that is not least a question for education in the belly of imperial intentionality that is the USA today. Certainly, hip hop "charges up" communication with a "voltage" that gives its bodily performance a spirited significance and that summons youthful interest beyond that of the typical classroom ambiance. And, clearly, it has emerged as an idiom of choice in many movements of the hour, putting bodies in the streets—such as in the Arab Spring and Occupy movements.

But our time is also peculiar, full of sleight of hand that is really an eclipse of the body—especially in its dismembered economy. Indeed, time itself— in our time—is under assault, leveled out in the commercialization of every seasonal and diurnal difference, flattened into daylights natural and electronic, compressed under flows of image and word into a ceaseless intensity of the visual. Today the eye is all—without being able either to see itself or see beyond its own garish imaginary. Where both Smith and Marx focused fittingly on the body part most metonymically signifying industrialization, in our day of consumption the sign reigns supreme. No longer is the manufactured object rendered "commodity fetish" in its mass availability; the product of our hour is quintessentially the meaning made to adhere to the surface. A mere swoosh is enough to fill the coffer. Its condition of possibility is visibility. The eye that equates is the postmodern preeminence replacing Smith's orchestrating hand. But as Jameson's epigraph quoted above ponders, the techno-enhanced visioning is itself a kind of blindness, a surfeit and sublimity of seeing that is imprisoned by the surface, unable to grasp the meaning of bodies and matter for being enthralled with facades and skin. But here I get ahead of myself.

The central contention of this writing is both that bodies encode political economies and that contemporary political economy, for all its secular self-advertisements, has its own peculiar rites of mythic combat anchored in a display of spatiality and an exhibition of the body that is finally animistic in its projections of power and meaning. This latter claim situates postmodern social ecologies on a continuum going back to hunter-gatherer investments of topography with ancestral vitality, tribal memory, and interspecial reciprocity, and insists that capitalism's fetishism of objects and postmodernism's sublimity of the environmental surround are of a mythic piece with the carnivalesque negotiation of human embodiment that hip hop culture represents at the turn of the twenty-first century. More concretely, I want, in what follows, to orchestrate a dialogue between Fredrick Jameson's solicitation of the Enlightenment sublime as pointing toward the inchoate horizon of late capitalist mystification of the economy—Paul Gilroy's construction of a "slave sublime"—to highlight creative black response to the unspeakable terrors of modern social "order," and Andrew Krim's reading of gangsta rap as articulating a peculiar and powerful "hip-hop sublime" by way of dissonant beats sounding out urban dereliction in the postindustrial. But I will also argue, ultimately, that such a dialogue of sublimities finds its force perhaps most adequately figured in a history of religions category given postcolonial currency in the work of Charles Long.

The visible hand of culture

But having begun with an invisible hand, I want to continue with a visible one. In the glare of today's hypervisuality, tiny gestures can open entire archives of memory and go bail for the harder work of discernment. During the 2004 election, a quotidian moment underscored for me a long-held intuition. There, a slight gesture repeatedly showed up on national media that conjured an invisible menagerie of power and its profiles, whose archetypal signs are suggestive for analyzing mainstream politics and hip hop performance alike. During the debates leading up to the vote, when John Kerry wanted to give emphasis to one of his points he would pump his fist with thumb arranged upwards alongside his forefinger rather than across the front of his knuckles. My own reaction was an involuntary "wince" at what I perceived to be a less than forceful gesture. In the canons of the country's hard-knuckled cowboy myth, it did not conform to type. It signaled a certain "softness" associated with east coast affluence. Just as in a later campaign, a "black" fist bump would unleash all manner of racist doubt; here, a "white" fist pump probably helped secure deep-held patriarchal suspicion. Postelection, on the other hand, poll after poll offered evidence of people disagreeing with George Bush's policies who nonetheless voted for him based on his "incarnation" of affability and resolve: he was someone they read intuitively as both "down-to-earth" and "decisive," easily reimagined as a drinking buddy at the local bar and "cowboy-in-chief" who gets things done. That fist pumps and grins and even gaffes are politically significant is not news. Body language is compelling. Communication studies analysis confirms the decisive role of rhythmic synchronicity or "somatic entrainment" in any effective exchange between people seeking to mediate conflicts or agree on agendas.[6] Somewhere between 50 percent and 80 percent of what we communicate happens below the tongue and underneath consciousness.

But what is not always underscored in such analyses is the broader coding implied. In its most archetypal articulation, my conviction here is that there is a hegemonic form of male embodiment ghosting institutional life in this country that serves as a template against which any given candidate for power is measured and either summarily approved or presumptively put under suspicion. And it is likewise significant for any forms of resistance that may arise contesting its crystallization of potency. It is a form of embodiment that incarnates a certain style of power, encodes an entire economy of assumptions about class, race, and orientation, and reproduces itself politically in a relentless, though often hidden and silent, sanctioning of "deviant" somatic styles. Its gendered indices are as inchoate as the relationship between a stabbing finger and a still-born trunk, as sartorially obvious as a blood-red tie shouting dollar signs between white shirt and black suit, as racially certain as light skin and un-knappy hair (see Tim Wise's argument that Obama's election actually confirmed white power and privilege to the degree that he had to displace the meaning of his skin by otherwise packaging himself as "white" and distancing himself from any pro-black agenda or demonstrative expression). Not only does that body win elections and preside in boardrooms, but even more cogently, it enforces empire and polices dissent. Correlated isomorphically with "imperial reconstructions of space," it holds sway today, as the taken-for-granted icon of "democracy" and "civilization," in the various theaters of international verbal engagement that mediate, announce, explain, and otherwise license militant initiatives to secure more resources and power.

Monitored spaces and surveilled bodies

But such a bodily apparition equally haunts the streets of this country like an Orwellian haint—nowhere appearing as such, yet everywhere querying any other mode of embodiment that shows any sign of refusing the hegemony. And it constitutes public space from within its own ghostly void, as the unspoken norm against which all other motions of bodies, in malls and universities, corporate offices and suburban residences, are measured by video or human monitors and evaluated for potential interdiction. Social theorist Thomas Dumm cogently outlined the operation of this particular spirit-persona in relationship to gated community governance, for instance, in the 1992 post-LA-uprising flurry of academic anxiety to explain the explosion.[7] Unlike previous modalities of patrolling spaces by way of surveillances on outlook for particular bodies carrying particular histories of crime, the new visual era is busy investing monitoring technologies (now gaining panoptical ubiquity in the form of drone efficacy) as the new armature of demographic organization prevailing over and constituting middle-class spatial congress. Within such venues, whatever is not white, middle class, and heterosexual in stereotypic "profile" is likely to draw down attention and intervention to the degree it piles up signs of otherness—a "dark" body, sporting dreads, with a cap perched sideways, swaggering in "pimp" step, "sagging" with attitude, and gesturing like an MC in battle, for instance, will not often move through such spaces untended.

At the heart of monitored space lurks a somatic hegemon, a normative body type ruling that space with shadowy precision. Its power of possession above the glass ceiling or in the halls of deliberation does not mean it does not morph on its way down through the rest of the social order. Power-suited females may inflect its sameness with a certain gendered flair even while reinforcing its basic game. Baton-bearing officials of whatever color may give blue-suited bluntness to its authority while enacting its agency. And white middle-class males may even play with alterity on the way to maturity with a certain degree of impunity (suburban youth enacting adolescent minstrelsy in sartorial and gestural blackface), only to re-enter white "normality" rather quickly when adult conformity demands its due. But the normative regnancy of the ultimate profile of power in this society is only thereby ramified in its masquerade. The axis between corporate boardroom and white house dome remains definitive of the archetype and proscriptive of difference. Growing up as any other kind of male body in this country, or experimenting seriously with a different profile of appearance, almost inevitably means encountering the silent tyranny of that norm and learning the intimate costs of not measuring up or conforming. Growing up female and not finding oneself desired by such a body likewise poses an interior question mark not easily erased (unless nurtured in an alternative economy of female identity as has been the case in many African American and Latina communities historically in this country or all manner of LGBQT venues of alternative expression and experiment).

On the other hand, labor historian Michael Davis has long detailed the revamped potencies of a surveillance interest concerned not so much with keeping certain spaces "ethnically cleansed" or unobstructed for overclass use, but rather with tracking other kinds of bodies moving through other spaces (such as the inner city) that are perceived as posing "statistical probabilities of threat"—and if necessary, doing so by way of linkage to LANDSAT satellite hardware bearing GIS programming that can transform any given neighborhood into an outdoor prison in a mere flick of a switch.[8] Here the watchword is crime and the archetype "dark" and bristling with muscle. The home space of such an "outlaw" body, in the dominant class imagination, is the incarceral cellblock—the great social-structural prophylactic constructed by white male fear to protect the bourgeois Barbie from an imaginary black organ on the prowl for suburban meat just outside the gate. That such a fantasy obviously (and pathologically) only inverts the actual historical practice of white males in slave quarters does not mean its mythic potency has not haunted and regulated the organization of social space in this country ever since the end of the Civil War. Its latest incarnation has been that of American Political Science Association President James Q. Wilson's "somatotyping"— the statistical profiling of the body most likely to commit crime based on current prison populations that was given academic authorization in Murray and Herrnstein's "Bell Curve" belligerence and economic implementation in the prison-industrial complex (think NYPD's "Stop and Frisk" policy).[9] In the analysis of social theorist Frank Wilderson, this black body is the Archimedean outside of American civil society, an ontological fungibility of physicality constructed not in the nexus of wage-labor, but in the despotism of terror, as the mutilated site of absolute dereliction, "magnetizing bullets" (or in female form, lying open-legged on its back awaiting medical "reformulation")—a "non-subjectivity" deputizing all whites, whether they know it consciously or not, as police and simultaneously authorizing and threatening the gendered space of the middle-class white home as "the beginning of the free world."[10]

Imperial hegemon meets hip hop icon

It is this "other" body that hip hop potency ventriloquizes and visually stages with profound effect. And here I am concerned not to lose sight of the corporeality articulating the lyrical sagacity or comedy, gesturing in time with the tongue, animated by the base-beat thump, opening the melody to spinning trunks and rhyme-chopping hunks of thigh, and fast-fingered scratch-tones plying the sky with cyber-moans, tattooing the eye with fly menace or an existential "Why" or a simple cry of "Damm!" Especially in gangsta rap—but even more generally cutting through other genres or subtypes of the music and weaving in and out of both lyrics and fashion—the archetype in play is the stereotype of black "illity" in all of the complex oppositional resonances that word conveys, "outlaw" and "exemplary" alike. This is quintessentially the post-Black Power male body, carrying all of its white supremacist marking, to be sure, but no longer trying to qualify for inclusion, flaunting the multiple illusions with which it is hung (not least through the convict gear, it often "sags" from its hips), occupying the stereotype like a badge of belonging and simultaneously ripping it, tagging the observing eye with irony and riots, both politically audacious and party-stupid, at the same time answering history and refusing to answer anything at all. So powerful is the paradox of the posture that Orlando Patterson can lament the result as a Dionysian triumph of culture over self-interest: the "cool-pose" lifestyle of hip hop grants young black males so much in-group affirmation and white adolescent respect that they now exhibit the highest levels of self-esteem of all ethnic groups even while failing or dropping out of high school at catastrophic rates.[11] But the tragedy thus demarcated is not so easily evaluated. It at once impugns corporate profit-taking on the backs of black male self-destruction and at the same time raises issue more broadly with our vision of success. Is conforming to corporatized educational priorities that too often plunge students into lower levels of self-regard, erode their creativity, and train them to serve (or run) institutions bent on imperial conquest of the world's resources the substance of our pedagogical hope? Or is there also a larger question at stake in the conundrum? What is the power of attitude and innovation that the archetypal hip hop body encodes for the culture at large and—beyond its (supposed) dead-end seduction for young people of color—why is it both economically marketable and politically dangerous for the corporate elite who now exploit it like a postmodern circus yielding profits and distraction?

From one point of view, it is possible to comprehend the overclass body of resolute action and the outlaw body of defiant rhythm as imperial correlates. The political backlash against curtailed executive powers emanating from Vietnam and Watergate, coupled with the late capitalist takeover of popular culture as an unlimited project of commodification and consumption, have found iconic broadcast in the corporatist body of imperial certainty—visceral in resolve to impose a neoliberal global agenda, set of jaw and sharp of tongue in excoriating alternative visions of reality, whether Muslim or gay, unabashed in asserting that the quintessential patriotic response to terrorist attacks is to "go out and buy," and male, straight, and white in its policing of the body politic, requiring extra conformity for any Obama or Hillary attempting to "crash" its party. I do not take this profile as merely that of an individual, nor as a matter of mere expediency, but rather as a moralized collective simulacrum, a virtual version of the ancient notion of the mystical body of the king, now spectral in its dissemination, into which the subjects of empire are interpolated by the media of the day.[12] It is unrelentingly a ritualized body, repetitively ramified in the collective eye, in sound bite soliloquies packaged in talking head apparitions that act like digitalized "mythemes" inside the national psyche, a visual mnemonic that functions as the spectral equivalent of George Creel's Public Relations dictum—from earlier in the game of manufacturing consent—that, "People do not live by bread alone; they mostly live by catch phrases."[13] We would simply add, and by fawning and unthinking imitation.

On the other hand, the hip hop body, I would claim, emerges as an eroticized counter-icon, historically rooted in a "good times"[14] party-ethic in the South Bronx, but nonetheless incarnating a social polemic,[15] subliminally as well as consciously trading in gendered and racialized code-images, partially contesting imperial space in graffiti logo and head-spinning acrobatics, brokering political resistance into winnable battles of cultural comeuppance that function like a return of the repressed from the unconscious of empire. Its "difference from" the imperial body is tangled up profoundly with an elemental "American" sameness, in the seething underground of a racialized national history, simultaneously defying and mimicking the aggrandizements and violence of the imperial context. Like its "boardroom" counterpart, it too is globalized in digital media, given performative articulation and transnational materialization as an obtruding corporeal signifier, not only in MTV daycasts and nighttime clubbing, but in outbreaks of political protest like the flame-shrouded Muslim exurbs of northern Paris in late 2005, or the more recent "boom-bap" YouTube send-ups of despised dictatorships in the Arab Spring.[16] Here, the bureaucratic bellicosity of imperial efficiency finds rejoinder in the animated bombast of a diasporic *banlieu* or keefa-ed square. Both are male; both are militant. But the latter, I would contend, also exhibits something else—what might be tentatively probed as a mode of rhythmic messianism, conscripting adolescent bodies of all genders, orientations, and color markings into experimentation with insurgent desires that neither entirely exit from nor fully capitulate to the marketed package of acceptable deviance.[17] There is more going on here than merely a ghetto version of the impulse to conquer in the mode of guerilla sound. The global uptake of this black somatic apparition as a template for imitation and embroider-ment, triggering an explosion of youth cult creolization while grounding the hybridity in a percussive vitalism, has yet to meet its spiritual vision, however.

And this is where pedagogy must become savvy. The circulation of the black body as a mode of cultural capital now bearing not only opprobrium-yielding white notions of supremacy but also prestige-yielding planetary profit is a sign begging synopsis and divination.[18] Just what is the crossover attraction of this body? Is its code of gesture and rhyme, hard times and raw crime, just Madison Avenue falderal—a knotting up of stereotype and exotica, white banality and black braggadocio, suburban triviality meets ghetto loquacity, peppered with Latin leg-swipes, Caribbean toasts, Puerto Rican roasts—answering to all the boasts of all the hosts of small-organ-ed wanna-be-like-west-coasters living in Oklahoma City and rural Georgia, fondling the lyrics like little boys with toys they have no instructions on how to assemble? My own experience and conviction tells me "No." There is an archetypal pattern underneath the patter that taps an energy source otherwise latent in global culture. When a white twenty-year-old stands up in the middle of a hip hop conference in Detroit in 1999 and says, serious as a roach in front of a baited trap, "I would die for this shit!," there is something on burn worthy of the flame that puts most pedagogy to shame. That kid likely has no clue what he is trying to channel, but the possession is symptomatic and the passion a resource for greater humanization—if it is given political organization and spiritual vision. There is a conjuration of something critical to human integrity in the "orgiastic"[19] effect of the beats in the body—memory of a way of being that civilization has merely displaced into restless anomie when the commodity reigns unimpeded or organized into genocidal ferment when fascist or missionary charisma finds opportunity.[20] It is imperial pretension itself that is potentially put in question in the awakened but confused and sublimated ferocity that limns hip hop performativity—a warrior fierceness that today finds little social authentication other than in one or another corporate buy-off or in misdirection into scapegoating or war.

Civilizing containment and carnivalesque release

Norbert Elias in the 1980s traced the gradual transformation of the old warrior classes of Europe into "tame" courtiers, as the state increased its monopoly on violence by way of duly authorized policing forces and war making.[21] As opposed to the medieval social demand for hair-trigger displays of violent self-defense, from the Renaissance forward, the body as the bearer of value becomes subject to expanding taboos, through processes of individualization, rationalization and socialization.[22] The civilized male body of European court societies became the site of hierarchical status distinctions, exhibiting keen sensitivity to the "war of position" negotiated in courtly intrigue by way of the subtle cues of proxemics (e.g., distance in the room from the body of the king), chronemics (the timing of communication), kinesics (the meaning of gestures and facial expression), and all manner of paralanguage, delimiting importance and political access.[23] The internalization of a demarcated set of rules about appropriate behavior, highly controlled emotional expression, extreme individualization over against the social and natural environments, and attention to the minutiae of behavior all became de rigeur for inclusion in the social concourse of middle and upper classes.[24] Pierre Bourdieu explores roughly the same phenomenon in terms of what he calls social and cultural capital "banked" in the body in the structuring calculus of a slowly engendered habitus, guiding behavior, in the contexts to which such a habit is calibrated, underneath the radar of conscious deliberation and forethought.[25] And Michel Foucault, among other body theorists, focuses his forays on exhibiting the modern Western "soul" as a constitutive effect of the body, itself increasingly constrained by technologies of supervision, laminating the corporeal surface as a mode of transparent incarceration and intruding an internal version of that gaze by way of its external ubiquity and unpredictable interdictions.[26]

Elias opens this exegesis of the "civilized" or "supervised" body toward our concern for hip hop in emphasizing the historical shift of violent display of emotion from social expression between persons in the Middle Ages to psychological forms of struggle against internalized supervisory controls in late modern social scripting.[27] The trade-off is one of danger for boredom. Along the path of this corporeal involution of drives and passions as population has increased and space has concentrated, Western institutions have also found it expedient to license certain modes and times of hedonistic release as actually reinforcing overall "progress" toward control and routinization. From Carnivale in the late Middle Ages to sports and leisure activities today,[28] the civilized body has found refreshment in carefully circumscribed forums of sensuous excess—momentary immersions in what Mikhail Bakhtin theorized as the "grotesque body," inverting social hierarchy, pillorying propriety, celebrating the "lower bodily strata" in wanton exchanges of fluids and sounds, foods and feelings.[29] Hip hop culture arguably functions for much of dominant white culture as the postmodern modality of such a carnivalesque intentionality, gone global. David Roediger (among others) has offered provocative analysis of the way blackface minstrelsy emerged in this country as the flip side of abolition in the 1830s, enacting white working class anxiety over changing social conditions and possibilities, channeling a convoluted "pornography" of freedoms (of bodily expression) lost in the move from the peasant fields of Europe to industrialized discipline and supervision in the United States.[30] At one deep level, hip hop simply perpetuates and extends this white adoption of blackface masquerade. As a kind of "theater of eroticized release," dominant culture consumption of "the game" all too readily only confirms old pathologies when not coupled with actual pedagogies of political dissent and organization to struggle for an altered social order. Such is not really news.

What may be important to understand in the mix, however, is the possibility that the hip hop body also expresses something primal and crucial—a potency in danger of atrophy, registering in early twenty-first century Western educational disciplines as symptom, itself addressed, pathetically, as pathology and suppressed with Ridalin. Imperial codes registered through psychiatric pretension to adjudicate normativity have even recently detailed a syndrome known in the Diagnostic and Statistical Manual of Mental Health Disorders as ODD: Oppositional Defiant Disorder, otherwise denoted by the reputed father of American psychiatry, Dr. Benjamin Rush, as "anarchia"—"an excess of the passion for liberty" that "constituted a form of insanity."[31] But it is actually the entire history of "civilization" that needs to be interrogated in its assumption that ever-greater control is necessarily "progress"—beginning in a southwest Asian "turn" toward domestication of plants and animals, yielding the nascent imperial venture of settled mono-crop agriculture 10,000 years ago, sweeping up hunter-gatherer sustainability into an ecologically disastrous impulse to grow populations and productivity without limit. This latter "revolution" has not ceased to invest itself in every nook and cranny of the planet ever since, "reducing" indigenous populations to one or another form of peasantry and then wage-slavery (or worse), going "hyper" in industrialization, waxing cyborg in its latest mutation, colonizing ever more minute dimensions of the biosphere, from the silicon of Sahara sands to the genome of the rainforest, from the imagination of infants (via pre-toddler versions of Sesame Street) to the unconscious of adults (by way of saturation advertising), from the nano-structures of the body to the frequency of fires in the forest or the rate of glacial retreat in the mountains (gold has now been discovered under an Andean ice pack, which, in consequence, being systematically drilled and artificially warmed as we speak). Indeed, the idea of ever-increasing control is itself utterly fatuous and profoundly dangerous—an impossible enterprise that would eviscerate its own basis in the very act of accomplishing its aim, as C. S. Lewis once carefully demonstrated.[32]

But in particular here, I want to tease out of this civilizing project a supposition augured by the postmodern fascination with sublimity. It is a supposition that at first sight might seem immensely strange, but at the same time imposes itself with ever more irresistible compulsion. And that is the degree to which human "being" is constituted in an irrepressible wildness. The loss of the wild,[33] both on the planetary surface and in the human psyche—say the likes of increasing numbers of scholars and poets—may be co-terminus with the end of humanity.[34] And at the heart of the encounter with wildness is arguably what the history of religions would call "the mystery that is simultaneously fascinating and terrible" (*mysterium tremendum et fascinans*).[35] Here I can only briefly query the supposition by way of a summary outline.

Battling sublimities

The chain of thinking begins and ends with Adam Krims' exposition of what he called the "hip-hop sublime" in relationship to gangsta rap in a paper written in the mid-1990s. His unique combining of Marxism and ethnomusicology—later extended in his book, *Rap Music and the Poetics of Identity*—is immensely nuanced and provocatively critical. As a sophisticated analysis of both pitch and timbre in the construction of the late 1980s productions of, in particular, Public Enemy (as well as The Bomb Squad's execution of Ice Cube's breakaway album from NWA, *Amerikkka's Most Wanted*), the invocation of the sublime references both its claim of un-representability and of a certain element of terror.[36] Krims finds each of these in the assault-scape of sound created by PE's layering of dissonant tones on top of each other, deliberately bending pitch and de-tuning harmony, to fashion a sonic membrane of harsh conflict and aggressive menace, working an element of fear into the very bodily experience of the phenomenon (as indeed a younger white friend of mine confirmed when casually telling me of his first encounters with a PE album in high school; his unprompted description of the initial listening was one of being "terrified"). On the other hand, Krims also underscores a certain rendering of the ghetto itself as un-representably "terrifying" in rap fetishism of street "hardness"—an aestheticized "un-representability" that, he laments, may exactly function to mystify the real operation of terror in the predations of global capital and the effects of brutal policing on inner-city survivability—amazingly rendering urban impoverishment's "lack of value" precisely as a new form of "surplus value" in transnational profit-taking from hip hop's rendition.[37]

But the point here is the capacity of hip hop to give expression to a certain form of sublimity. The sublime itself, of course, first begins to materialize as an identifiable and distinctive mode of monitoring reality in Enlightenment celebrations of the titillation of perceived terror (such as a mountain height or a sea storm) from a position of relative security.[38] For Kant and Burke, the "sublime" referenced a physiological thrill (in Kant's case, having moral implications in awaking reason to its capacity for infinite mastery over sensorial surfeit) in the experience of vertigo, when confronted with what would otherwise be overwhelming, from a position that allowed passive "consumption" of the experience and mitigating reflection on the effects.[39] In this formulation, "sublimity" thematizes the packaging of terror as fascinating and useful "object."

This Enlightenment version of sublimity finds a kind of postmodern updating in the work of Fredrick Jameson and Francois Lyotard. For the former, the category serves to characterize the conundrum of a late twentieth-century takeover of popular culture by political economy, rendering experience itself "commodified"—a "possession" of the life-world by commerce that so colonizes perception as to compromise political imagination before it can even glimpse an alternative.[40] Jameson speaks of global capital's unfigurable presence as a quotidian and insuperable (at least for the present) sublimity that yet awaits a genre of representation from within its own peculiarities that might grant traction to political resistance.[41] Lyotard, on the other hand, reorients the word away from its rootage historically in spatial magnitude and visual incomprehensibility to speak of an alteration in postmodern temporality—now crescendo-ing into an ever-quickening succession of decontextualized "intensities" that, contrary to more durable experiences of affect, all but eclipse the capacity of emotion to leverage action or even orientation.[42] In either of these post-Enlightenment invocations, sublimity remains beholden to its background condition of spectation and distance—an apprehension of abysmal alarm yet held at arm's length (and more) in the privilege of a powerful interdiction.

Paul Gilroy, on the other hand, appropriates the category in a manner that stands the reference on its head. For Gilroy, sublimity is theoretically useful especially in connection with slave experience—where once again it underscores a terror that overwhelms representation.[43] But here the invocation is not of a spectacle, but rather of a dimension of real bodily experience that is yet made to yield knowledge if not beauty. The terror is certainly the gratuitous and wholly unpredictable violence constituting the very shape of slavery as an institution and governing its social continuation as white racism. But it is a terror partially displaced by communal arts of memorialization, in Gilroy's characterization, that actually seek to conserve and transvalue the energies of the experience in dramaturgical moments of recurrent visitation and exorcism.[44] Sublimity here refers to an unavoidable exigency of sheer evil that is survived—if it is survived—only in collective acts of shamanic jujitsu. This is no mere titillation, passively observed and "aesthetically" consumed by an individual psyche positioned in bourgeois safety, but real violence wreaking havoc on actual bodies, that must thereafter nonetheless re-collect their integrity inside the ontology of rupture. The ritual alchemy so referenced finds expression only in the ineffable and phatic struggle to speak the unspeakable in a collective conjuration elaborated through agonistic antiphony. Sublimity here is rendered a bodily art—terror made the subject of knowing by way of physical sweat and psychic distention. Hip hop, in its earliest decade, is simply its latest rearticulation.

But then we hit a wall of paradox, born of a history of irony. Unlike the originary work on terror inside the rupture of slavery and its segregationist aftermath (both South and North), hip hop crossover of the later 80s begins to confuse the categories as Krims notes. A new moment in the national morality play fractures the seeming clarity, as product moves into the suburbs and artists into the mainstream. Sublimity as labored survival meets sublimity as rendered fetish. Ice Cube in a family flick, Jay Z in the penthouse, 50 Cents as boardroom exec, or even just Chuck D in "real" middle-class life invests the "the hip-hop body" inside the very dominance its vitalism seemed to contest. The ghetto archetype "bleeds" cool in the mogul's lair. And the temperature rises in spite of the ice. Likewise, in the re-packaging of hip hop for white titillation, transnational capital in the late twentieth and early twenty-first centuries has merely once more rendered real terror a controlled datum for middle-class fascination. Like Kant contemplating the Swiss Alps from a bourgeois apartment, the white suburbs consume their sublime now not only in vacation packages, but CD remixes and MTV. The black body gives white pleasure like an unclimbed mountain, or a coming storm.

But for all that, I would still argue that its gesture is not mere posture (though often enough in New School, that may also be the case). And the terror here is neither that of Nature nor Divinity. It is human made and propagated. In historical trajectory—a logic and terror of domination, as Lewis argued in his warning about the fatuity of human aspiration to absolute mastery, in which human control over nature is really the control of one group of humans over another group of humans with nature as a means.[45] The mystery of wildness—of being in reciprocal exchange with other life forms by way of metabolism, living by eating and dying by way of becoming food for others in turn[46]—today meets its arch-nemesis in the machine, the elaboration of ever-more predictable motion and technique in service of ... what?[47] A destiny for humanity of never having to die or deal with the reality of such a metabolic exchange?

Wild style and global crisis

What has actually happened is rather an attempted division of the mysteriousness of being alive—in its compound ecstasy of fascination and fear—into a monopoly of fascination for a few at the expense of unrelenting terror visited on the rest.[48] Commodity culture, at one level, represents the reign of fascination, a mobilization of the surface of the planet for a ruthlessly stimulated appetite, rendered insatiable in growing numbers of Westernized human bodies, for experience now fashioned as consumable material object. The toll on the environment is now irrefutable and in grave danger of becoming irreversible. Slavery in such a view shows up as the quintessence of the reign of terror, the conquest and "consumption" of certain bodies marked by racialized (or otherwise differentiating) ideologies as disposable generators of surplus value, and their existential positioning as a form of prophylactic, for the enslavers, against the terrors of natural predation and mortality. The remedy for this ever more complexly ramified attempt at bifurcation—10,000 years in the making in the machinations of so-called civilization—is not the sheer abolition of terror. It is rather recognition of its pedagogical function, coupled with fascination, for all of humanity, its schooling, not as absolute experience, but as the real sign of the actual destiny of all bodies on the planet—including postmodern ones that live encysted in the machine-surround embodying all of the dead and coerced labor of the past—as food for others.[49]

This, I would claim, is the ultimate power of the hip hop body over global youth, even when not consciously recognized as such. It serves as an adumbration of destiny, a codification of memory, a percussive rendition of the sheer ferocity and eloquence and end of all living, itself labored into celebratory being out of a context of radical desperation and dismembered ontology, a facing and parsing of both the fascination of eros and the terror of demise into rhythmic frequencies that relativize each with respect to the other, and signal human beauty as always a momentary innovation, elaborated out of the heritage and detritus of the past, animated by the risk of finding oneself cantilevered over a void.[50]

This is "the real" when hip hop does manage to keep it real. It is also what the boardroom body will never be able to signal in any believable form as archetype of the imperial—even if ironically that body now carries the name of "Baby" or "50." Whether pedagogical vision in our time is capable of transcending the seductions and imprisonments of empire and giving radical vision to the kind of animation hip hop at its underground best reflects is a question only the future will answer.

History has already weighed in with a continuous recitation of peoples responding to the throb of truth and emergency of their time, and going renegade and feral from their captivities inside the imperial matrix to give flesh to something better. From the Egyptian slave "walk-out" memorialized in the ancient Hebrew tradition to the peasant "Occupy" movement of Jesus in the first century Palestinian Temple; from Muhammad's Bedouin resistance to Meccan hegemony in the seventh century to maroon resort to the American outback in existing New World slavery in "modernity"; from Ghost Dance visioning on the plains of the Old West to rainforest rubber-tapper refusals of ranching interests of yesterday (and multitudes upon multitudes of examples un-tellable in so small an effort as this)—the litany of insurgence in the quest for modes of living and relating adequate to the impulse sounding in human depths has never been entirely eclipsed.

Arguably, hip hop was born of such a blood beat—just as, arguably, its "wild style" has been incarcerated in a commercial. But its siren is not yet silenced as even relatively "ignorant" white skin can sometimes recognize—like the kid confessing immortal love and mortal risk for such mentioned earlier, rather than just a desire to party. The immediate issue is not whether such a confession is serious; it is rather that it is conscious enough to be expressed. A depth has indeed been sounded. But if it is to realize the possibility of its destiny, its schooling must come from the frontlines of crisis of our time. Cree Indian rights to refuse Alberta drilling or Egyptian freedom to gather (or vote) in Tahrir; Detroit resistance to Citibank foreclosures and corporate takeover or Chikpo tree hugging and seed-banking in India; Roma insistence on recognition in Austria or the Palestinian version of the same in the West Bank—the cry for redress and a different future is ubiquitous. A collapsing global economy and an ecology on rampage to be heard and respected before it is too late—these are the seismic upheavals the beat could probe and serve. And here and there, it does. For this writer, the game encodes this level of ferocity and interrogation. It is indeed a throb to die for. It channels a dying planet. The question of commitment it hints is a question for all of us.

9

Bun B on religion and hip hop: An interview (by Biko Gray) with Bun B

Biko Gray

[handwritten: Bernard 'Bun B' Freeman]

[handwritten: Bun B: 1/2 of UGK & also successful solo]

[handwritten in margin: Hip hop religion commodity]

Bernard "Bun B" Freeman, along with the late Chad "Pimp C" Butler (1973–2007), formed one half of the influential rap duo UGK (Underground Kingz) and also became a successful solo artist. As an artist, Bun B understands hip hop and religion as both deeply human cultural productions, which means that they both can occasion one to lead a life of corruption and exploitation, or they can provide the space to "speak the truth"—to tell one's story in a way that will hopefully provide help for others. Brought up in a deeply devout household, his early years were heavily structured by the church that he and his family attended. But his family's faith was only as strong as his father's; when his father left the church, Freeman and his brothers followed suit. It would be hip hop that brought him full circle.

Freeman speaks of hip hop as an entertainer, and therefore sees hip hop as a profitable industry as well. With cultural and financial success came multiple kinds of temptations (like illicit sex and drug use), and Freeman eventually found himself at a low point in his life, pushing him to return to the faith of his youth. This return to the faith, however, would look different. Observing the devotion of members from other worldviews (like the Five Percent Nation and the Nation of Islam), Freeman realized that he did not have to understand his faith and his identity as an artist as distinct and separate realities. He learned

[handwritten: Now sees hip hop & religion as 2 sides of same coin]

to merge the two identities—personal and musical—and now sees hip hop and religion as two sides of the same coin.

Recently, Bun B added another dimension to this work, by co-teaching (with Anthony B. Pinn) a course on religion and hip hop culture, at Rice University. In this interview—conducted by Rice University PhD student and teaching assistant for the course, Biko Mandela Gray—Bun B shares his perspective on the relationship between hip hop and religion, as well as the experiences that have come to shape this perspective. *[handwritten: In this interview, Bun B talks about hip hop & religious connection]* *[handwritten: B]*

Biko Mandela Gray: **How were you brought up religiously?**

Bun B: I was raised in a very devout family on both sides. Both sides of my family were always practicing Baptists, so I was brought up Christian. My father's side was more devout than my mother's; my mother's side would gather on the weekend, they would dance and play cards, but my father's side, not so much. They would gather, they would commiserate, and we would have a good time, but it would not be the same kind of gathering. My father was a high-ranking deacon in the church, and so all of my brothers and I were ushers every Sunday, it wasn't even a question—my brothers and I used to have matching suits. There aren't a lot of early pictures my family and me coming up, but the ones I do remember seeing are those weekend photos. I was in play shorts, or we were in church clothes. This lasted a long time until my father strayed, and once my father left the church, eventually we left the church, you know. So that kind of separated us as a family from the church, which was very different for us. We went to bible study. All the people I knew outside of my family—all of the people I knew—I knew from church. The church community was very small, very tight-knit. It's a very small church in the fifth ward [of Houston]; my family still attend this church to this day. My cousin got married recently. My uncle's going away [funeral] ceremonies were there. When my father was a deacon, the Skinner family was the preaching family at the church, and so when the elder Skinner first became ordained as minister at the church, I was his first baptism.

[handwritten right margin: Father was a deacon, he was an usher]

[handwritten right margin: when father left church, whole family did]

[handwritten right margin: From 5th ward of Houston]

BMG: You said you and your brothers would dress up in the same suits for church. How important was dressing for you as you were growing up?

BB: I don't think it had much to do with how I felt about it; my parents insisted upon it. I didn't grow up in a house where my parents would say, "Look, go in your closet and find you something to wear to church." It would be like, "Hey, you're wearing this suit today. Everybody go in the closet and get your burgundy suit, you're wearing your burgundy suit today, or y'all are wearing y'all's blue suits today," you know. That kind of a thing. So that regimen was already implemented.

BMG: **So your family—and more specifically, your father—implemented the regimen of dressing for Church on Sunday?**

BB: Absolutely, it wasn't even a question. And then he had his burgundy suit, too. So he was the deacon and we were the ushers. Yeah, yeah, those were some of the fonder memories I have of my family back in the day, because my parents divorced when I was probably about eight or nine, um, so yeah, a lot of our early family days, our early family gatherings, I remember, kind of revolved around the church.

BMG: **You mentioned you were Rev. Skinner's first baptism. How important was that moment for you.**

BB: At the time, I didn't really understand the poignancy of it, obviously, you understand. I loved to swim, so the whole point of the baptism, for me, was cool, you know. But I was very young, so I'm not really sure, you know, how knowledgeable I was about everything that was happening at the time. I know I was very studious; I could recite all the books of the Bible when I was young—don't put me on pocket for that one right now [chuckles]—but it was, um … I was very proud, you know, that I knew different stories in the bible and the different books of the bible, you know, because those were ways to impress my father, at that time. As I got older, there were other ways of doing that, and then, at some point, I was no longer concerned with impressing my father. But that's another story for a different time.

BMG: **What gets you into hip hop? I will return to your religious upbringing later, but I want to get to the connection between hip hop and religion.**

BB: You know, when I first got into hip hop, I had no … I was not trying to be an artist. I was purely a fan. So, practicing hip hop was never in the cards for me; um … I never considered myself an athletic guy, I never considered myself, you know, terribly good looking, or anything like that. I figured I could get by, but, you know, I always felt like entertainment and, you know, at those times, I thought that was for different people—for a different class of people, a different type of person. You know, me, I was just more appreciative of the art of hip hop. I couldn't fathom how these guys were writing these rhymes and, you know, talking about all of these incredible experiences, and I was like, "man, it would be ill for me to be able to talk about that kind of stuff, but I'm not a rapper," you know what I'm saying'? I felt like rap was, like, a very special gift that was only given to a few people. So um, so I just kind of sat back and listened to it, and just appreciated the art form, until I started seeing people around me, in my own little small Port Arthur town, who were starting to rap and were actually good at it. And so I was like, "Damn, so we have special people like that, here too," and it was cool to watch them do it. And then, I saw somebody doing it—and I know this is going to sound a certain way—but I felt like I was smarter than this person. So that if this person could acquire the skill to rap, and it's all about words, and I know more words than he does, and I'm better at putting words together than he is in normal English conversation—if I converted that to rhyme form, I should, in theory, be a better rapper than him. Because I have a better command of the English language, which couldn't be further from the truth. Just 'cause you're bigger than somebody doesn't mean you can beat 'em up, you know? And so, it took a lot of time and a lot of practice, and um—you know, because I was terrible for a long time. I was terrible. I started rhyming in the summer between my sophomore and my junior year, during summer school, um, and that whole summer I was garbage. Just garbage, like the first 40–50 rhymes were just terrible, because I was just thinking, I'm trying' to … my whole life as an emcee was about trying to incorporate language that wasn't normally heard in rap music, so initially I thought that meant big words. But what it ended up coming down to was being able to speak what's in your heart without having to curse through it. Cause a lot of times when you're speaking and you don't have the right word that you want to use—nine times out of ten you use a cuss, you know what I'm saying'? You can't really tell a person how mad you are at them, you say, "Fuck you," you know what I'm saying'? [Laughs] So, for me, my thing was, how do I say, "fuck you," without saying "fuck you?" How do you know that what I mean—what I really mean at the core of what I'm saying is "fuck you," you know what I'm saying'—so that's when I started concentrating on, junior year, sophomore year. And then, um—and at this time I was not partnering with Pimp C; this was me formulating my own style of rhyming. When I eventually started working with Pimp, um, I realized it was just, you don't have to think of a crazy way to say something, you don't have to reinvent the wheel, so to speak, just speak your truth, you know what I'm saying. As long as you're being honest with yourself, you're going to always be honest with other people, and as long as you stick to the truth, you don't have to remember the lie.

BMG: **So you're brought up in the church, which is articulating a truth. And after you meet up with Pimp C, he tells you to speak your truth. So you have this truth in the church, and this truth that Pimp C has advised you to speak. Do you see a connection between religion and hip hop as ways of speaking the truth?**

BB: It's kind of that reverse fork in the road, where instead of being on one path and trying to figure out which way you want to deviate, I'm on

⚹ Back & forth btwn God truth & truth of dat day Flesh

these parallel paths, you know what I'm saying, kind of going back and forth, you know what I'm saying, between the truth as I know God wants me to live, and the truth of the flesh, and my day-to-day, what I'm dealing with. It takes me a few years before I realize the only way to deal with the matters of the flesh is to go to the truth of God, and it takes me a while and years of dealing in the flesh and really doing a lot of things that I only was doing because I had the ability to do it—you know, the drugs, the random sleeping with the women—all these things I was doing because I could do 'em and there was no reason for me to not do 'em. Then the repercussions of these things came—STD's, you get dissed by girls, you know what I'm saying, and things like that—and you get far removed from who you really are. And the only way to get back to who you really are is to get back to who you really are.

Realizes can deal w/ Flesh thrugh God after being off track

BMG: **Do you think hip hop offers you a way to get back to who you really are as well?**

BB: I think—oh absolutely, because what happens is, is that hip hop is my job; it's the way I take care of my family. But sometimes, I can't get caught up in just being me. I tend to forget I got a day job. So I have the kind of job that allows me the freedom to go home and not do anything for three weeks; but that's not a good thing if I'm not doing anything for three weeks! [Chuckles] Something's wrong, I should be contributing, you know what I'm saying? So—and then in my earlier years I thought those two had to be separate—that through the music I had to serve the world, and through my prayer and faith, I served Christ. You could do both, as long as you're being honest and true about it. So as I got older, I started realizing that, you know, you don't have to say what you think they want you to say, you know what I'm saying? What is true to you is what they really want you to say. So you start off being very true to yourself; as you learn the industry, you learn that, you know, if I do this or if I do that, or if I make songs about this or if I project myself like this or market myself like this, I can go much, much further. But, at some point in time, you're going to compromise yourself, you know what I'm saying, as a person. So there was always that fight to not, you know, man I want to go to the other side—I really would love to have this huge house and have all of this fame, but at what cost? So as appealing as everything seemed to Pimp [C] and me about really taking our careers really into the next stratosphere, we couldn't compromise ourselves; we wouldn't be able to look at ourselves in the mirror if we did that. So, a lot of times, when a lot of people thought we should've been bigger than we were or more famous than we were, we just refused to go down certain roads. We just refused to go down those roads.

⚹ Refused to Compromise certyn Parts of himself—sacrificed some material success to preserve that

BMG: **But you are Bun B. So somehow you got the notoriety. Or, to put it differently: do you feel like you got the notoriety, and does hip hop remain a space for you to fully express yourself with integrity, or do you feel like now you have to compromise? In what way does hip hop still allow for you to be you?**

BB: Once I stopped worrying about notoriety, once we stopped worrying about being famous, once we stopped worrying about, "Should we have to try to impress certain people," that's when everything changed. Once we took those shackles off, it gave us the freedom to truly speak about things we really wanted to speak about. One of the things that we always loved about Rap-a-lot and the Ghetto boys was that on every album, outside of all the crazy gangsta shit that they spoke, they had one song that had to have some kind of social commentary. And it had to be true to what they believed. So, I remember they made an anti-abortion song, and it was during the time when, you know, this was a very volatile conversation we were having in our country—doctors were dying—but, you know, this was what was true to them, this was what was true to their beliefs, um, you know, rap-a-lot as a label, many people don't know it, but they're very … J. Prince [the owner and CEO of rap-a-lot records] has very strong opinions about shacking up, not being married, you know, and children being born bastards, and things like that, so, you know, growing up and looking up to these guys, I looked up to them for their music, but then, I look at the other side, you get to know them as people, and they're still, you know, they're still trying to let you know where their character—all of this is about character: how you carry yourself as a person. So a lot of what we talk about is how we carry ourselves. But then, as UGK, our thing was to pull the curtain back on—pull the curtain, you know, back on the wizard and show you what it really looked like. So a lot of what people were talking about happening on the street was the "good things" about it—the money, the cars, the women, the clothes, and the lifestyle. What we wanted to tell people was, "Hey, there's a flip side to all of this. These dudes you see ballin' in the club and all of that, they go home and they cry, they pray, they worried about gettin' into heaven just like you, you know? So then, our music, you know, we wanted our music to reflect both sides. As we got older, and we understood better, we could implement it more, you know? The first couple of albums, there may be one song; there may be two songs. Then as, you know, right before Pimp went to prison and we started having these conversations, as he goes into prison, these conversations become more significant to us, you know? We were asking these questions before, and now we're living these questions out in real time. So when he came home, he was like, "yo, we have to let people know how we feel and how we view the world because people are looking to us to grow," because there are things people are wanting to say, things that people feel, but they're unsure how to express it, because the streets don't allow you to express it that way, you know? Even up until the point when Pimp C passed away, I made it—I kind of felt, I was grieving, you know, I was grieving very rough. But, I called in the radio station, and I talked and I cried, and I let people know that the young black man, or young men in general, it's okay to grieve. It's okay to cry and let it out, because, all that's going to happen if you keep it inside is you're going to let this pain out in a way you can't control, and in a way you're going to regret. So, I know a lot of times, we're taught not to cry about a lot of things, especially young men, you know, you're to "toughen up," suck it up, but that's more of a physical thing. [Death] is the only time we're taught to deal with tears and situations like that. We're very seldom taught to talk about emotions and how to deal with emotions with our young men, you know what I'm saying? So I felt obligated to show people that it's a good thing to release like this. You don't have to take a stiff upper lip. When people you love leave you, this is what you're supposed to do, you know?

BMG: **And was it hip hop that offered you the space to do that?**

BB: I realized that I no longer had to differentiate. It got to the point where I realized that who I was as an artist and who I was as a person were not different anymore. The character and the author came together. So I'm not writing about someone else; there's no alter ego anymore, you know? There's no "Bernard Freeman, a.k.a. "Bun B"; it's just "B" now, it's just—this is my reality, my reality as an artist—because at this stage in my life, the music business has been figured out. A lot of the early days were trying to figure out how to maneuver between the music business and the real world. I've mastered the music business; now I'm trying to master the real world, you know what I'm saying? And the better I am at one helps me to be better at the other. So it's just a matter of really just keeping a left hand and the right hand together. Which is how we pray.

BMG: **So you see a way for your identity as an artist and your religious identity to be merged together?**

BB: There is no other way at this point, because, whether as an artist, or as a person, I was always trying to save lives. As an artist, you know, I'm trying to make sure that the musicians that follow after me don't have to make the mistakes I've made … the people I represent, to let them know that they're being cared about. And as a person, you know, I'm actually trying to do my due diligence as a Christian, trying to be that Good Samaritan as often as possible. Well, isn't that what I'm doing in music anyway? I'm still playing those same roles, you know, on the stage or off the stage, so there's no need for me to differentiate anymore.

BMG: **We're going to go back in time, for a bit, to the 90s, where the Wu-Tang Clan and other groups were explicitly melding their religious identities with their musical expression. Help me to understand where your perspective was on these different religious orientations within the context of hip hop.**

BB: Or even before the 90s ... one of the very first real rap friends that we made in hip hop was Lord Jamar [of Brand Nubian]. So our awareness and understanding of Five Percent [Thought] came from one of the earliest practitioners in hip hop who was incorporating the Five Percent Nation's mind state. So ... and there was a certain point in hip hop where, if you didn't try to find some frame of reference within the Five Percent, you were missing out on some of the best music, you know? If you didn't have self-awareness, you couldn't really understand the X-Clan albums, or the Poor Righteous Teachers' albums, you know, or the Brand Nubian's albums, which was some of the best music out there? It goes from talking about maybe clothes or a party to speaking about mind-self-body, or Arm, Leg, Leg, Arm Head [the Five Percenter break down for the term "Allah"], but you don't have a frame of reference for these things. Sometimes, we would go to Lord Jamar's house, all the time, his wife would say hello from upstairs, but we never saw her, you know? And this was something that would never come up until, you know, the third or fourth visit, you know? She would be upstairs, they would be in a two-story townhouse, and she would be upstairs.

BMG: **Was [Lord Jamar's] wife allowed to come downstairs, or this was just the way they lived?**

BB: I don't know if it was allowed, I think it was more of a respect thing, like, you know, I think, at home, in their space, she's allowed to be as comfortable as possible. So, for her I think it's easier just to stay out of sight, like she's not—definitely not allowed—if she's at home, and it's 8 o'clock in the evening, she maybe got on a shirt and some shorts. She's not allowed to be dressed like that in front of other men. So, instead of her getting all super dressed up and coming down, she'd just say "hello" from upstairs and it's all good.

BMG: **Yes. So what does that say to you about hip hop? How do you understand the relationship between hip hop and these particular religious orientations?**

BB: As you grow as a person, and become more aware as a person, in the midst of that search to become more aware of yourself as a person, the higher power comes into play. Because what happens is, is that, you're sitting down wondering how to figure out why are things happening, and why are things not happening, and who controls this, you know? And once you run through all of the conspiracy theories of everything, the only thing that's left—the only real actuality that's left for you—is God. And we see it in so many other people, and we start to ask, if these guys can be as cool as they are, but as deeply religious and faithful as they are, then why can't we do the same? Initially, the Five Percent Nation just seemed like a club that you wanted to be a part of, but then when you realize how incredibly devout these people are, then you go, "You know what? I used to have this kind of connection with my higher power, and I walked away from it because I thought it wasn't something I could incorporate. But for these guys, it's the foundation! Why isn't that our foundation?" And it's not just a New York thing, because again … and I got to go back to rap-a-lot and the ghetto boys; they're doing it too! They're Baptist, just like us. They're letting it be known. The same way that they're like "I'm not afraid of no man?" [They're saying it] not just because "I'm a gangsta" but because "I have this faith behind me!" It's the faith that makes me walk around with my chest out!

BMG: **Right. But let me ask you this, though: the very people you're talking about—the church today—doesn't necessarily say, "look, come on in" to the people that you're talking about. That doesn't seem like a disconnect to you, between hip hop's way of being, and what the church—religion in the form of the church—is preaching? How do you handle that?**

BB: I'm flawed. You know, we always hear these things about, "I'm a work in progress," you know? I'm not perfect, none of us are perfect, and who's to say that I couldn't find something to point the finger at the people in the pew about? The reality is that I was born into my religion, and I eventually became a hip hop artist. But that doesn't mean I'm not still who I was; that just means I'm presenting a different side of myself, or wanting to present what I feel is a different side of myself. But at the end of the day, I'm not put on earth to please no preacher. I'm not here to please anybody, you know? If you choose to hold the good book that says, "judge not, lest ye be judged," and use that book to stand in front of your church and judge me, I'm just going to go—I'm going to cut out the middle. Especially if I know you ain't right. We talked about this before—the fact that there was a preacher (who will remain nameless) that we knew, personally, preaching at day, and at night was trying to mess with the same girls we were messing with! Okay, so now I know you're a man just like me; you're flesh just like me. You're fighting the good fight, just like me, you know what I'm saying? And it kind of … how can you preach to me about my testimony when you have no testimony to give? You trying to sit up here and tell me you've been perfect all your life? You're trying to sit up here and tell me that at 50 you're looking at me at 22, and judging me, at 22, when you know at 22 you were a different man than you are now? I mean, how many … what's the percentage of preachers who grew up in pastoral families? How many preachers today are the sons and daughters or grandchildren of preachers? So, you know, the church I go to … the reason I'm proud to go to that church is because if you come to my church, and you walk in, you're not going to know who the pastor is until he starts the sermon. He's not dressed different than any of the deacons, he's not driving any better car than any of the deacons, there's no big stupid chair at the front of the church that you sit in, and the junior ministers … it's basically like they "bigging you up," like saying, "Now, are you ready? Are y'all ready? Well get on your feet for pastor so-and so!" you know, and you got your theme music, you know? It's almost the same presentation as Richard Pryor in *The Carwash*. But to get back to your original question, man, it's like we worried about how the church will look at us for a long time. Until we realize that the church is not God. It's a place to worship God, but it's not the end all, be all about what happens between you and God. It's more of … say, if you go to a football game, then you're going to wear the jersey, you're going to put on the sports clothing, you're going to act accordingly. But that's kind of what church is like, you know? You dress a certain way, you going to come in here, you're going to sing—especially when you get into Catholicism, you know? It's very, very routine, very ritualized. But when does the ritual overtake the faith? When it's really more about just … you know, when does going to church stop being about, "Oh yeah, they saw me at church today?" Or when does it really become about you going to church as a place of worship for you to really connect with a higher power. Or is that somewhere where you go to say, "I took my kids to church—I'm a good mom because I take my kids to church." But you ain't getting the message, you can't relate the message to [the kids], you just took 'em to church.

The Church is not God, it's a place to worship God

BMG: **So whether you're in hip hop or in the church, people are people, is what you're saying?**

BB: Absolutely, you know? We shouldn't judge the church, we shouldn't sit back and judge you as a person, but you have to quit judging us. We have hip hop artists from within the church now that come out, who question the church. Because the church … for you to not accept a person who, his entire thing is about praising God, uplifting the name, sharing his experience, but you don't like the way it's done? You resent it? You don't want to let rap in the church—and not even Christian rap or gospel rap or rap that uplifts and praises his name—you don't want to let it in the church because it looks like and sounds like something else that you don't like? That's like saying you don't like—hold on, let me get a good analogy for this—that's like saying you don't like the Temptations because they sound too much like the Isley brothers.

We got to change ... so what happens now, the millennials, and people like yourself want to get closer to God, but don't want to go through the church.

BMG: **Last question: can hip hop be a religion by itself?**

BB: In my eyes, as I see the world—which probably may not agree with many people—I truly believe that religion should make you a better person. The virtues of the religion you follow should only make you a better person, and draw you closer to people. Religion was designed to bring people together in faith; it was not designed to be used as a weapon to separate people. Same thing for hip hop: hip hop was created to bring people together. Not to separate. So, if hip hop makes you a better person than the religion that you practice—or the way that you've been practicing that religion—then I would rather you be a part of hip hop than a part of an organization. For me, if a religion makes you a better person than hip hop does, then I would ask you to put the mic down, turn the turntable off, walk off the stage, and go get on your knees and pray somewhere. And if you can be mutually a part of hip hop culture, contributing in a positive way, affecting people's lives, and also be a part of an organized religion, affecting people's lives, speaking truth to people, then there's no duality and there's no reason for you to have choose either way. In that sense, religion is hip hop, and hip hop is religion.

nanism:

ew

ms[1]

A

relig

on the margins

of political and social life in the United States and around the world. While my most immediate focus is religious fundamentalism—in particular, the new resurgence of religious fundamentalisms, it is not exclusively so. I note also the political and cultural dimensions of fundamentalism, for example, the persistence of "market fundamentalism," or a rigid adherence to free market principles even in the face of countervailing evidence as to their effectivity or the unparalleled quest for "purity" among resurgent Rightest movements in the United States and around the world.

In this paper, I locate hip hop as a transformative cultural force—not a transcendent one, nor one with a clear moral teleology. Hip hop evidences a deep engagement with the everyday—the aforementioned "this-worldly." Participants have, over the last several decades, actively invented, reinvented, embedded, and re-embedded hip hop in myriad spaces—from clubs to bedrooms to cars to street corners to parks—in emergent and unpredictable ways. Hip hop has continually (often explicitly) rejected narratives of moral closure, and struggled against fixity and purity in a world that is increasingly looking for fixity or purity in all aspects of life—secular and otherwise.

In his careful treatment of the late Edward Said, "Transformation, Not Transcendence," Stathis Gourgouris explores Said's "secular criticism," as "an intransigent intellectual position that seeks to critique and *transform* existing conditions ... without submitting to the allure of otherworldly or *transcendent* solutions."[3] Gourgouris highlights the relentlessly "contrapuntal" nature of Said's critique, his effort to read texts (literary, musical, and otherwise) against each other without recourse to any sort of absolute authority. Said places us in the world, struggling toward a future that cannot be predetermined in advance. In so doing, he critiques what he sees as the dangers of thinking that would lock the world into preordained and predetermined forms and parameters. On this point, he writes, "The faith that certain policies and courses of action, whether directed by the will of God or the pseudorational analysis of national security specialists, will unilaterally transcend the contradictions of the present and be fulfilled in a redemptive future means lack of thinking critically, historically. It actually abdicates humanity's responsibility and self-consciousness in the making of history, making the future a mere game of power in order to confirm the status quo of power in the present."[4] For Gourgouris, "transcendence" looks to will away contradictions of the present in favor of a predetermined future, while "transformation" looks to the self-conscious, human making of history. If nothing else, hip hop evidences this self-conscious making of history—the work involved in investing and reinvesting deep, embodied meaning in the everyday in ways that can transform "this-worldly" experience.

Transcendent thinking—including authoritative faith in predetermined futures—has very much been a part of fundamentalist belief systems. As Malise Ruthven reminds us, the term "fundamentalism" came into wide use only in the early twentieth century with the publication of *The Fundamentals: A Testimony of Truth.*[5] Among other things, fundamentalism has come to rely on authoritative and fixed modes of transcendent thinking. Drawn together by two Christian brothers beginning in 1910, the tracts were meant to support the dispensationalist version of American Protestantism, one that affirmed the "inerrancy" of key beliefs including creationism and the imminent return of Jesus in the so-called End Times. The term has since become more widely used to describe a "religious way of being that manifests itself in a strategy by which beleaguered believers attempt to preserve their distinctive identities as individuals or groups in the face of modernity and secularization."[6] Indeed, as Ruthven and others such as Arjun Appadurai[7] have made so clear, fundamentalism is a modern phenomenon, often marked, I argue, by a need to reassert an authoritative tradition in the midst of what may be a disorienting cultural heterogeneity. In the Christian context, tradition "conveys the sense of a cumulative body of ritual, behavior, and thought that reaches back to the time of origins." In the Islamic context, tradition "means the accumulated body of interpretation, law, and practice as developed over the centuries by the *ulama*, the class of learned men who constitute Islam's professional class of religionists or clerics."[8] In both cases, tradition implies something firm and stable and long-standing.

Asserting tradition in its most literal and selective form, fundamentalism has become a bulwark for many against a world that is increasingly complex and messy. As Appadurai reminds us,[9] the contemporary flow of money, people, ideas, technologies, and images has worked to produce new kinds of localities all around the world. Multiple traditions and ways of life are now living side by side in hyper-diverse cities like London and New York. As Paul Gilroy has argued, this lived heterogeneity can produce a kind of everyday "conviviality" that makes the negotiation of difference "ordinary."[10] This everyday negotiation of difference can produce a sense of being "at home" everywhere—or a sense of cosmopolitanism. While they are produced by the same social, cultural, and material dislocations, fundamentalist responses are quite different. Fundamentalism here is anchored "in the responses of individual or collective selfhoods, of personal and group identities, to the scandal or shock of the Other."[11] In this sense, rigid and authoritarian fundamentalism is as much a product of globalization as is cosmopolitanism.

The quest for ideological and historical certainty has its parallels in other kinds of rigid, ideological dogmatisms that so mark our moment. For example, Appadurai compares the faith in free market principles to religious ones with free market faith emerging as something of a new religion—"the new religion of the market treats the market as the source of certainty, as the reward for disciplined focus on its messages and rhythms and as the all-embracing power that rewards its own elect, so long as they obey its ethical demands."[12]

In the first edition of his book on globalization, Manfred Steger noted that free market principles have formed bedrock ideologies for structuring popular understandings of globalization.[13] Free market principles were seemingly "natural" forces, outside the control of individuals, sorting winners and losers in inexorable ways. In the second edition of his book, Steger added "jihadist globalism" to "market globalism" as ideologies giving structure and meaning to many around the world today.[14] That these phenomena can be treated in a parallel fashion only underscores (as Ruthven writes) the kind and range of "extremism, sectarianism, doctrinism, [and] ideological purism" so apparent today.[15] These ideologies often rely on notions of worldly transcendence—the rigid belief in a future that can unilaterally resolve any contemporary contradictions.

In contrast, the humanisms I will discuss here rely more on transformative approaches to change, on an understanding of human beings as active, self-conscious makers of history who do not take recourse to ideological purism or rigid doctrinarism. These are the tendencies I see most pronounced in hip hop and ones that I see most valuably understood through various frameworks of humanism(s). Of course, I use the plural here advisedly. Some forms of humanism in the singular can be as narrowly conceived as some forms of fundamentalism. For example, Enlightenment humanism tended to make an authoritative religion out of reason and was conceived along strictly Eurocentric lines. The "human" at the core of this humanism was the white, property-owning male—a fiction enforced through various forms of overt and subtle power.[16] Understanding humanism in the plural allows us various angles of vision on hip hop as an evolving set of transformative "this-worldly" social practices that allow participants to make meaning in and of the world in complex, heterogeneous ways.

I draw on two different treatments of humanism—Said's "secular humanism" and Pinn's "African American nontheistic humanism." Both locate critical energies in the secular or everyday but have somewhat different concerns. A Palestinian American, Said's form of criticism was avowedly "worldly" and he wrote as someone who lived most of his life in exile. Said's concern with humanism was broadly informed by his stance on world affairs (including the plight of the Palestinians), and he was centrally concerned with expanding notions of democracy and democratic criticism. Pinn's version of humanism is located more closely in the experiences of African Americans in the United States, and is centrally concerned with the role of religion in African American life. For Pinn, however, religion should be delinked from its often assumed home in Christian churches and instead evoke all the spaces in which people can critically engage, articulate, and discuss *the deep existential and ontological issues endemic to human life.*[17] Looking at both forms of humanism together further underscores the idea that humanism itself can best be seen as multiple—not the exclusive possession of one group or another.

Edward Said and Anthony Pinn on humanism

I begin with Edward Said. Said is broadly concerned with a kind of critical, intellectual practice that looks to broader democratic possibilities in world affairs. Said's work is marked by the impulse to make more and more of the world available for "critical scrutiny" as a basic part of democratic intellectual practice.[18] While he was concerned with literary texts, the impulse to make more and more work available for scrutiny will be helpful for understanding the proliferation of regional forms of hip hop in ways I discuss below. Indeed, throughout his work, Said did not close off engagement with a range of texts and practices but famously called for "contrapuntal" readings. Ideological purity was less important to Said than particular, critical dispositions toward a "worldly" body of texts and practices. As Said wrote, "the essence of humanism is to understand human history as a continuous process of self-understanding and self-realization."[19] He noted that the purpose of humanism is "to make more things available to critical scrutiny as the product of human labor, human energies for emancipation and enlightenment, and just as importantly, human misreadings and misinterpretations of the collective past and present."[20] This kind of "critical scrutiny" opens up a range of texts for exploration—wherever one can locate human energies and labors as part of the ongoing human project, and it guards against the kinds of intellectual control and determining clarity that often accompanies "fundamentalist" approaches to critical scrutiny—religious, political, intellectual, or otherwise.

If Said's vision of humanism was a secular one, Anthony Pinn's version engages more directly with the debates in religion though remain rooted in the worldly. In his book, *The End of God Talk: An African American Humanist Theology*, Pinn looks to challenge what he calls "God talk" in contemporary religious discussions. For Pinn, African American humanist theology pays attention to the "search for meaning in its most significant form(s)." This search for meaning does not "look for transcendence *beyond* this world" (a theme I will pick up again below).[21] Rather, it forces our attention to the everyday ways in which people look for meaning, and make meaning in the world. Pinn's move turns our attention away from what he calls "God talk." For Pinn, such talk is too easily wrapped up in symbolic ideals—the most obvious being so-called Imago Dei the notion of a singular god who will provide personal transcendence. Pinn argues, "God has never been anything more than a symbol—an organizing framework for viewing and living life in 'relationship to....' This symbol has run its course, and it is no longer capable of doing the heavy lifting required for the contemporary world."[22] Of course, such "God talk" tends to focus attention on specific homes of worship—churches. For Pinn, "God talk" typically centralizes discussion of religion in ways that pull attention away from the broad swath of everyday activity where people look for and create meaning for themselves. Pinn argues for a kind of theology that would recast "God talk" in less transcendent or metaphysical terms, allowing for a kind of humanist recasting of religion as the search for ontological and existential meaning in this world.

Both approaches to humanism are helpful for understanding hip hop today. In what follows, I look at two key currents in hip hop history, and see how they can be understood through various strands of humanism(s). I first look at the ways southern hip hop challenged the bicoastal hegemony of hip hop by continually pulling participants into a variety of everyday spaces—cars, clubs, street corners, bedrooms—where the bodily rituals could be enacted and reenacted. Said's democratic impulse to make more and more of the world available for critical scrutiny is useful for understanding this tendency. I then look at how hip hop artists Jay-Z and West reflect on the limits of worldly transcendence—the ways the gods of wealth and fame do not deliver on their promised ideals, particularly for African Americans in the United States. Pinn's discussion of "God talk" proves useful here for highlighting how Jay-Z and West reflect on the limits of rigid narrative and moral closure, as well as worldly transcendence. In both cases, I look at how humanist approaches to hip hop highlight how the art form has continually resisted conscription in various efforts at ideological purity or discursive clarity. In both cases, I look at hip hop as a transformative not transcendent social and aesthetic force.

Southern hip hop

I begin here with Amiri Baraka's (then LeRoi Jones's) classic *Blues People*.[23] Baraka's book was an attempt to trace out a particular trajectory for African American music in the US—from early slave music up through bebop jazz. Baraka rooted African American music in an oral tradition, one that privileged face-to-face communication and interaction. Baraka argued here that the Western preference for composed music, and the performance of scores in concert halls—high European classical music—was largely a political artifact. That is, the notion that written traditions were valued over and above oral ones served to marginalize the cultural productions of groups that did not have historical access to or preference for composition. Baraka argued that art in African American communities was stitched into the everyday life of oppression—both in terms of form and function. In his discussion of "serious"

Western music, Baraka writes, "One would not think of any particular use for Haydn's symphonies, except perhaps the 'cultivation of the soul.' 'Serious music' (a term that could only have extra-religious meaning in the West) has never been an integral part of Westerner's life." He goes on to say, "It was, and is, inconceivable in the African culture to make a separation between music, dancing, song, the artifact, and a man's life or his worship of his gods. *Expression* issued from life, and *was* beauty." A "dreadful split between art and life" allowed for the distinction between "'art' music" and "something someone would whistle while tilling a field."[24] For Baraka, the everyday is a site where music and art can be re-ritualized—music, dancing, and song are part of everyday life and cannot be separated from the religious. As above, Baraka resists the idea of authoritative texts that have sacred meaning, outside of their contexts of use—hence his reference to Hayden. Indeed, the very separation of a Hayden symphony from something someone would whistle while tilling a field was part of a deep split between "art and life" that Baraka saw as problematic to the core. In what follows, I call particular attention to southern hip hop and the impulse to "re-ritualize" it at every turn, to bring it back to everyday or "this-worldly" contexts of use evoked above.

If nothing else, hip hop's history has been a testimony to the pull to bring art and culture into the everyday. Hip hop began in the context of social interaction—in New York City basements, parties, and clubs, where DJs like Kool Herc and Grandmaster Flash mixed and cut records to get crowds dancing and moving. Through the late 1970s and early 1980s, hip hop was a music conceived largely in the context of live parties. MCs were originally used by DJ's to hype the crowd though they eventually came to take central stage. With the rise of hip hop as a recorded medium, "rapping" fully came to the fore, and skilled MC's did more than enliven parties. For many years, hip hop was a bicoastal affair between the East and West Coasts. The former was associated with rap's origins and claimed many of the most sophisticated lyricists. The latter was associated with the wildly popular genre of "gangsta rap" and claimed a kind of "realness" rooted in gang life. Indeed, authenticity or "realness" was always a central part of hip hop. This concern with authenticity or "realness" was taken up most fully by Imani Perry in her excellent *Prophets of the Hood*. She writes, "Realism in hip hop is an artistic format inextricably linked to the material conditions of black American urban communities," though this, I argue, "realness" has taken on different valiances for different groups over time.[25] For those on the East, hip hop's authenticity claims were located in the genre's roots and the skills of its top lyricists. For example, artists like KRS-One, Rakim, and Kool G Rap displayed verbal and poetic dexterity that defined "real" hip hop for many self-proclaimed aficionados. Popular criticism tended to stress the aesthetics or politics of the genre. For those on the West, authenticity claims were located in the lives of its narrators. For example, artists like NWA, Ice Cube, and Ice-T narrated first-person tales of gang life that defined "real" hip hop for others. Popular criticism of West Coast hip hop tended to be more sociological in nature.[26]

The south was largely ignored by mainstream hip hop artists and journalists until the mid-nineties. In the absence of support from mainstream commercial outlets, southern hip hop developed from the "ground up," largely satisfying a poor, African American base of fans. Southern hip hop would come to dominate commercial sales beginning in the late 90s, leaving many critics and artists trying to sort out the implications.

While hip hop was a commercially successful music form with broad popular appeal, it never lost its regional roots. Indeed, a kind of regionalism became increasingly pronounced in the late 1990s and early 2000s just as "scenes" and "crews" became more important than individual rappers. As hip hop circulated nationally and internationally, communities around the country reclaimed it in particular ways. For communities in the south, reclaiming or reasserting hip hop's roots as a club-based music—a music about social interaction—was paramount. While the themes were ones that emerged in hip hop at this time (that is, the ones associated with so-called hardcore rap), much of this music was influenced by a distinctly southern flair.

For artists in New Orleans, this meant a sound often called "bounce"—a music rooted in dance. Influenced by hard, percussive hip hop beats, as well as the big band, jazz inflected sounds of "second line" Mardi Gras music and dance, "bounce" artists made music for block parties and clubs. For artists in Houston, this meant a music rooted in the "mix tape" aesthetic of DJ Screw and others. The sound was distinct to the region—sprawling, laid back, and hypnotic. For artists in Memphis, this meant the "crunk" music of artists like Three-Six Mafia and Eightball and MJG and the accompanying "gangsta walk" dance and riotous live performances. Each of these scenes reclaimed hip hop and returned it to its roots in everyday social interaction.

Atlanta was, in many respects, the Southern scene that received the most initial national attention in hip hop. In a iconic moment in hip hop history, Atlanta rap group Outkast won the "best new rap group of the year" award at the Source music award ceremony at Madison Square Garden in 1995. This event is largely remembered for its role in the evolving feud between East Coast label Bad Boy (headed by Sean Combs, most prominently featuring Biggie Smalls) and West Coast Death Row Records (head by Suge Knight, most prominently featuring Tupac Shakur). The event was marked by a clash between the camps and onstage comments by Knight and Combs. Of course, both Shakur and Smalls would later be killed in still unsolved homicides.

Less noted (for a time, at least) but perhaps as important was Outkast taking the stage to win the "best new rap group of the year" award. The group won the award in the wake of the platinum success of their album,

Southernplayalistic, now considered a classic of the genre. The largely East Coast crowd booed the group, crystalizing the anti-South sentiment common on both coasts. While group members Big Boi and Andre 3000 were initially dismissed, Andre 3000 proclaimed, "The South got something to say!"—a phrase long since remembered as marking the South's ascent into the national stage. Reflecting back on the moment and its importance for the South and Atlanta, Big Boi notes, "Back then, we said, 'The South got somethin' to say.' That was back in '94, '95 or whatever, and you skip fast-forward, and look at what the South has done: from OutKast and Goodie Mob, we got Ludacris and T.I. ... , 2 Chainz, Gucci ... you know what I'm saying? Atlanta music, Atlanta artists, Jeezy ... it's a certain brotherhood that we got out here in Atlanta."

In addition, Atlanta played a large role in mixtape culture. In fact, Atlanta was also home to one of the most noted mixtape DJ's in the genre, DJ Drama. Drama would go on to release mixtapes for Atlanta artists including T.I., Young Jeezy, and Gucci Mane on his noted "Gansta Grillz" series. These mixtapes existed in a kind of legal gray area—they were not official studio releases and often had numerous supposed copyright violations. While they were technically "for promotion only," these mixes helped commercial careers of T.I. and Young Jeezy and DJ Drama would eventually produce a mixtape with Gucci Mane. As with the mixtapes noted earlier, these mixes were produced and circulated outside of the normal industry chains of distribution. These tapes helped solidify one of the many "signature styles" that would mark the South—trap rapping.

The South disrupted what many saw as a bicoastal hegemony. That is, southern hip hop underscored the culture's impulse to embed itself in the everyday lives of its listeners, particularly in the context of dance. As noted, the East had long been marked by a stress on complex, lyrical sophistication, as well as keen political sensibilities. The West had been marked by a stress on a kind of narrative "realness," rooted in seemingly accurate descriptions of inner-city life. If one considers the broad swath of popular and academic criticism to be a part of the hip hop industry, then this criticism helped to solidify this bicoastal bifurcation.[27] In contrast, southern hip hop encompassed a large and complex geographic region, marked by a plethora of styles that were produced and disseminated through a whole host of local modalities.

As Roni Sarig notes, southern hip hop remained firmly rooted in social interaction. The South is a place "where chanting and unabashed party songs are still part of hip hop's social fabric. The music's foundation—from booty dancing in Florida to gangsta walking in Memphis—has always been tied to its listeners, and fulfills a social function. Unlike the too-hip-to-dance stance of New York hip hop heads, the provincials down South are still unselfconscious enough to enjoy the music."[28] In this sense, the music allowed multiple opportunities for a kind of re-ritualization for what had once been a music rooted in social interaction. In this respect, hip hop is in the long line of music that Baraka treats—music that is a part of everyday life.

Said's version of humanism gives us another angle of vision on this music and culture—the "worldliness" of humanist criticism that makes more and more of the world available for critical scrutiny. For Said, the goal was to understand the evolving human story wherever it could be located or found. This could only be accomplished by a continual pushing out of the boundaries of what can be considered part of human accomplishment. "Humanism is not about withdrawal or exclusion."[29] One must remain "open to the presence and still unresolved, still open to the presence and the challenges of the emergent, the insurgent, the unrequited, and the unexplored."[30] One can understand the coastal evolution of hip hop through this lens. If West and East Coast hip hop scenes looked to pull hip hop into certain authoritative social, political, or aesthetic readings through the work of key, high profile recording artists (several of which I noted above), southern hip hop resisted this impulse, and continually placed hip hop back into the everyday lives of its listeners in various and unpredictable ways. In this sense, one can understand this particular "genealogy" of hip hop as one of human transformation, of the impulse to make more and more regions in the United States available for creativity though more and more creative modalities—from cars to bedrooms to street corners to parks through various media such as mixtapes.

Holy Grail

I turn now to the work of Pinn. For Pinn, a reconceptualized approach to theology would push us outward into the world, to look for the places where people find meaning for themselves. As Pinn points out, "although traditional geographies such as churches can play a significant role for some humanists (particularly those referencing themselves as religious humanists), nontheistic humanism can actually be expressed in the very living of life within the broad plans and hidden corners of mundane existence."[31] Importantly, this notion of "the very living of life" forces us into complex spaces that do not have a specific, preferred teleology. "There is no determined need to even think of humanist religiosity in terms of good and bad—with good being liberative and bad meaning oppressive."[32] Pinn's reconceptualized version of African American nontheistic humanism offers a useful framework for understanding hip hop. He argues, "It is argued that religious experience is *religious* in that addresses the search for meaning in its most significant form(s), also called complex subjectivity. It is humanistic in that meaning does not entail transcendence *beyond* this world, and it is African American because it is shaped by and within the context of African American historical realities and cultural creations."[33] This complex subjectivity highlights "the fractured and fragile nature of the subject"—the human condition of contingency.[34] We see this struggle with this world (as opposed to another one), as well as the articulation of complex subjectivities in key hip hop artists like Jay-Z and West, who have produced work (individually and collectively) that meditate on these themes, and often articulate them in specifically religious terms. Both need to be understood more broadly in the context of hip hop.

Rappers have long talked about their everyday struggles, as well as the legal and illegal ways they have tried to transcend quotidian struggles with poverty. On the one hand, this constant concern with wealth as a way to transcend poverty has reinforced the notion that hip hop is a highly individualized genre, one that accepts and even celebrates the ethic of capital accumulation so endemic to neoliberalism. On the other hand, to struggle for the rewards of capitalism in a deeply unfair society can be a profoundly allegorical endeavor. The struggle for material rewards in such an unequal society can both highlight persistent inequities and offer ways of vicariously coping with them—a key part of their appeal.

I recall here Jay-Z's long body of work that has struggled with these concerns explicitly. For example, Jay-Z's first album *Reasonable Doubt* (1996) chronicled his own efforts to turn from illegal hustler or drug dealer to legal hustler or rap artist. Throughout, his goal is fairly straightforward: to achieve material wealth. For example, on his song "Dead Presidents II," Jay-Z talked about being "out for presidents to represent" him. Jay-Z underscores here the long-standing concern in hip hop around "representation" as a complex motif—what Marc Lamont Hill calls "representin(g)."[35] If hip hop is about representation, that representation for Jay-Z is fairly straightforward—dollar bills in all their multiplicity. This search for money is girded by the filmic narratives of *Scarface* and *Carlito's Way*, open album tracks. Both films are often referenced in hip hop—especially *Scarface*. In both cases, the films feature characters who have "come up" through the drug trade—achieving something like the "American Dream," albeit illegally. Jay-Z would solidify his allegiance to this alternative form of the American Dream, in his soundtrack to *American Gangster* (2007), a film about drug kingpin Frank Lucas. These films were largely about the goal of personal and social transcendence, providing a clear narrative backdrop for hip hop as genre, while "mainstreaming" the acquisition of wealth that has so preoccupied the music and culture.

In the years hence, Jay-Z would produce more complex autobiographic works with more deeply personalized and psychologized themes. Perhaps most significantly, his 2003 album, *The Black Album*, was conceptualized as a personal meditation on his life. The track "December 4th" is instructive, putting his life into a clear narrative arch, complete with an explanatory, psychological subtext. Jay-Z begins by noting his conception between parents

Gloria Carter and Adnis Reeves, before rapping about being "torn apart" when his "pop disappeared." He raps about increasing rebelliousness and anger, noting that nothing could make up for "the pain of my pop not seeing me." In addition, Jay-Z notes feeling "worthless" because of his poor, mismatched clothing. Life appears better when he starts dealing drugs—he's with the "in crowd" with women and "swag" all around him. While he could rap, it came second to drug dealing. But the "stress" became too much, with the threat of police, other drug dealers, and the danger of "drought" in the available product. Jay talks briefly about returning to rap full time, or trying "this rap shit for a living"—the fruits of which he will demonstrate throughout the album.

This complex personal and familial narrative deepens on later tracks, such as "Moment of Clarity." If "December 4th" was about his anger at the loss of his father, this track details coming to terms with his death. While his father was absent, and Jay-Z raps about seeing his own face in his father's face—like him, his father got "caught" into "the same game" he "fought", a game that many others lost. Jay-Z survived by moving into the music business, however. Here, he talks about the concessions he had to make to be commercially successful—about deciding not to rap like "conscious" hip hop rappers Talib Kwali or Common after seeing how much his own, popular style sold. The goal above all else is material wealth. "I can't help the poor if I'm one of them," he raps, noting that he "got rich and gave back"—a "win, win."

One can usefully posit *Magna Carta Holy Grail* (2013) against these earlier efforts. If *Reasonable Doubt* was about the struggle with the transcendence of material wealth and fame on the horizon, and *The Black Album* was a personal, complex meditation on that life, MCHG was about the death of those gods—the gods of wealth and fame. The opening track, "Holy Grail," underscores this disappointment. Indeed, in the very first verse, Jay-Z raps about seeing what the "lights and cameras" did to MC Hammer, as well as what the "bright lights" did to Mike Tyson, and noting that he looked for fame the same way Kurt Cobain did. These references are telling. All three of these figures—Hammer, Tyson, and Cobain—index the danger of fame and wealth. That he would call this song "Holy Grail" underscores the dangers of worldly transcendence when focused on single, culminating ideals.

West is another important example here. West's earliest work did not focus on drug dealing, but he was well-known for songs that pushed the aesthetic and lyric content of hip hop. For example, his early song "Jesus Walks" (2004) from his first album, *The College Dropout*, was a very straight-forward song about his faith. West would achieve a remarkable degree of financial and critical attention in the wake of this album, and he quickly became one of the most prominent and successful artists in the industry. Ironically, he also mediates on the ways this religious theme might stop the track from getting radio play. In a stunning reflection, he raps, "They say you can rap about anything except for Jesus," including "guns, sex, lies, [and] video tape." We see here a theme that would resonate throughout his career—his ambivalent relationship with mainstream success. Indeed, West has always been somewhat uncomfortable with his public fame, and has had numerous run-ins with paparazzi and others.

Interestingly, West would call his latest album *Yeezus* (2013), which contains tracks like "I Am a God," where he details his own godlike status in the industry. On this track, he calls himself a God, and tells his imagined listener to "hurry up" with his "damned croissant." Clearly, he sees himself as a larger than life figure, having achieved fame, fortune, and critical accolades for his music. West raps that he is both "a man of God," even as his life is "in the hands of God," before summing up—"Y'all better quit playing with god!" This latter point begs the question: whom is the listener supposed to stop playing with—West or God (with a capital "G"). In many respects, this conflation seems part of the point here, the way West moves theological discussions into the everyday material world. West asserts his godlike status even as he meditates on the limitations of success in this world.

Tracks like "New Slaves" are even more explicit in articulating frustrations with worldly fame. West begins the track by talking about his mother's struggles during the civil rights era, a moment in time when people collectively struggled for collective rights—the so-called promised land of Martin Luther King Jr. "My mama was raised in the era when clean water was only served to the fairer skin!" Yet, this song is not about racial uplift per se, though it clearly comments on racism. West goes on to detail all the ways in which he is still something of a "new slave" to the industry—still victim to stereotypes about wealthy African Americans. "Y'all throwing contracts at me, you know that n**** can't read, throw em some Maybach keys!" The victories of the civil rights era are not entirely apparent here. "I know that we the new slaves." His material success has only opened up new avenues for struggle.

In using the pronoun "we," West underscores a larger point about the persistence of racism in the United States. In a number of well-publicized interviews and appearances, West has critiqued what he sees as a "glass ceiling" in the entertainment industry—one that has allowed him to achieve fame and fortune as a rapper but not parlay that success into other areas such as fashion. He has been a vocal critic of fashion brands and outlets such as Louis Vuitton, Nike, and others who have not accorded him the space he perceives he needs to "branch out" from music. In this sense, his own personal fortune has not accorded him the kind of social and cultural mobility that he might have expected or anticipated. In "New Slaves," he asserts that the fashion industry would never accept him "unless [he] picked the cotton" for the clothes himself. The seeming permanence of racism in the United States is key for West in "New Slaves" even as he asserts his godlike status.

In both of these cases, we see extended meditations on the struggles to transform this world. This everyday struggle is melancholic or tragic (in the classic sense), emerging from a sense of the world as deeply flawed and without utopias on the horizon. The humanism of Pinn proves useful here—particularly Pinn's impulse to end "God talk" (in the traditional sense) and push us into a space (or spaces) of a humanist theology where complex subjectivities can be enacted. God talk does not provide an organizing framework here for either Jay-Z or West but rather a humanist theology that asks both to consider their subjectivities in a world where such organizing frames have been decentered. In fact, this notion is explicitly commented upon by both Jay-Z and West on the first track of their collaborative album, *Watch the Throne* (2012)—"No Church in the Wild." On this track, both Jay-Z and West evidence their complex relationship with religion in the context of a hyper-material world. While many tracks on this album detail hyper-materialism, this song begins with a sobering refrain that highlights the existential condition of life lived without "gods" of any kind—"What's a mob to a king? What's a king to a god? What's a god to a non-believer?" Here, mobs, kings, and gods are all trumped by the reality of the nonbeliever who does not "believe in anything." This pushes us into the "wild" and away from "churches." In this sense, the large questions of life cannot be addressed wholly in specific, sacred spaces, but must be taken out into "the wild."

Indeed, Pinn's challenge to "God talk" seems a challenge to those who would look for such certainty in sacred texts and spaces alone. Like other humanists, he pushes us outwards into the world. There is very little moral certainty in this move. He writes, "The very yearning for complex subjectivity itself and the various responses and yearnings are more complex than that and cannot be lodged within the conceptual frameworks suggested by qualifiers such as 'good' and 'bad.'"[36] If nothing else, this has been the space of hip hop.

Conclusion

As noted, fundamentalism is best seen as a modern response to the "shock of the Other," "the crisis for believers that inevitably follows the recognition that there are ways of living and believing other than those deemed to have been decreed by one's own tradition's version of the deity."[37] As Ruthven and others have noted, the contemporary moment has seen a series of revivalist religious movements, movements which claim special access to universal truths, often found in the literal reading of foundational "sacred" texts. These fundamentalisms are verily the response to the complexity of the global world, as Appadurai writes, "the uncertainties about identity that global flows invariably produce." These fundamentalisms "may be seen as part of an emerging repertoire of efforts to produce previously unrequited levels of certainty about social identity, values, survival, and dignity."[38] Contemporary global flows have been met with vicious fundamentalisms that aim for new and brutal kinds of clarities. The quest for certainty has produced rigid and dangerous dogmas and ideologies, often rooted in claims to worldly "transcendence."

Various forms of humanism become important correctives here—the democratic humanism of Said, or the nontheistic African American humanism of Pinn. In both cases, we are pushed past this quest for certainty, out into the messy complexity of the world. Understanding hip hop through these lenses allows us to see that the art form is best understood as "transformative" as opposed to "transcendent." Such an understanding of hip hop gets us away from discussions about "positive" versus "negative" hip hop—indeed, it provides a critique of traditional sources of morality and their claims to authority, and takes us outwards to the world in all its complexity. This transformative impulse is enacted in southern rap and its unique history and is articulated more explicitly by artists such as Jay-Z and West. In all cases, we see an art form resistant to transcendent ideals. The wise participant in contemporary global affairs would do well to attend to this very basic impulse.

11

Conspiracy is the sincerest form of flattery: Hip hop, aesthetics, and suspicious spiritualities

John L. Jackson, Jr.

Beauty and the beat: From social to antisocial contracts

It was 1997, and even as a native New Yorker (a native Brooklynite, no less!), I was in the midst of my very first pilgrimage ever to Marcy Projects, also known as the Marcy Houses, a 28-acre and 27-building New York City public housing complex in Bedford Stuyvesant, Brooklyn, first opened in 1949.[1] And yes, I called that short visit (only a couple of hours long) to those almost-identical six-story buildings a kind of pilgrimage, a journey to one of hip hop's holiest shrines. There are other sacred sites, certainly, older and more venerable locales, but for a discussion about hip hop's current center of gravity—not to mention its most commercially successful public spokesperson, Jay-Z—all roads lead through the newly constructed Barclay Center downtown and into the heart of "Do or Die Bed-Stuy," the historically poor and black neighborhood that ongoing gentrification has been making a little more "do" than "die" every single day.[2]

[handwritten margin notes: "Marcy projects in Bed-Stuy - hip hop shrine", "Jay Z's old stomping ground"]

I do concede, however, that other hip hop heads equally invested in the musical genre's potential sanctity might describe this same trek as something closer to an anti-pilgrimage, an excursion into the realms of the decidedly non-sacred. In fact, it could be described as a visit to one purported birthplace for a reincarnated version of the profane and demonic within contemporary popular culture. In Christo-centric terms, certain naysayers would consider any trip to Marcy, Jay-Z's old stomping ground, a search less for truth, beauty and divinity, than for their quintessential opposites: for clues to newfangled and seductive evils purposefully aligned against the forces of good. Cultural critic Hortense Spillers, for one, is working on a book about "the idea of black culture" that defines hip hop as antithetical to (and excluded from) the constitutive core of that very idea.[3] Such a position is of a piece with those that would condemn hip hop for its much-discussed commitments to violence, drugs, and hyper-sexuality—an undeniably unholy trinity. These kinds of criticisms disqualify hip hop culture, without singling out any particular artists, but there is often specific condemnation reserved for the likes of Jay-Z, one of the most financially successful hip hop artists in the history of the genre. And that same exceptional success might be part of the reason why Jay-Z is consistently linked to conspiracy theories about Satanic attempts at world domination, conspiracy theories that might help to tell us something useful about how hip hop continues to function as a space for fascinatingly existential questions about life and death, right and wrong, good and evil, heaven and hell.[4]

What does it mean to wonder aloud about this new—and old—conspiracy theory, found in hip hop music, and in black culture more generally (though clearly not just "a black thang" by any stretch), a conspiracy theory that links popular cultural performers and major musical celebrities such as Jay-Z to claims about a global cabal of devil-worshipping members of an occult group, the Illuminati, secretly attempting to control earth's population? This particular conspiracy theory might be one powerful example of what anthropologist Michael Taussig (retooling the "base materialism" of surrealist Georges Bataille) claims about the fundamental (seemingly universal) significance of beauty and aesthetics to any and all questions of sociopolitical power/contestation and to what he calls (following Max Horkheimer and Theodor Adorno) "the domination of nature."[5]

This brief essay is an attempt to ponder how a kind of vernacular semiotics of conspiracy—a hermeneutics of hyper-suspicion—constructs such conspiratorial claims in racially and aesthetically meaningful ways, claims that circulate far and wide on the internet and on network television. Similar to how accusations of secret homosexualities become the ubiquitous narratives around which many successful black public figures (from Will and Jada Pinkett-Smith to Jamie Foxx and Eddie Murphy) are defined as duplicitous and potentially inauthentic in their meteoric rise to fame, dismissed as mere sell-outs bowing to the backroom logics of Hollywood's secret codes, public invocations of hip hop's complicity with the Illuminati (about which, more later) and its supposedly Satanic agenda are windows into folk readings of contemporary life that tell us something about how certain forms of control, authority, and power are vernacularly conceptualized in an early twenty-first century America growing increasingly unequal by most economic measures. I want to examine this particular conspiracy theory with recourse to Taussig's claims about beauty's constitutive and inextricable links to terror. Considering the aesthetic coordinates of these hip hop conspiracy theories might help to explain how powerful logics of exclusion and exploitation have long been predicated on the recognition of racism's undeniably aestheticized historicity.

For Taussig, working in contemporary Colombian contexts, a notion of "the beautiful as force" grounds his concerted attempt to think about the links between plastic surgeries of various kinds in Latin America—from bikini-donning runway models augmenting their breasts and straightening their noses to fugitive drug criminals disguising themselves from law enforcement agencies through purposeful (and sometimes extreme) facial modification. Taussig wonders aloud about whether or not beauty's irrepressible "force" and "energy," a force and energy that serves, he implies, as something close to a central organizing principle for our species-being, also helps to regulate supposed contracts with the devil (literal Faustian pacts) that some poor laborers in the southern Cauca Valley region have been said to enter into when working for exploitative agribusiness firms. These "devil contracts" allegedly allowed cane cutters to double their wages over the short term, even as the accursed transactions eventually decimated livestock on their lands, ultimately rendering those same patches of earth completely barren. According to Taussig, the luxury items purchased with such occulted income easily presages the kinds of consumptive excesses that power the beauty industry and the cosmetic surgery that exploits it. The stories Taussig collects and relates about cosmetic surgeries, what he calls "cosmic surgeries," stories that usually seem to end in tragedy, dashed hopes, and the most grotesque of injuries, speak to the same sorcery-based logics that fueled devil wages, logics that ushered in the end of work itself for those wage-earners; there would be no contracts to sign, demonic or otherwise, if there was no longer any cane growing from the ground. This represents the central irony of Taussig's contention: beauty is not tragedy's or the ugly's or the beastial's *opposite* so much as their constitutive core—the grotesque but a culmination of beauty's completed and holistic logic.

Current conspiracy theories about hip hop icons and their links to the Illuminati pivot on a similar discussion about subjects willfully signing demonic/devilish contracts in a most decidedly literal sense. And there is something about the aesthetic energies and forces that seem to swirl around the semiotic ones in this particular instance that also meshes with Taussig's contention that beauty "saturates the arts of survival" and helps to spin "the motor of history" itself:

> If hunting and gathering technologies, making bows and blowpipes and canoes, spinning fibers, weaving clothes, building houses, and the great galaxy of the arts of kinship and ritual are bountifully present [in societies that anthropologists study], so is being gorgeous and handsome and fastidious about one's appearance. In what the celebrated Marcel Mauss called archaic societies, the economy (based on the gift) is at once religious, magical, political—and aesthetic.[6]

Specifically invoking Bronislaw Malinowski's work among the Trobrianders, Taussig goes on: "It was all so aesthetic, not only the dances with the oiling and perfuming of the body and the sculpture of the gardens, but the kula ornaments too, the red shell necklaces and the white shell bracelets[.]"[7] The point is not just that those hip hop artists allegedly linked to Illuminati plots of Satanic dominance are simply driven by a will to look beautiful, physically appealing, in their billboard ads and magazine articles. Instead, part of Taussig's suggestion would be to recognize how much of the evidence about these purported conspiracies are predicated on hyper-aestheticized renderings of their photographed and videotaped images. Indeed, much of the data for this Illuminati conspiracy evidence a commitment to streamlined and purposeful design or artistry, which might be productively flagged for just these aesthetic appeals and fixations. The fact that much of the conspiratorial documentation is being mined from carefully composed advertising campaigns, music videos, and other hyper-aestheticized genres only remind us that there is something about the centrality of beauty and the aesthetic to these images and iconic figures that only further implicates them in this ugly plot to turn the planet over to antihuman and self-destructive forces.

"Can't Truss It"[8]: Malcolm X, Manning Marable, and the stakes of race-based paranoia

Hip hop has long held its religiosities and spiritualities close to its albums' sleeves—if not on their covers, then certainly in their liner notes.[9] There have always been explicit "shout-outs" to Jesus and invocations to "the church" as a formative institutional space for MCs' early familial lives. At the initial stages of its public emergence and corporate institutionalization and co-optation during the 1970s and 1980s, some of its most provocative musical offerings were famously organized around the seemingly techno-paganist longings of DJs like Afrika Bambaataa of the Zulu Nation and Afrika Islam, host of the radio show Zulu Beats. Early hip hop was always more than just the slapstick revelry of groups like the Fat Boys and the Sugar Hill Gang. Spiritually inflected Afrocentrisms have long been fertile ground for hip hop iconography, even when some of those rap acts are glossed as (and conflated with) so-called conscious hip hop in ways that sometimes downplay their religified cores.[10] Figures as diverse as Sun Ra and Malcolm X were foundational muses beyond "party crowd" versions of hip hop's supposed superficialities, and their influence on a great many hip hop acts was predicated, in part, on the ways in which they steeped existential and political claims in unabashedly spiritual and religious registers.[11]

One common meme or theme of hip hop's masculinist self-description, for instance, includes the reimagining and recontextualizing of an iconic Malcolm X pose: the Muslim minister purposely peering out of a household window, curtains held to the side with one hand, and a rifle clutched in the other. Malcolm X's fusion of spirituality with radical racial politics has long served as justification for commitments to armed and organized self-defense, as well as for proud assertions of individual independence and autonomy. Cultural producers as diverse as KRS-One, Spike Lee, and Nicki Minaj have recast this recognizable photograph in their own ways. It is an image that links prophetic vision with militant action to instantiate a claim about the inextricable ties that bind cosmology to contested sociality.

Given ongoing rhetorical investments in Malcolm X's sociopolitical significance, it is not surprising that his imagery and legacy are carefully policed. It might be legitimate, for example, if KRS-One reverently cites the aforementioned image as grounding for his own religio-cultural politicking (which would eventually morph into his "Temple of Hip Hop" project), but Nicki Minaj using the aforementioned photograph of a rifle-clutching Malcolm for her song "Lookin' Ass Nigga" is deemed, predictably enough, wildly inappropriate.[12] Is Malcolm X peering out of that window an iteration of the "lookin' ass nigga" she disparages throughout her tune? Detractors recoil. How dare she proffer such analogics?

Amiri Baraka's withering critique of Spike Lee's cinematic rendition of Malcolm X's life for, among other things, its middle-class intonations and appropriations, anticipated the more recent (and even more scathing) dismissal of late historian Manning Marable's Pulitzer Prize-winning biography, *Malcolm X: A Life of Reinvention*. This hostile take on Marable's reading of Malcolm X's life is predicated on an even more cynical interpretation of mainstream and middle-class expropriations. One telling version of that critique, *A Lie of Reinvention: Correcting Manning Marable's Malcolm X*, edited by Jared Ball and Todd Steven Burroughs, is an anthology of criticism about Marable's book's political and historical shortcomings.[13] Marable's rendition of Malcolm X is dismissed as a manipulative narrative put in service to the logics of a decidedly depoliticized neoliberal moment. Marable gets cast as part of a

[handwritten margin note: photo of Malcolm X used by hip hop producers (spiritual + radical racial politics)]

concerted effort to remove the radical edge from Malcolm X's life story. As a function of Malcolm's ongoing sociopolitical importance, especially among the so-called hip hop generation the editors maintain that the minister's biography and ideology are purposefully neutered so as to model a much-weakened and purposefully inaccurate form of political subjectivity.

The editors frame their criticism within the specific register of conspiracy theorizing, with the late Marable, who died only a few days before the book's official release, directly implicated in, denounced for, and charged with embellishing Malcolm X's story as part of a larger project aimed at the docilization of contemporary Africana political actors. Ball and Burroughs toggle back and forth between a structural critique (of Marable's class positionality over-determining his historical interpretations) and a more explicitly conspiratorial and paranoid reading of Marable, with his editors, and other cultural gatekeepers (including reviewers for newspapers and awards committees) actively plotting to defang Malcolm's image, so that it could no longer be enlisted in the production of a radically antiracist social agenda—a social agenda most forcefully articulated through the lyrics of hip hop's politicized spokespeople.

[margin note: Criticism of ~~~~ Marable's reading of Malcolm X's life.]

But just because you are paranoid, the saying goes, does not mean that someone is not also out to get you. (Malcolm X's watchfulness by that window serves as a prime example of such a truism.) Paranoia is more than its own best critique. It is also a response to larger sociocultural contexts, whether or not that response seems proportionate to those contextual realities in some objective sense. Moreover, racial categorization per se, "race" itself, has always been about paranoia and conspiracy from the beginnings of its sociopolitical development and deployment. The very notion of race is, at heart, a distillation of paranoid fears mapped out onto an embodied hierarchy of social difference operationalized with self-interestedly imperial zeal and purpose by a constellation of forces and interests we have shorthanded with recourse to labels such as "the West." My brief discussion begins here with the idea that lines can be constructively drawn—even if just in broad strokes—between the irrationalities that ground race qua colonial conspiracy and the irrationalities that turn racialized hip hop artists into purported lapdogs for Satan.

[margin note: Race as a distillation of Paranoia.]

Racial Paranoia: The Unintended Consequences of Political Correctness was misread by some (purposefully so, the would-be conspiracy theorist in me thinks) as a call for the mere friending-away of America's racist history and contemporary racial problems.[14] *Racial Paranoia* does ask readers to interrogate their most intimate social networks and closest friendships for degrees of racial diversity and eclecticism, but anything they find, I argue, is an epiphenomenal extension of other issues—an indication of deeper historical and structural concerns. Indeed, I even spend time in the book talking about how interracial friendships can provide cover for the reproduction of racist performances and discriminatory practices. There is the example, say, of white college softball players donning blackface for a campus costume party, blackface dutifully applied and endorsed by some of their black friends at school. Friendships does not inoculate us from racist longings, nor from the extensive reach of racialist reasoning. That is all true, but it is also the case that we can not even begin to imagine a world of truly post-racial possibility if many of our most intimate networks are still stuck in the pre-Civil Rights Era's segregated parameters. *2 Points in Racial Paranoia*

Racial Paranoia had two main points. First, the abovementioned idea that "race," the very concept of race, at its core, is almost completely reducible to paranoia, especially, though not exclusively, as mobilized in "the West" to clear the way for psychically unfettered colonialisms linked to skin-color gradations and other observably physical human variations. The "grab for Africa" relied on race-based chattel slavery to justify and execute its motivations on ontological grounds (these are different and inferior and dangerous species/beings)—just as it leaned on Christianity to provide an empyrean alibi. Race is a way to dress up xenophobia and paranoia in the garb of natural threat—cultural distinctions read as irredeemably pre-cultural. So, the notion of "racial paranoia" is already redundant, a way to mark the addition of more and more layers of fear atop the ones that first organized the logic of racial exclusion and exploitation to begin with. Moreover, it is not a mere trivialization to argue that the history of race-based chattel slavery might be accurately framed in the language of global conspiracy, even as many would continue to dismiss such talk as nonsensical, irrational, and unproductively paranoid.

Paranoia inherent to race [margin annotation]

The second point I tried to emphasize in *Racial Paranoia* is predicated on the idea that we might actually be able to learn something from paranoiac postures—from concerns about concerted worldwide plots and backstage plotters organized around profound hatreds. Anthropology provides license to imagine that the cliché of a political scientist's plausible answer to wild conspiracies of all kinds (of Mexico's imminent plot to attack America and reclaim land, of the UN's slow-moving "Agenda 21" plan to seize southern states and transform them into communist oases, of Common Core's ulterior intention to turn young test-takers into anti-Christian and anti-American homosexuals, and of Jay-Z working for Satan's attempt to take over the planet), as a fleeing from the political and a distraction from actual politics, isn't the only possible response to talk of pending Mexican attacks or homophobic responses to national education standards—not to mention theories about literary agents, book publishers, and dead authors making a clear attempt to steal an icon from his adoring black counter-public.[15] And that is all before we even get to the fact that some of hip hop's most prominent figures (not just Jay-Z but, Kanye West, Rihanna, Nicki Minaj, and Eminem) are most often invoked as key culprits in the fascinating contemporary—and age-old—conspiracy theory about Satanists secretly running the world, or at least actively plotting to do

We can learn smth from concerns about worldwide plots [margin annotation]

so. Hip hop is also the discursive space wherein many of the links between Satanic conspiracies and hip hop acts are explicitly articulated.

"Secret Society, Trying to Keep their Eye on Me": An introduction to the Illuminati

R&B singer Aaliyah's plane crashes in the Bahamas in 2001. Kanye West's mother dies after plastic surgery in 2007 (particularly ironic in the context of my abovementioned discussion of Taussig's investment in plastic surgery's Faustian implications). The triangular symbol for Jay-Z's Roc-a-Fella records. Beyonce's alter ego Sasha Fierce. Nicki Minaj's alter ego Roman. Eminem's alter ego Slim Shady.[16] A music video that includes Lil Wayne calling himself a beast and then sitting on a throne inside a church. Entertainers striking media poses with hands or hair obstructing one of their eyes.

[margin handwriting: Facts strung together form implication about the Illuminati]

These seemingly discrete and disconnected facts and observations are sometimes strung together as clues to a deeper and more dastardly story about conflict in American society and all around the world, a tale that is said to go back to ancient Egyptian Freemasonry and to include several of America's Founding Fathers within its diabolical orbit. Hip hop music and culture have become the frontlines for ramped up accusations (and ostensible evidence) about this age-old story and its most recent incarnations.

[margin handwriting: Egyptian freemasonry & the founding of America]

My personal introduction to the Illuminati, Freemasonry, and the founding of the American republic dates back to my first year of college at Howard University (a year that I most often spent with the offerings of Public Enemy and NWA as a kind of everyday soundtrack) and to my reading of Anthony Browder's *From the Browder Files*, a book that asks readers to take a second look at certain common facts of American history.[17] Browder's premise seemed simple and compelling: if one pays a little more attention, one should have so many serious questions about the ubiquitous symbols of Americana that have always defined the recognizable iconography of our nation-state. Why, he asks, is an obelisk one of our most cherished and secularly sacred buildings in Washington DC? What do obelisks (or any of the other symbols of ancient Egyptian culture) really signal vis-à-vis power and patriotism in the United States? Why would our forefathers have made that structure so prominent— and without spending a lot of time publicly explaining their choice? What, he asks, does this fetishization of classic Egyptian symbolism tell us about the "hidden history" of our nation and its ties to the occult?

One short answer to Browder's interrelated questions, questions we debated into the wee hours of the mornings in our freshman dorm rooms, was that the forefathers were practicing Freemasons, just about all of them, and that Freemasonry is a secretive fraternal order that ostensibly controls the world. As if such global conspiring were not enough, Freemasonry, we found out through further reading in similar genres, was also nefarious in terms of its ulterior agenda for the wielding of such international power. Some rank and file members do not know, the theory goes, but the Freemasons are supposed to be in league with other groups, such as the Illuminati, that are hell-bent on taking over the planet—hell-bent, quite literally, since they were said to be working, unabashedly, for the devil himself. Every Freemason might not know this little fact, various conspiracy theorists claim, many Freemasons might even consider themselves to be doing good and ethical work, but to ascend to its upper echelon, its highest precincts and degrees of initiation (positions some of our Founding Fathers would have occupied) was to be made aware of the true nature of the organization's global aspirations.[18] That line of reasoning is exactly what is supposed to make the Masonic references found in American political life so troubling: they are said to function as telltale signs of the ultimately demonic "contracts" that the American social compact is founded upon. Hip hop acts from Public Enemy, X-Clan and KRS-One to Dead Prez, Lupe Fiasco, and Nicki Minaj have written a plethora of lyrics trying to decipher such secret codes, which they consider hidden in broad daylight from their many listeners.

As adherents to Illuminati conspiracy theories will tell you, there are a lot of Masonic references in America's political landscape. The dollar bill's Masonic and Egyptian symbolism probably gets invoked (and deconstructed) by such conspiracy theorists most of all. That piece of currency is constantly exhibited as evidence for subliminal, half-hidden messages about the global forces at work in the founding of the United States. Given the speed with (and range over) which conspiracy theories travel in the contemporary digital moment, I assume that many readers already have some familiarity with this discourse on the demonic dollar, so I just want to quickly highlight one of the elements on the bill that provides it with its evidentiary status within such conspiratorial claims, an element that I would hear invoked again (after graduating from college and those dorm room discussions) during my preliminary graduate student research with several spiritual communities in Harlem and Brooklyn, New York, during the 1990s.[19]

The logic of symbolic revelation in American currency begins with that triangular eye on top of the pyramid on the back side of the dollar bill, the all-seeing Eye of Providence (which dates back to Freemason symbolism in the late nineteenth century) an image that is the basis, conspiracy theorists maintain, for the symbol of Jay-Z's Rockafella Records (an eye positioned between a triangle or diamond formed when the index fingers and thumbs from both hands are put together). What Taussig asks us to remember is the ornate design of this symbol and of the entire bill, its aesthetic particularities and decorative excesses, its flowing curves, spirals, and floral flourishes. There is clearly an investment in the beauty of the imagery and design, from the encircled pyramid with the floating eye peak to the severe and symmetrical eagle on the other side. One may not agree with the aesthetic choices made, but it can hardly be denied that the aesthetics of it have all been closely considered.[20]

And the evidential landscape always expands beyond currency. George H. W. Bush's aspirational talk about "1,000 points of light" was famously linked to the New World Order, *Novus Ordo Seclorum*, also explicitly declared on the dollar bill—a cloaked reference, conspiracy theorists maintain, for a commitment to post-national, global governance. This fear of a "one world government" is a central plank in Illuminati discussions. It is the same fear that animates anti-UN discourse of various kinds. Indeed, the United Nations gets invoked as a mere consolidation and fast-tracking of the one-world-government project spearheaded by the Illuminati's many demonic and untrustworthy ambassadors. And several hip hop acts spend a lot of time trying to call out these ambassadors. For instance, Dead Prez (in the song "These Are the Times") uses the phrase *Novus Ordo Seclorum* as a kind of mantra throughout the track's chorus, ostensibly to shake listeners out of their apolitical stupors. And MC Prodigy has an entire song dedicated to calling out the Illuminati, the chorus of which starts, "Illuminati want my mind, soul and my body/Secret Society trying to keep their eye on me." This singular eye is the same one that adorns US dollar bills, ostensibly explains why iconic artists cover one of their two eyes in photos, and directly implicates Jay-Z's Rockafella hand gesture.

The Illuminati conspiracy theorists' premise is that opaque symbols on dollar bills or throwaway lines in presidential speeches are not harmless or innocent. The semiotics of statehood are not arbitrary. They have productive force, and a history. They are attempted incantations to demonic spirits, evidence of "devil contracts" and explicit demonstrations of public power by a secretive international organization invested in destroying people by facilitating pathology and dysfunction all around the world.

Of course, there are discrepant readings that the varied and inter-citational literature proffers about links between the Illuminati and the Masons, even though by its very nature conspiracy theorists tend to use the same terms in somewhat divergent ways and to believe, occasionally, mutually exclusive things about how such groups are organized and interrelated. But most iterations of the story put the Masons and the Illuminati in cahoots even if they are not always reducible to the same entity. And those conspiratorial formulations of pending one-worldism often add the Council on Foreign Relations, the Rockefellers (after which Jay-Z's crew/label is ostensibly named) and other wealthy families into the conspiratorial mix.[21]

Such conspiratorial commitments are also usually not simply partisan projects in the sense that they have adherents on both sides of the proverbial Left-Right politico-ideological divide, people whose views even short-circuit such too-easy bifurcations of American political possibility. Some conspiracy

Pretty
Interesting
conspiracy
examples
that some
left &
right
leaning

theorists link these self-destructive Illuminati moves to the abomination of genetically modified foods from transnational outfits such as Monsanto, and they read global warming as a concerted attempt to destroy God's precious creation, earth, which human beings were ostensibly designed— and placed in The Garden of Eden—to protect. But other conspiracy theories linked to Satanic world domination tend to tie discussions about one-world governments to hidden American concentration camps and the need for guns to fend off Federal over-reach and tyranny in ways that seem much less linked to environmentalism than militia-based contrarianism. Moreover, the racially inflected populism that invokes Barack Obama as the prophesied "anti-Christ" (which was much more prominent during the run-up to his first presidential campaign but has not completely disappeared from certain crevices of public discourse) has been fueled not just by opportunistically partisan media outlets or crackpot televangelists, but by the wider backdrop of Illuminati-like concerns. Even the idea of Obama possessing the technology and cabal-like organizational secrecy to fake an official birth certificate (to hide the fact that he was supposedly born in Kenya) represents seemingly uncanny and supernatural powers akin to the kinds linked to Satanic conspiring.[22] One should not read the anti-Obama birther-movement's antics without understanding the ground cleared for its conspiratorial claims by herculean feats long imputed to Freemasons and members of the Illuminati. Positing the reality of secretive groups so powerful and untouchable and invisible (even with much would-be evidence available in plain sight) provides the very ontological premise that makes Obama's seemingly implausible cover-up believably non-falsifiable.

Again, it is not quite enough to argue that conspiracy theories trivialize and confound real sociopolitical concerns.[23] I will not spend too much time talking about the extent to which questions of conspiracy theorizing teeter between discussions of mental health and social sincerity, to concerns about whether or not adherents are psychologically imbalanced or self-consciously disingenuous. I want to argue that both poles underestimate the extent to which conspiracy theories work because the believers themselves can incorporate these seemingly cockamamie beliefs into the rest of their everyday lives without it demanding all of their undivided attention. That some people can believe Satanists are using hip hop acts to subliminally control the minds of young people while still seemingly going about their everyday business is the best indication of just how normalized such thinking has become.

This
kind
of
thinking
is
normalized

Whether it is activist Stokely Carmichael writing, matter of factly, about his theory that the CIA might have found a way to give him cancer or the commonly accepted arguments about a purposeful and intended "conspiracy to destroy black boys," African American existence is often predicated on a certain "cool-posed" acceptance of massive conspiratorial forces aligned against you.[24] Part of the point of conspiracy theorizing is to articulate a vision of the world that is purposeful, motivated, and causally secure. Everything serves as piece of a larger puzzle, and all the pieces are necessary, equally valid, and volatile. Or course, such a flattening is the very logic of conspiracy itself—like the cannibalistic organizing principle of capital, devouring everything in its way, bending social processes (and their interpretations) to its mandates. The flattening of difference—all difference—is exactly conspiracy's forte, its stock-in-trade, to the point where sincerity and insincerity (do folks really believe some of these seemingly bizarre claims?) almost seems beside the point. We are in a topsy-turvy world where accusations are constitutive of verdicts themselves. Or we can think about that Baudrillardian notion that a conspiracy may be real, regardless of whether or not its perpetrators exist as stipulated by adherents, whether or not Satanists are secretly pulling world leaders' strings.[25] (And one does not even have to be a Baudrillardian thinker to imagine that the public discourse on, say, "mass incarceration" is a ruse for occluding and ignoring the fact that certain masses have effectively been incarcerated in places like the Marcy Houses even before the prison-industrial complex's seemingly unstoppable ascendancy.)

But this dangles, admittedly, very close to the position attributed to a conventional concern in the sober political science of conspiracy theorizing: the conspiracy theory's misguided power is said to pivot on a too-easy capacity for covering up even larger and more real conspiracies by trucking out Satanic aspirations to paper over market-driven global inequities and to justify electoral apathy. Conspiracy theories close the sociopolitical circle so tightly that absolutely nothing gets left to chance or chalked up to happenstance. Instead, everything is reified into self-evidential binaries: black or white, good or evil, godly or demonic. This is the very neatness that guides sociocultural critiques through the self-assured sifting of Christianities (at least in some of its forms). Even before any public talk of hip hop's potentially Satanic proclivities, I remember hearing one of my aunt's Pentecostal readings of hip hop's unmitigated demonism. Her son, my cousin, attempted to scratch on a turntable and write rhymes in his marble notebook—when he was thirteen years old—only to find himself rebuked by pastors brought in to cast out his demons and to pray over his penchant for listening to the devil's music. Of course, my cousin would respond to such interventions by doubling-down on his rap commitments and eventually hitting the road as tour manager for the hip hop group Brand Nubians, which popularized its own brand of Islam-inflected politics in the early 1990s.

There may also be something arguably "post-racial" about some of this Illuminati talk, post-raciality being a much overused concept in certain circles these days. The Illuminati conspiracy theories seemingly implicate contemporary recording artists of all stripes, from hip hop artists like Jay-Z to pop rock celebrities such as Lady Gaga. In this sense, it seems to function as a kind of equal-opportunity accusation with little regard for the social valence of American racial categories. At the same time, there is also a decidedly racialized underbelly to these same conspiracy claims, usually linked to decidedly anti-Semitic contentions about historic Jewish complicity in this global conspiracy and concerted efforts to keep power away from the world's black masses. One of hip hop's most recognizable and adamant conspiracy theorists is Richard Griffin, better known as Professor Griff, former "head of security," "hype man," and background member of the group Public Enemy. Griff represents one of the most concerted and codified attempts to frame the talk of a global Illuminati conspiracy in terms of hip hop's aesthetic and political transformations since the late 1980s, arguably the height of political/conscious rap music, and the time when Public Enemy was one of the most well-known hip hop acts in the world. I want to end by offering Griff's formulation of the Illuminati conspiracy's impact on hip hop music, a formulation that borrows from other conspiratorial claims but provides for a distinctive lens on things from the perspective of contemporary hip hop cultural praxis.

"Professor Griff knows ..."[26]

The Nation of Islam and the Five Percent Nation of Gods and Earths over-determined (and were over-represented in) the early two decades of hip hop's public dominance. Many of the most popular acts consisted of people who were members of these two related religious groups, including Public Enemy.[27] Professor Griff was one of PE's most public voices, a raconteur whose very title, "Professor," was meant to speak to his intellectual investments and authority. Even though front men Chuck D and Flava Flav were the main lyricists for the act, Griff would become a controversial public figure for statements that were deemed homophobic and anti-Semitic, comments that would get him fired by the group (before he was later rehired).[28] He backed-off of those original statements years later, while also arguing that they were taken out of context. Even still, Professor Griff's basic contribution to that iconic hip hop group (and its fans) has been to serve as a kind of critical, analytical foil for the act's provocative and polemical songs.

Professor Griff is still associated with Public Enemy these days (making appearances with the group on stage throughout the 2000s), but he is also actively cultivating his own independent public voice, a voice that he uses to rail against (among other things) the problems with contemporary hip hop music, and what he considers its precipitous moral fall. According to Griff, this fall is a function of the genre's co-optation by the forces of evil, its active and unknowing (for some) realignments with Satan, making Griff a somber disseminator of current theories about hip hop's semiotics of Satanism.

One can find Griff taking his argument on the road in local black bookstores and community events all around the country, a tour pitched to a distinctive black reading community, an alternative black public sphere organized around a deep-seeded skepticism about common American claims of racial inclusion, fairness, and justice. It can be misleading to search online for these theories about the Illuminati's impact on contemporary hip hop artists, mostly because the claims are plentiful and easy to find, which may overstate the actual prevalence of the beliefs themselves. One of the powers of the internet is that it can make the erstwhile "fringe" look glossier and more mainstream than it actually is, providing an inflated sense of its actual followers.

Video clips of Griff's lectures are all over the Internet, including slide shows that he prepared specifically on the Illuminati conspiracy within hip hop. He has collected many of his theories on the issue in a fascinating and eclectic 2011 book, *The Psychological Covert War on Hip Hop: The Illuminati's Take Over of Hip Hop*.[29] The book is an assemblage of quotes, interviews, photographs, bible verses, news briefs, and letters that are carefully interpreted and contextualized by Griff, interpreted and contextualized with recourse to his theory about the Illuminati's attempt to actively depoliticize hip hop music (a contention not that different from the aforementioned one leveled at Manning Marable's treatment of Malcolm X). The organizing principle of this book is actively conspiratorial, as is its very layout—a mix of font styles and sizes, varied image formats and design motifs. There is an entire page that reproduces the back of the dollar bill and its hidden Masonic significances. Jay-Z is one of hip hop's most prominent supposed Illuminati conspirators, and he does get many mentions in Griff's treatment of things. Some of the most damning evidence he presents links his wife Beyonce's jewelry to classic symbols of Satanic worship (including a figure named Baphomet), with clear implications for Jay-Z's active complicity. However, Jay-Z and Beyonce "are not the Illuminati," Griff maintains. Rather, "... they are the workers of iniquity. Foster children of the bloodlines of the Illuminati."[30] This is a distinction that Griff does not spend much more time parsing.

Griff's book is committed to telling an all-encompassing narrative that tries to leave very little out of the story. It is an alternative history of the world told through the lens of Illuminati-related claims, which means common sense notions of the past must be recast by Griff's interpretive machinery: the entire empire of Walt Disney, the disappearance of JonBenet Ramsey, the controversial black occult leader Dr. Malachi York (who allegedly taught Jay-Z his deceptiveness on the streets of Brooklyn), the United Nations, the trilateral commission, Hegel, the FBI's cointelpro operations, the grab for Africa, Helen Keller's theosophically inspired "I love you" hand sign, even the death of Run-DMC's DJ Jam Master Jay.[31] Conspiracy only works when matters of scale and seemingly segregated silos of sociocultural life are brought together as ironic and inescapable bedfellows.

In Griff's treatment of things, much of what defines the Illuminati's dastardly plot pivots on what Taussig would describe as the inextricable link between "beauty and the beast," the undeniably aesthetic coordinates of all this talk of demons and devils, of secretly satanic celebrity cabals. Griff's arguments and accusations are tethered to stylized images of national monuments and opaque organizational symbols, celebrity headshots and magazine fashion spreads, fancy jewelry and expensive automobiles. Indeed, the point is that style has distracted hip hop audiences from the self-evidently evil substance of the music's currently hegemonic ethos. The images that animate just about every page of Griff's book (of hip hop royalty donning t-shirts with nihilistic slogans from notoriously Satanic characters, of just-so coifed artists posing with one of their eyes covered by locks of hair or hands or dark shadows, of the intricately designed occult signs that help to serve as a testament to the aesthetic value of the evidentiary ground that Illuminati claims rest upon) are all readable as homages to the value of self-consciously designed and stylized symbolism. Part of Jay-Z's problem is that, as he puts it, he has "the hottest chick in the game wearing my chain," which is another version of Taussig's inextricable "beauty and the beast" scenario, the ugly underside of jealousy over other people's good fortune.

In *Decoded*, part autobiography and part analysis of his own hip hop lyrics, Jay-Z includes an annotated reading of his song "Lucifer," a tune that he admits fans the flames for all the Illuminati conspiracy theorists targeting him. "Some people have used this song as evidence that I worship the devil," he writes, "which is another chapter for the big book of stupid. It really is just laughable."[32] In fact, Jay-Z wants to maintain that all this talk of his links to the devil are simply a function of people being blown away by his poetic gifts, his lyrical abilities. "They can't believe this much skill is in the human body," he raps in the song "Heaven." They are responding—with awe—to his performance of poetic mastery. Jay-Z wants to read these Illuminati accusations as flattery offered up in the register of jealousy, all predicated on his aesthetic prowess as an MC. Whereas Professor Griff excavates the hyper-aestheticized landscape of contemporary hip hop culture for evidence of its postlapsarian status, Jay-Z points to the inescapable envy that (specifically lyrical) beauty seems to breed, especially for those who succeed in making an improbable escape from places like the Marcy Houses.

There is always an aesthetic to exclusion, from the ornate metalwork of literally gated communities to the lines outside of fashionable nightclubs that separate would-be insiders from outsiders by assessing everything from physical attractiveness to sartorial style. Some might describe hip hop as the art of turning exclusion into opportunity, mere noise into a potentially empowering soundtrack for the streets. It can also be quite skeptical when that same soundtrack starts to sound far too good to be true.

12

Constructing constellations: Frankfurt School, Lupe Fiasco, and the promise of weak redemption

Joseph Winters

Introduction

It might seem strange and inappropriate to juxtapose Frankfurt School-style critical theory and hip hop culture.[1] For most people, the first generation of the Frankfurt School invokes troubling notions of elitism, Eurocentrism, and the general dismissal of popular culture. When one reads, for instance, Theodor Adorno and Max Horkheimer's (in)famous chapter on mass culture in *Dialectic of Enlightenment*, it appears that music, radio, television, and the entertainment industry are merely sites of repetition, conformity, and subjugation. The "culture industry," Adorno's term signifying the mass production of culture and entertainment, secures the assimilative logic of late capitalism by foreclosing images, sounds, and ideas that are unsettling, dissonant, and subversive. In addition to this general attack on entertainment and popular culture, Adorno's scathing critique of jazz music (as a repetitive and predictable musical genre) would make most people suspicious of using Adorno's ideas to interpret and reimagine rap, hip hop, black cultural practices, and so forth.[2] How could a critical approach that privileges and even exaggerates the commodification of cultural creations be fruitful for discussions about rap and hip hop? How could an author so widely recognized for dismissing possibilities of everyday resistance and agency be "useful" or relevant for thinking about the complexities—both the dangers and potential openings—of hip hop? By juxtaposing critical theory and hip hop music, how might we engage these complexities in a more rigorous manner and potentially rethink the contemporary relevance of abstract/high theory?

In what follows, I go against the grain of standard dismissals of Frankfurt School-inspired critical theory as irrelevant to contemporary cultural practices. In the process, I highlight two related tropes that are prevalent in the writings of Theodor Adorno and Walter Benjamin—the constellation and weak redemption—to spark a conversation/cipher with the controversial, Chicago-born rap artist, Lupe Fiasco. As I flesh out below, a constellation is a tension-filled arrangement of concepts, ideas, and images—an arrangement that is marked by both dissonance and affinity. It is also a reminder that signs only make sense in playful relationship to other signs and meanings, that words can be used against their ordinary meanings, especially when placed in unexpected contexts and relationships. Weak redemption is a term, often associated with Benjamin, that refers to the possibility of rescuing legacies of suffering, loss, and oppression from triumphant narratives, narratives that would explain away or mitigate the tragic qualities of history and human experience. I argue in this piece that Lupe Fiasco performs a constellational style in his songs, a style that is directly related to his tendency to trouble neat, overconfident accounts of history, especially those accounts that exist under the guise of American exceptionalism and the idea of a post-racial America. By examining Lupe's "American Terrorist" and "Bitch Bad", I underscore the relationship between constructing constellations, weak redemption, and remembrance of tragedy and loss. By creating this conversation, my aim is to demonstrate not only the political and ethical relevance of critical theory but also to continue to show hip hop's layered complexity, especially in a juncture when this complexity is often difficult to hear. In addition, by underscoring themes like weak redemption and loss, this piece aims to further assess and map the place/function of the "religious" within hip hop and hip hop scholarship.

Adorno, Benjamin, and the redemptive quality of the constellation

Walter Benjamin introduces the constellation motif in his obscure but important work, *The Origin of German Tragic Drama*. In the midst of a discussion around truth, knowledge, and representation, Benjamin offers an enticing analogy: "Ideas are to objects as constellations are to stars."[3] Here, Benjamin suggests that ideas and concepts don't merely subsume and integrate corresponding objects as part of the all-too-human endeavor to master and control the world. Rather, like a constellation, an idea brings to light the multiple ways that objects can relate to each other; an idea can illumine and express the affinities, connections, and differences among various objects and concepts. Adorno adopts Benjamin's trope, even though he rejects the Platonic residues in his companion's thought. Performing a constellational style, Adorno configures and juxtaposes concepts, images, and tropes, in ways that do not always seem to cohere. In other words, he arranges concepts and images that relate to one another through affinity and difference, coherence and discord. These playful tensions undo familiar meanings, reminding us of the flexibility and open-ended quality of language. His conceptual arrangements perform the "labor of negativity," resisting desires for closure, stability, and reassurance; they disturb, unsettle, and motivate us to think against the grain. In general, the constellation bespeaks two fundamental commitments that resonate throughout Adorno's corpus: (1) That the world always offers us "More" than our concepts can handle, that there is always some excess or remainder that cannot be assimilated into our language, narratives, and patterns of thought. (2) That the form of expression (essay, aphorism, atonal music) reflects the content in some way. A world that is broken and damaged, according to Adorno, prompts genres, styles, and forms that are characterized by dissonance and tension (which in turn can alter and transform how we see, hear, and experience the world we cohabit).

It is important to think about what Adorno is resisting through his use of the constellation. In his coauthored text, *Dialectic of Enlightenment*, Adorno (and Horkheimer) contend that modernity's prevalent forms of thought and practice (capitalism, science, instrumental reason) operate to minimize difference, dissonance, and individuality. The proverbial modern subject is shaped to preserve itself against "threatening" forms of otherness. For Adorno, the desire for coherence and the desire to render the world lucid and manageable are all too human and not necessarily bad. Yet this desire harbors an underside insofar as it can lead to an aversion to and repression of objects, ideas, desires, or realities that undercut yearnings for coherence and assurance. The constellational style is one expression of what Adorno calls a "persistent sense of non-identity," a heightened awareness of those dimensions of the world that are opaque, that resists being integrated into established narratives and frameworks of meaning—such as death, trauma, contradiction, and novelty. Many commentators, most notably Jürgen Habermas, refer to this emphasis on nonidentity as part of Adorno's negativism or his naive commitment to the nonconceptual or irrational.[4]

According to Habermas, Adorno accepts the idea that modern thought is thoroughly marked by domination and violence. For Adorno, reason is thoroughly distorted and damaged, merely a means to coerce and subjugate others. Therefore, Adorno can only find possibility or hope in some space outside of language, discourse, and the conceptual realm. Because language and thought are realms and spaces that necessarily seek to impose unity and identity onto the world's plurality, Adorno places his faith in that which opposes identity and unity, that which exceeds the creation and use of "rational" concepts and thoughts. While there is some truth in Habermas's accusations, he downplays the significance of concept creation and play in Adorno's thought. In other words, Habermas underestimates the ways in which Adorno uses and plays with language and concepts to show both the limitations and possibilities of our words, concepts, and ideas.

Therefore, Adorno does not simply focus on the violent quality of language, the ways in which language and grammar impose unity on the world's plurality. He also creates and juxtaposes concepts in ways that attempt to be more receptive and open to the world's complexity—plurality, contradiction, tragedy. (For Adorno, the tragic quality of modern life and human existence more generally demands styles, arrangements, and ways of thinking that are layered, messy, and unsettling.) Even as our concepts and ideas can be used to both underwrite and conceal violence, they can also be used to illumine the damages internal to our lifeworlds, and the possibilities that we tend to ignore. Think, for instance, of his description of constellational thinking in *Negative Dialectics*, when Adorno writes:

> The model (for constellational thinking) is the conduct of language. Language offers no mere system of signs for cognitive functions. Where it appears essentially as language, where it becomes a form of representation, it will not define its concepts. It lends objectivity to them by *the relation into which it puts the concepts*. … By themselves, constellations represent from without what the concept has cut away within: the "more" which the concept is equally desirous and incapable of being.[5]

This is a difficult passage. What does Adorno mean here? As intimated above, Adorno is suggesting that language is defined by a playful set of relationships and interactions between concepts and ideas. Prefiguring Derrida's notion of difference, Adorno suggests that a particular sign makes sense because of its multifarious relationships (affinities and differences) to other signs and words. As he puts it, "When a category changes, a change occurs in the constellation of all categories, and thus again in each one."[6] At the same time, Adorno introduces the notion of a "more" in the above passage; he alludes to an excessive quality internal to the world that language cannot fully grasp or illumine. As I take it, Adorno acknowledges both the playful possibilities within language—words can be used in myriad ways and for different purposes—while also reminding the reader of the limitations of language (in addition to the ways in which language can become congealed, thereby blocking or "cutting" possibility). This "play," as I show below, is a defining quality of rap music, a crucial part of how emcees like Lupe Fiasco use language to trouble and undermine ordinary meanings and definitions.

While bringing concepts and ideas together can illumine crucial differences, it can also draw our attention to unexpected similarities. Think about Adorno's claim in the first chapter of *Dialectic of Enlightenment* that Enlightenment thought has become increasingly like its putative other, myth. While Enlightenment thought is typically defined by its aversion to the qualities associated with myth (fate, sacrifice, violence, aversion to individuality and creativity), Adorno suggests that these qualities can be found in the Enlightenment project. Enlightened reason, like logic of myth, *sacrifices* or suppresses individuality, thereby reinforcing the smooth flow of things. Throughout the first chapter of the (in)famous text, Adorno shows the affinities between Enlightenment and myth. Odysseus, for instance, is akin to the proverbial bourgeoisie subject who is taught to manipulate the external world in order to preserve himself or herself. (This self-preservation depends on denying or assimilating forms of difference that threaten to destabilize my sense of identity and self-assurance). Notice what Adorno does here—he identifies two concepts (myth and enlightenment) that many would place in a binary; like Derrida, he shows how this imagined binary conceals important similarities. He therefore puts these categories into play, compels the reader to think about them differently, and resists inclinations toward frozen meanings and rigid binaries. By juxtaposing these concepts, he uses language to show both disavowed violence within Enlightenment thought and to show and perform the flexibility and instability of our words and categories. The resistance to frozen meanings and rigid binaries is important in a world that often imagines and creates these harmful binaries—us/them, self/other, hip hop/American values. Acknowledging similarities and affinities among ostensibly radically different things, as Lupe does in his track "American Terrorist," can be just as subversive as being more aware of difference.

For Adorno, there is an intimate relationship between constellational thinking/practice and art. As Romand Coles points out, Adorno underscores the ways in which art both captures the tragic qualities of human existence, as well as possibilities for a more promising world.[7] For Adorno, there is a dynamic, yet incongruous relationship between art and the empirical world. While art always finds part of its content in the empirical world, art also places the elements of the empirical world into new and unprecedented configurations. As Adorno puts it, "The basic levels of experience that motivate art are related to those of the objective world from which they recoil. The unsolved antagonisms of reality return in artworks as immanent problems of form."[8] This is another way of saying that the form of an artwork can reflect the fractures and breaks within the social world; the style of an artwork is related to the content being expressed. Here we might think of the novelist Toni Morrison's work—the style of her writing can be disjointed and unsettling, in part because she is dealing with content that is traumatic. We might also think of Tricia Rose's claim, in her groundbreaking investigation of hip hop, *Black Noise*, that the language of cutting, breaking, and bombing in early hip hop was inspired by the violent, broken conditions that marked The Bronx and other urban spaces in the 70s and 80s.[9] But as Imani Perry reminds us in *Prophets of the Hood*, to reduce artworks and hip hop more specifically to their social and historical conditions would be to minimize the importance of imagination, fantasy, pleasure, re-signification, and exaggeration within the world of art.[10] In other words, art does not merely reflect reality; it also reimagines reality, and it can disrupt and unsettle our relationship to reality by placing familiar ideas, objects, and images into unfamiliar relationships. According to Adorno, "The nonexisting in artworks is a constellation of the existing."[11] Artworks incorporate images, ideas, relationships, and conditions from the world (and therefore are always bound up with the world) even as they reconfigure these elements into something slightly other than the existing world. This reconfiguration involves imagination and fantasy on the part of the artist and the audience. Fantasy and imagination, however, are not simply forms of escape. Even fantasy, according to Adorno, traverses the conditions and contradictions internal to social life but with the aim of envisioning and constructing something different and new. As Adorno puts it, "If everything in artworks, including what is most sublime, is bound up with what exists, fantasy cannot be the mere capacity to escape the existing by positing the nonexisting as if it existed. On the contrary, fantasy shifts whatever artworks absorb of the existing into constellations through which they become the other of the existing, if only through its determinate negation."[12] As this passage suggests, the power of art is not only its ability to express and make us aware of violence and suffering. Its power is also located in its capacity to open our imaginations to the possibility of a different kind of world, a world, for instance, in which more people flourish, a future state in which currently suppressed desires and pleasures are satisfied. Art, according to Adorno, "draws its credit from a practice that has yet to begin."[13]

Adorno suggests that art provides a weak redemption with regard to the world insofar as art places objects, ideas, and relationships (typically reduced to the logic of instrumental reasoning and capital) into new configurations, configurations that unsettle and disturb the viewer and listener, that gestures toward a different kind of world. Although there are serious differences between Adorno and Benjamin, I argue that this weak redemptive power of art resonates with Benjamin's understanding of history in "Theses on the Philosophy of History." In this important aphoristic essay, Benjamin suggests that resistance to the present order of things involves a struggle over how the past is interpreted and used in the present. In opposition to progressive, triumphant notions of history that erase or mitigate the tragic quality of history and human experience, Benjamin urges endeavors to seize images and events from the past in ways that disrupt what he calls the continuum of history. When legacies of oppression become the "tool of the ruling classes," when they get placed in neat, linear narratives, the dead die a second time.[14] These legacies, in other words, get used and interpreted in ways that reinforce current configurations of power. The proverbial example here is how Martin Luther King's image has become what Vincent Harding calls a convenient hero, used by George Bush, for instance, to champion and justify war and empire. Or one might think of how black freedom struggles have been read as precursors to Obama's presidency and a post-racial America. According to this vision, historical struggles for racial equality have culminated in the first black president, an achievement that reinforces America's collective self-image as an exceptional nation and the accompanying march of progress trope. For Benjamin, critical readers and interpreters of history must retrieve—and even rescue—images of the past and place them in dissonant, tension-filled relationships with present ideas and conditions (so as to avoid the amnesia associated with Progress). For Benjamin, the past can disturb, haunt, and open up possibilities within the present; in addition the past is always unfinished to some extent and can be reinterpreted and read against the grain of dominating discourses and imaginaries.

Lupe Fiasco and the mournful redemption of the past

How might Adorno and Benjamin's reflections on constellational thinking, weak redemption, and art be useful for thinking about hip hop, rap lyrics, the flows and ruptures associated with the MC? How do MCs use words against their ordinary meaning, play with the meanings of words, or place images and concepts together that do not cohere in any ordinary sense? How is rap music both the site of congealed meanings and ideas and a site that makes audible the flexibility and fluidity of language? How do artists use language in ways that compel us to reimagine everyday realities and conditions? What is the relationship between the aesthetic and ethical/political dimensions of hip hop? How does the verbal play within hip hop and the tension-filled quality of this play complicate our understanding of religion, the sacred, and so forth? While I obviously cannot adequately answer these questions in the space allotted, I want to begin to respond to these questions by showing how Lupe Fiasco performs a constellational style, particularly in his well-known tracks, "American Terrorist" and "Bitch Bad." Other artists might provide an illuminating comparison with Adorno and Benjamin's style and strategy—think of Ghostface's ability to juxtapose and organize images and words in discordant ways in a song like "One" or Bahamadia's fascination with word-play and spontaneity in her appropriately titled album, *Kollage*. I intentionally focus on Lupe's "American Terrorist" and "Bitch Bad" because of their political implications and the significance of remembrance and mourning. Lupe's music provides a helpful way of thinking about the contemporary relevance of critical theory while also gesturing toward new paths and trajectories for critical theory.

It is important to briefly consider the moment—September 19, 2006—that Lupe released his first album *Food and Liquor*, which includes the track "American Terrorist." The album, which boldly addresses topics like television addiction, racism, and misogyny in hip hop, drops five years after the 9/11 attacks and the beginnings of the war against terror. American citizens are in the middle of George Bush's second term and directly participating in two wars, in Iraq and Afghanistan. Although many Americans resisted the kinds of narratives and images about Muslims and Arabs used to justify and make us comfortable with these invasions or wars, the political landscape has increasingly been defined by dualistic language—either with us or against us: Axis of Evil versus the Forces of Infinite Justice, American Democracy versus Terror. In addition, Barack Obama, at this time a United States Senator from Illinois with strong attachments to Chicago, was ascending through the political ranks. This is important, considering the vivid and harrowing depictions of Chicago throughout the album, beginning with the opening poem by Lupe's sister.

"American Terrorist" is a fascinating song that complicates prevalent conceptions of Islam, while also troubling reassuring notions of American history. Here it might make sense to linger with the title of the song insofar as it brings together two signifiers—America and Terror—that many people imagine as incompatible. Lupe therefore destabilizes the binary relationship between American democracy and (Muslim) terror, a contrast that has become more rigid within the cultural imaginary after 9/11. This is not all that different from Adorno's attempt to trouble the binary relationship between enlightenment and myth. By juxtaposing these two "incompatible" terms—American and Terror—the title prepares the listener for a different kind of narrative, one that will unveil the affinities between the two (or at least that will address different kinds of terror). Lupe continues to unsettle the listener's understanding of terror in the first verse as he assembles concepts, sounds, and images that connect traumas of the past with more recent atrocities. He introduces the image of a noose, a smallpox blanket, an airplane landing on the Pentagon, and an anthrax lab.[15] In other words, he invokes and juxtaposes images of slavery, lynching, the decimation of Native Americans, the September 11 attacks, and recent examples of bio-terrorism within the United States. By bringing these disparate, but related, images and memories together, he expands and broadens our conception of terror beyond its association with Muslim/Arab resentment toward American ways of life. Because these different historical events are alluded to in a couple of bars, this opening verse suggests some level of continuity between these different forms of terror. Yet this continuity should not let us ignore the dissonant quality of the invocation. Images of slavery and genocide can be disruptive to a culture attached to progressive narratives that downplay the traumas of the past and present. I therefore argue that Lupe, similar to Adorno and Benjamin, unhinges the past from triumphant, progressive narratives and creates an alternative constellation of concepts, tropes, images, and memories, a constellation that troubles the pervasive assumption that terrorism and American democracy are incommensurate. It is also important to mention that he begins the song with an allusion to traveling through a storm. Although Lupe is most likely alluding to the Middle Passage, this opening line recalls Benjamin's claim in "Theses" that "the storm is what we call progress."[16] Social and human progress, in other words, is never as smooth as its proponents suggest; it always occurs as a catastrophe for some group or community, leaving behind a pile of wreckage and debris.

As the listener immerses herself into Lupe's imaginary landscape, she is confronted with images, events, and memories that trouble any well-defined boundary between past and present. Adorno, like Benjamin, cautions against rigid notions of time and history that "intend to liberate the present moment from the power of the past by banishing the latter beyond the absolute boundary of the irrecoverable and placing it, as usable knowledge, in the service of the present. The urge to rescue the past as something living, instead of using it as the material of progress, has been satisfied only in art."[17] In "American Terrorist" past forms of terror haunt the listener and work against present attempts to associate terror primarily with "radical" Islam. An allusion to burning tepees in the first verse, for instance, reminds the listener of the traumatic underside of the nation's birth—the destruction of Native American bodies and lands. Notably, this image of "burning down tepees" flows from a preceding reference to the fire department using hoses to quell civil rights protestors. The final command in the verse to "Move" is an allusion to the Philadelphia-based black liberation movement whose community was fire-bombed by the police in the early 1980s. Using the image of fire or burning,

Lupe connects several events and experiences that constitute a part of American history. Freedom and democracy, in other words, are intertwined with histories and experiences of destruction, loss, and terror. The point is not that America, as an idea, place, and national community, is reducible to this terror, or that America is exceptionally evil, cruel, and malicious. The point is that America, like any nation-state, has a messy, ambivalent history, a quality that, when artistically represented, might disturb triumphant images of America or the idea that terror is not internal to democratic modes of life, but rather only located elsewhere, away from us, in foreign territories and spaces.

Lupe underscores this messiness when he raps, "Nigga they ain't livin properly, break em off a little democracy, turn their whole culture to a mockery … give em gum, give em guns, get em young, give em fun." Notice the repetition of the term "give" here. As many authors, including Adorno, have demonstrated, giving is often an attempt to impose our will onto someone else or another community. The language of charity and gifting can often conceal or justify invasion, dispossession, theft, and the consolidation of power.[18] The use of the term "break em off" already signifies this tension between giving and rupturing; the attempt to fix those who are not living properly, by breaking them off with a piece of authentic democracy, ends up reproducing damages and losses in those communities that supposedly need to be saved, rescued, or fixed. (But perhaps Lupe is suggesting that our democracy is broken and fragmented as well.) As Matthew Santos suggests in the song's hook, making and taking, accumulation and theft, are connected and intertwined. In the final hook or segment of the track, Lupe continues to reiterate this language of giving. He mentions black people being given drugs and guns while being deprived of food. He also makes a reference to Native Americans being offered liquor and slot machines, the latter as a kind of compensation for centuries of dispossession. The listener is also reminded of Chinese immigrants building railroads under harsh, dehumanizing conditions in the nineteenth century. Here, we might want to think of the different functions of this "bring it back" motif. On the one hand, he is anticipating a repetition of the hook, yet he might be suggesting that the various atrocities and injustices he is recalling tend to repeat themselves in the present and approaching future. Or in bringing these events back through song and remembrance, by reaching back so to speak, Lupe hopes that the listener might relate to this history differently and work for an alternative kind of future.

One might claim that Lupe Fiasco's verses on "America Terrorist" are pessimistic, cynical, and that he leaves no room for hope or possibility. These are the kinds of accusations that are typically hurled at Adorno. But, similar to Adorno, I suggest that Lupe gestures toward a melancholic kind of hope, a hope that is made possible by remembrance and attunement to loss, by reimagining the relationship between past and present. In addition to a kind of lament, this reimagination involves play, creativity, re-signification, and even moments of sarcasm—such as when Lupe mentions the Ku Klux Klan members who cannot afford gasoline to burn the cross. By creating an unexpected constellation, by organizing and juxtaposing images, words, and events in ways that disrupt standard depictions of our social worlds, Lupe's track reminds us that we are not simply constrained by the prison house of language and grammar. We can also use language against itself to trouble, undo, and broaden horizons and frameworks of meaning. This predicament is not an occasion for optimism but does encourage selves to struggle, resist, and cope during inescapable moments of despair. If the constellation always includes a tension-filled quality, then perhaps one of these tensions is the play between hope and tragedy, or possibility and loss. This is important in a culture that frequently adopts progressive narratives and that uses black culture and the "success" of hip hop to reinforce these kinds of narratives. *Maping onto "Bitch Bad" now....*

In addition to "American Terrorist," Lupe's 2012 track and video "Bitch Bad" creates a constellation between the past and present in a way that compels the viewer and listener to think critically about the representation of black bodies in the entertainment industry. Among other things, I am interested in the interplay between word and image in the video, and how this interplay, among other effects, resists the idea of a post-racial America—of an America that is somehow beyond race and racism. Each verse in this song connects to tell a disturbing story. In the first verse, the listener is introduced to a five-year-old boy and his mother, riding around in a car, listening to a popular rap song. Because the mother sings along and repeats a line about being a "bad bitch," the boy begins to conflate his mother with the bad bitch image. In other words, he sees this term as a potentially favorable appellation and subject position. He associates this term with his provider and source of life. In the second verse, Lupe envisions a group of "malleable" young girls watching music videos, particularly images of women who are reduced to sexually available objects, women who are "acquiescent" to the desires of the male artist. In the "Bad Bitch" video, we see one of the young girls mimicking the dances and bodily movements of the "paid actress" on the screen. She wants to be a bad bitch, but what this term means for her does not cohere with the term's signification for the boy in the previous scene. In the third segment of the narrative, the boy and girl from the first two verses meet at a later stage in their lives. Because they have different, conflicting conceptions of what it means to be a bad bitch, or what it means to be an attractive, powerful woman, they cannot communicate. Or, more precisely, their line of communication is distorted.

On the face of things, this seems like a conservative song with a fairly simple argument—children without proper direction and guidance (a responsible mother, or parents that monitor their children's viewing habits) will end up confused and lost. In addition, Lupe seems to be placing a large onus on the black female subjects in this song and story. The ostensible source of the distorted communication between the innocent male and the deluded female in the third verse is the internalization of the bad bitch trope and mantra by women. In addition, the multiple uses and connotations of the term—the fact that the b-word can be used as a form of empowerment as well as an expression of denigration—simply leads to confusion and disorder. In other words, we have to get a handle on the meanings of words and tropes, tame the proliferation of meaning in the same way that bodies need to be tamed and disciplined. While this is certainly a plausible reading, I do not think it is a very interesting. In fact, Lupe cautions against any facile interpretation of this track, any attempt to draw a simple lesson from the song. At the beginning of the third verse, he reveals that he is not using the term "bitch" as a lesson but as a psychological weapon. He is admittedly trying to "mess with" the listener's conceptions, patterns of thought, and ways of seeing the world. To mess with something is to disturb and unsettle; it is to perform what Adorno might call the labor of the negative. This labor, this "consistent sense of non-identity" reveals tensions, contradictions, and fissures in spaces, discourses, practices, and subject positions that appear coherent and stable.[19] (Therefore the multiple uses and meanings of the term "bitch", not unlike the n-word, both express and introduce tensions. Yet, the track is not necessarily calling for a simple solution but rather an alternative way of thinking about and relating to these tensions and predicaments.) This labor also reminds us that no matter how smoothly an arrangement of power seems to operate, "there is no system without its residue."[20] Any system, in other words, both generates and conceals tensions that threaten to undo that system and that gesture toward something different.

The video to "Bitch Bad" provides a harrowing depiction of how one particular arrangement of power, the culture/entertainment industry, operates on and shapes subjects. In several shots during the first verse and scene, we see the young black male in Lupe's story in a movie theater, visibly amused by whatever images are being emitted from the screen. In one shot, the theater is filled with replicas of the same child. In another shot, he is alone, taking in the iconography. This strategy is repeated in the second verse/scene as we look at the young black girl looking at images alone in one shot and with replicas, or duplicate images, of her and her friends in another shot. Here, the video/narrative seems to be reminding us how the culture industry produces conformity and sameness, even as this sameness is troubled and mediated by gender difference. But even as television, film, and music videos have regular and patterned effects on cultural consumers, the repeated shots of the isolated individual spectator suggests some gap between the collective and the self. Or, as the Marxist tradition and its Frankfurt School offspring teach us, the isolated individual, who enjoys music and television in private spaces, might itself be the product of conditions and modes of being that render lifeworlds fragmented and selves alienated from each other.

While the video visualizes the connection between entertainment, pleasure, and conformity, it also explicitly racializes this relationship by invoking images from the legacy of blackface minstrelsy. In the beginning of the third scene (or Act Three), we see fragments of previous blackface performances in the background (dancing, singing, clowning). As this scene continues, the viewer is unsettled by a configuration of images. For instance, we see a video actor playing the role of the proverbial thug, a video girl dancing provocatively, and then we see both of these characters in black face. At one point, the male actor, still in blackface, is crying; the viewer, for a brief moment, experiences this anguish. In another shot, the actress, with a melancholic look, wipes off the black paint, an image that is juxtaposed to her trying on a butt enhancer and taking an injection to make that part of her body more appealing. Throughout this scene, a mysterious white male is seen carrying and distributing cash money, reminding us that this kind of entertainment is profitable. More generally, there are forces and powers involved in the production of hip hop's visual culture that prosper from black bodies, while remaining buffered from criticism, public accountability, and so forth. To be sure, Lupe is not the first person to imagine a relationship between hip hop and blackface minstrelsy. Many people, including filmmaker Spike Lee (*Bamboozled*) and cultural critic Stanley Crouch, have located the exaggerated, stereotypical—yet lucrative—behaviors of some rap artists within the blackface tradition. What is interesting, however, is how Lupe's video invokes this past, how it juxtaposes the past and present, how it shows affinities and differences between certain dimensions of hip hop culture and minstrelsy. By creating a configuration of fraught images, memories, and tropes, "Bitch Bad" works against the idea that America is in a post-racial state, that a legacy of degrading, one-dimensional depictions of black bodies is somehow behind us and irrelevant to the present. The track does not redeem the minstrel tradition in order to revive and affirm it (in any simplistic sense) but to cut against the grain of linear narratives that too easily smooth over race-inflected tensions and losses—in the recent past and present.

The interplay between word, sound, and image in "Bitch Bad" also compels the viewer to confront her or his own complicity in watching reductive and frequently pernicious representations of black bodies. As I watch the two characters in the first two scenes consuming hip hop videos, I am forced to think about the kinds of pleasures and satisfactions (and repulsions) that

I experience while watching scantily clad women gyrating in front of the camera; or I am pressed to reflect on the fact that the video thug might be a persona that enables me to project fantasies of being invincible, or at least existing and behaving with fewer constraints. In addition, by juxtaposing shots of characters donning black paint with shots of these characters preparing for a hip hop video (putting on a bandanna and gold fronts, practicing how to use and carry a gun; putting on butt and breast enhancements), the video renders explicit what visual productions tend to conceal or downplay—the constructed, fabricated quality of any aesthetic work. This is what Lupe is suggesting in the second verse when he claims that behind the bad bitch is a paid actress, performing according to certain expectations, norms, and fantasies. By broaching the language of fabrication and performance, I am not suggesting that we can ever get outside of social constructions. I am claiming that by becoming more aware of just how much goes into the production of things, how much energy, work, and pain go into making certain images and performances seem natural and given, we can begin to deconstruct and reconstruct the world we cohabit.

Conclusion

In this piece, I attempted to create my own constellation. By juxtaposing Adorno, Benjamin, and Lupe Fiasco—and admittedly focusing more on affinities than differences—I aimed to rethink the Frankfurt School's contribution to critical theory and to highlight aspects of Lupe's music—word play, tension, remembrance, loss—that are promising and exigent. By playing with words and images, by reconfiguring tropes and memories in a manner that unravels linear narratives and rigid binaries, Lupe urges the listener to think about history, experience, terror, racism, and misogyny against the grain of prevailing imaginaries. To conclude, I suggest several future trajectories and paths of inquiry that this constellation might make possible. For one, I hope that, by placing Adorno and Lupe in a cipher or conversation, scholars might move beyond the tendency to reduce Adorno's significance within black cultural studies to his critique of jazz music. While suspicions directed toward Adorno's occasional elitism and Eurocentrism are certainly warranted, it is time to identify other dimensions of Adorno's corpus—mourning, the expression of suffering, labor of the negative, irony, hope draped in black— that might allow for a fruitful discussion with black literary discourses. Through this discussion, one would hope that both critical theory and hip hop studies are reimagined and developed along more generative lines of flight. While critical theory can illumine tropes and categories within hip hop that tend to be downplayed by participants and scholars, "down to earth," so to speak. Hip hop culture and theorist to think about modern practices and legacle by the tendency to concentrate on more acceptable sub and classical music (as important as these subjects and continue to be).

Secondly, the idea of the constellation should enable us to th ways about the relationship between form and content within hip hop and rap music. A dissonant style—a style that organizes words and conce in order to unsettle linear conceptions of time and history—might be related to subject matter that is tragic, messy, and disturbing. Similarly, the constellation trope exhorts hip hop scholars to think more critically and substantively about the ambivalence of language. On the one hand, language can become rigid, frozen, and confining. Not only is it used to block possibilities but it is often used to master, dominate, and subjugate certain communities and bodies. Lupe suggests that the b-word is part of this legacy of subjugation, especially for (black) women. Yet language can also be used against itself; within linguistic structures, patterns of flow, and hip hop grammar, there is always room, no matter how cramped, for play, improvisation, resignification, and rupture.

Finally, by grouping critical theory and hip hop, and paying attention to motifs like weak redemption and loss, I hope to broaden, contribute to, and "mess with" scholarly attempts to rethink the relationship between religion and hip hop. Scholars like Anthony Pinn and Monica Miller have recently urged scholars to think more critically and extensively about the religious dimensions of hip hop. Pinn, for instance, demonstrates how these religious qualities are not reducible to traditional or institutional modes of piety. By defining religion as the search for complex subjectivity, or the search for meaning in the face of oppression and dehumanization, Pinn urges listeners to be more sensitive to lyrics and artists that appear antireligious, nihilistic, and so forth.[21] While operating within the space that Pinn's work opens up, Miller contends that Pinn's focus on subjectivity and meaning downplays the ways in which discourses and cultural arrangements shape and structure our understanding of religion. She also worries that the emphasis placed on meaning and coherence problematically identifies religion as a site where life's contradictions and tensions might be overcome.[22] A return to authors like Adorno and Benjamin pushes this conversation in fruitful directions.[23] Like Pinn and Miller, these authors acknowledge that any rigid distinction between religion and culture, or the religious and the secular, is misleading and unhelpful; in other words, one can find religious tropes and themes in spaces and practices outside of the church, mosque, synagogue, or temple. In addition, the Frankfurt School is very aware of the ways in which historical and cultural contexts shape and frame human understandings, interpretations, and desires. Religion, in other

erience but rather a product
More importantly, concepts
constellation, suggest that
of meaning and coherence.
can also trouble and frustrate
ty.

hip hop can bring critical theory
rap music prompt the critical
s that get overshadowed
jects like Kant, Hegel,
bjects of thought
ink in new
culture
pts

13

Zombies in the hood: Rap music, Camusian absurdity, and the structuring of death

Anthony B. Pinn

How does it feel to be a problem?
—W. E. B. Du Bois, from the *Souls of Black Folk*

Walkin' talking dead, though we think we're living (black zombies)
—Nas, from "Black Zombie"

W. E. B. Du Bois frames as a "problem" the presence of African Americans in the United States, and he maps this out in terms of the color line defining the twentieth century. In words that continue to haunt life in the United States, Du Bois wrote,

> The Negro is a sort of seventh son, born with a veil, and gifted with second-sight in this American world,—a world which yields him no true self-consciousness, but only lets him see himself through the revelation of the other world. It is a peculiar sensation, this double-consciousness ...[1]

African Americans, as he observes, struggle to maintain in tension two dimensions of themselves: they are African and American, and only their determination and "dogged strength" keeps them from being (ontologically) torn apart.[2] In this chapter, I want to extend the notion of African Americans as a problem, but I have in mind the manner in which African Americans have been made to reflect the meaning of death. In this way, I maintain the idea of African Americans as constructed in relationship to a discourse of anxiety, but I propose they are constructed as a way to address this anxiety over death. In other words, the construction of black bodies and black being is meant to isolate death for the larger population, in something other then themselves. By so doing, blackness and black bodies take on death so that others (i.e., members of the dominant social group) are able to operate without a particular fear of death. I am suggesting that white Americans, in this case, work to construct existential arrangements and ontological structures that make visible and "manageable" death by projecting it onto black bodies. This is not to say that white bodies do not experience death, but rather they are able to "attach" their worse fears about death, the most grotesque dimensions of their anxiety of death—a type of projection—on black bodies. This happens with respect to two geographies that define the two-dimensional "stuff" of death, for the larger and dominant social group: (1) death as physical demise, and (2) death as ontological meaninglessness.

I elsewhere address African Americans and the meaning of physical death, but here I intend death as the end of meaning, or meaninglessness—as an ontological and epistemological rupture in its most graphic form.[3] My basic argument is this: African Americans are positioned as the very embodiment of death—or meaninglessness. As such, they have been rendered epistemologically and ontologically the un/dead—zombies.[4] Yet, my argument does not end there. I also suggest this remaking of African Americans has not gone unchallenged, and in these pages, I outlined ways in which rap music seeks to address the "zombification" of African Americans.[5]

The nature of death

I share a question with Sharon Patricia Holland—"What if some subjects never achieve … the status of the 'living'"? Holland frames the question in light of Toni Morrison's brilliant *Beloved*, and raises the specter of some existing with the dead, being "at one with the dead."[6] For Holland, African Americans are perceived as ghosts.[7] Not so for me. I suggest, they, African Americans, do not achieve this status of the "living," because they are categorized not with the dead—the ancestors for instance—but rather they are the

In Between space

un/dead. They are neither fully objects nor fully subjects. Put another way, they have a particular materiality—an embodiness—that produces discomfort and anxiety in the general population; but, they have limited metaphysical importance in that their presence is without deep epistemological and ontological significance, in that they have no will that matters. They, through socioeconomic and political arrangements, for example, put in place and monitored by the dominant population, occupy an in-between space, of sorts. The artist Nas describes and laments the nature and meaning of African Americans without existential—for example, social, economic, and political—meaning in "Black Zombies."[8] He chronicles the disregard heaped on African Americans ("... they say we ain't shit ...") in ways that capture the tone and texture of physical existence within a capitalist system. And while he appeals to a critique of Western knowledge by pointing in the direction of ancient Egyptian epistemologies as a corrective, Nas's presentation of the zombie entails the manner in which African American private and public life is subscribed by socioeconomic and political arrangements, that limit the significance of black life through a denial of black will and agency, to advance within the workings of the larger society. The marker of this zombie-status, this movement through the world as the un/dead, is the effort of African Americans to buy into the systemic arrangements of white supremacy. In his words, "We just copy-cat, followin' the system (black zombies)."[9] This take on the nature and meaning of the zombie is important; however, in this chapter I am more interested in the zombie as a response to metaphysical (e.g., epistemological and ontological) concerns over against existential issues of meaning. In making this argument I am less concerned with quantitative claims—that is, the number of African Americans who are trapped in this complex over against the number who see the problem and manage to negotiate it. And I am more concerned with zombification as the intent of a particular system of meaning making, with African Americans as the target of this system.

The dead must also be "alive"—present, ever present—if the meaning of whiteness (the larger population) is to have meaning. But they can not be so present as to cause epistemological and ontological discomfort on a fundamental level for those (e.g., advocates of white supremacy) depending on this particular arrangement of the dead. Put differently, African Americans must be recognizable—"human" enough to be visible, or regarded—but not able to demand so much attention (e.g., significance in time and space) as to threaten those who advocate modalities of white supremacy. One might think of Trayvon Martin's death as representing this visceral desire to maintain the placement of black bodies, so as to keep intact the framing of safe and "death" fear life for advocates of white supremacy.[10] The logic of life, in fact, is death. To talk about death—to understand it on some level within and beyond

Nas in "Black Zombies"

meaning of Zombification here

Example of Trayvon Martin's death

its most superficial dimensions as confrontation of the senses in the form of physical demise—is to talk about life.

Death, within the context of my chapter, is not primarily a marker of biological boundary, and, more importantly, it is not a material condition primarily. It is a way of thought, and of structuring reality. It is not the end of vital functions such as heart activity or brain activity that I have in mind. Nor do I mean the end of spiritual vitality in a traditional religious-theological or "spiritual" sense. This is not death as a physical or "spiritual" condition, but rather death, more fully, as an ontological positioning and an epistemological rupture regarding knowledge of being, of life integrity, of dignity, etc. It is the loss of meaning more generally as opposed to the particular ending of a particular person's mattering. It has something to do with the nihilism feared by Cornel West, but is not limited to the paralysis of justice work embedded in a sense of worthlessness he means to avoid.[11]

The physical body, the biochemical reality whose functions end, can be ritually addressed upon death. It can be mourned, represented in a variety of ways, and then set apart from the living in a clear and "final" manner. It can be presented and available to the living—for example, cemeteries and urns—but still at a safe distance from the living; confined, managed, epistemologically docile.[12] It, the dead, must be apparent, in place, exposed to life so as to differentiate it from that, which is not meaninglessness. In this regard, practices related to the material body are fairly sure across cultures and social dynamics. However, this shared structuring of death is not the case, with a particular take on the culturally constructed black body that is death (i.e., meaningless)—that presents the physical body as a symbol of this death, and that renders a particular ontology of death normative in order to maintain sociopolitical arrangements. African Americans are made zombies epistemologically and ontologically in that there is great effort put into controlling their presence in order to avoid total destruction of the logic of social organization and relationships so important to the maintenance of white supremacy and to preserve the dominant population's ways of being, of thinking, of doing.

What is a zombie?

Others have noted the manner in which some bodies defy traditional or normative configurations of life due to sociocultural and other factors. Elizabeth Hallam, Jenny Hockey, and Glennys Howarth, for instance, have written about the vampire as a category of body that resists easy classification as alive or dead.[13] This is because such bodies have markers representing both categories, resulting in a unique configuration as non/being.[14] Unlike the zombie, the vampire, however, is superhuman—a creature with the capacity to hunt humans (e.g., higher on the food chain) and without limited mortality and, unlike the zombie, with will and agency. It is a heightened self, but a non-reflexive self (e.g., no image in the mirror). The "mirror" serves as a reminder to humans that our days are numbered, making visible the fragility of the body as it changes over time.[15] Vampires can extend their "gift" to others in a way desired and sought—not so much the case for the zombie, the un/dead, with its aesthetic of decay and its clumsy movement through the world. With respect to encounters with zombies, the stance for the living is awareness, visual contact, confinement, and distance. African Americans, hence, have not been cast as a type of vampire unleashed upon the world to the extent they do not feed off the system as beings higher on the "food chain," and do not have strong will and agency that must be respected, but rather as zombies bent on consuming the content and meaning of human life, without any process of discrimination and selectivity as is the case with the vampire. Hence, the vampire might terrorize society, but the vampire's work takes place within the context of a set of ground rules based on a logic and set of restrictions. But the zombie moves through the world, consuming it without logic and without rules (e.g., in a way that is uncivilized and chaotic). With the zombie, by and large, there is the absence of contact with human society that is not destruction and death dealing.

Putting aside the vampire as a proper conceptual paradigm for understanding the imposed relationship of African Americans to death, Russ Castronovo's intriguing notion of "necro citizenship," also fails to fully capture what I mean to represent in this chapter. His sense of a citizenry rendered docile, disengaged, corpse-like, entails some of the consequences associated with the ontological-epistemological death of African Americans, but I also have more in mind—more than the sociopolitical spheres of life. For Castronovo, there is something about the recognition of morality as political capital that says a word about the "democratic existence within the state." Social death, also discussed by Orlando Patterson, that defines the position of enslaved Africans positions death—metaphoric and biological—as a point of significance within US democracy.[16] The corpse—the body—for Castronovo can be dead, or can be reanimated through particular shifts in political ideals, practices, and sensibilities. This sense of death, of the final disembodiment, understood within the context of "necro citizenship" has something to do with the sense of privitization that so many have understood as the modern turn regarding the dead, while the political is public. This separation is not certain and it is not fixed, when, for instance, one considers the political importance of the social death of enslaved Africans. Furthermore, Castronovo argues that US democracy enjoys nonresponsive citizens—African Americans—who do not react to political developments, who are passive and who still are … corpses.[17]

While not the same idea, my sense of death shares something with Castronovo's depiction of death as it does with Patterson's sociological discussion of social death.[18] However, I also mean something more fundamental by epistemological and ontological death over against the "dis/embodied experience, social position, and political metaphor" intended by Castronovo and Patterson. The death I describe is the structuring of knowledge about black bodies in spheres of collective interaction (e.g., educational ability and criminality) and the very meaning of black bodies that undergirds these other historical patterns of individual and collective life. It, death so conceived, is one reason we can talk about bodies mattering.[19]

Finally, when I argue that African Americans have been constructed as zombies, I do not have in mind the zombie of the movies, or of the religious traditions growing out of West Africa. Those about which I speak are not religio-theological zombies in a strict sense. Zombies, as I understand them, are epistemological and ontological in nature, in a way that cuts against and across this more limited sense of the zombie found in film, stories, and religious arenas. It is not a process, orchestrated by a (religious) bokor or (spiritual) ritual expert, of placing a person in a limbo space of ego docility through incantations and chemicals (as Wade Davis suggests[20]). No, zombies, as I discuss them, are created to maintain the basic framework and logic of collective life writ large. As Albert Camus notes, humans wrestle with meaninglessness—both trying to destroy it while reinforcing it—a dilemma, for sure. The construction of the African American as zombie—the un/dead representing meaninglessness rendered external to "human" life—gives texture to this dilemma. The zombie becomes residue of a "Unity" (sought by supporters of white supremacy), to borrow another concept from Camus. I am referencing his sense of the human desire or hope for conclusion, for wholeness, cohesiveness and certain value—for a unity of ideas.[21]

Why zombies?

This fixing of zombies by supporters of white supremacy serves to push human life closer to, and more in line with, the ultimate "Unity" of life. In a word, the presence of the zombie helps to authenticate a fundamental and expansive meaning (either theological or ideological in nature matters little), something greater—a greater "good"—and more significant that any particular person and her wants or needs. This "good" that demands zombification of African Americans as its safeguard might entail the substance of religious salvation or the beauty of democracy. Either way, it pulls at humans for obedience and complacency.[22]

The zombified African American marks the absence of substance, the complete destruction of social sensibilities and communal connection. One might think of the zombie as the symbolic and ideological container for all that is despised and feared, for the loss of meaning as waste. It is both despised (un) and needed (dead). Put another way, African Americans were constructed as enfleshed *vanitas* through which meaninglessness is abated, and the fragility of "life" captured (or controlled) in time and space.

Finally, it is not the case, nor need it be, that all agree to the merit of African Americans so constructed. The manner of structuring African Americans as such is not dependent upon consensus. It only needs to become the dominant logic, with people benefiting directly and indirectly from its normativity, and this does not preclude slippage regarding when and how African Americans are so understood. So, the presentation of this logic must be compelling or at least presented in light of a shared need, and with time, it will become the unspoken reality, the assumed condition of life. This logic, to borrow and apply in a different context a phrase from Camus, entails "solidarity against death."[23] The cause of the zombie phenomenon is hidden in the larger narrative, but this is its power: it does not need full conversation, but rather must have ritualized consent—for example, the discourse of criminality and the extreme right's fear of the destruction of the very fabric of life in the United States. And those given authority—either religious or secular—are best positioned to prophesy the need for this structuring of reality. Both sermons (religion) and speeches (politics) have the capacity to explain and fix this logic, to make appealing— that is, to establish deep need—the structuring of reality that fines African Americans.[24] They, sermons and speeches, can numb the mind, slow critical thinking, enhance emotion, and make counter argument more difficult.[25]

Undergirding this is a prior epistemologically grounded and ontological move: zombies are needed in order for meaning to be, and to be lodged in the "life" of the non-zombies. Within this narrative of meaning, the zombie is a cautionary tale suggesting the importance of accepting the dominant structuring of individual and collective existence—of safeguarding against contamination. Letting one's guard down in the presence of zombies can only result in the destruction of social existence as vital, vibrant, and humane. Death is meaninglessness, in that it restricts one's life force to memory. That is to say, it subjects one to the caprice of others, to the will of others who determine to what degree one has presence.

Zombification involves more than other-ing, of rendering African Americans as objects. Objectification is vital, but zombification marks recognition that the work of objectification cannot be finished as such. African Americans cannot be rendered, in a strict sense, objects—without impact on subjects.

To fully render black bodies objects means that white Americans lose the subjects they need in order to produce the objects. There is something about the fluidity of subject/object distinctions that is necessary. And to this equation is added always the fact that blacks are human, and in a variety of ways push against their reconstruction (e.g., political protest promoting social change).

Making zombies

As I have worked to establish above, African Americans were not simply positioned as the personification of evil, but rather, their construction and placement meant that they were meaninglessness (e.g., death or demise) grasped and harnessed, to the extent it can be handled in this manner. Personification of evil would mean African Americans became a way of addressing the sociology and economy of enslavement and modern discrimination. The latter, construction as meaninglessness/death, however, draws attention to a more fundamental challenge: elemental and ontological meaning in the "world" that humanity both does/doesn't create. This problem would have been in place without enslavement. It would have found another form of expression, and it would have required another way to externalize death. We know this process in the Americas vis-à-vis race and racism, for instance. This focus on death informs racial dynamics, but it is not confined to that particular structuring of human interaction.

Still, the very construction and presentation of black bodies already and always hints to death, or meaninglessness.[26] Death is never unassociated with difference. Put another way, anti-black racism, as philosopher Lewis Gordon names it, was modernity's virus, rendering people of African descent ontological and epistemological zombies—those whose being is unfinished, unfulfilled, and therefore marked by a bizarre rendition of death and life.[27] As zombies, African Americans give conceptual and metaphorical clarity to a necessary dimension of the life and meaning of white Americans; hence, African Americans are alive, a presence. Yet, they also house the fear of meaning lost; hence, they also connote death: they are the un/dead. That is to say, sociocultural structures tied to race and racism are not meant to destroy death, to wipe out death as a threat, but rather to confine death into something more manageable—to confine death in time and space in ways that take away its "sting." The threat is the uncontrolled zombie that hungers for human flesh and brains (body and mind).[28]

This is not simply a statement regarding alterity—the other as a "presence" to be recognized and addressed. Such cannot be the case when African

on anti-Black racism [margin annotation]

Americans are ontological and and meaningful, who moves through human being will not be addressed by simal and traditional theological assumptions recognize the dominant mode of hunThis does not wipe out consideration of of African Americans from zip coon to Thistorical and practical consequences another way in which the African Americandiscussion on his part. Kanye West represented in and by the cultural frameworksbecomes the creator, and in this public.[29] It is in thinking about African Americansbification.
them in this fashion, that white Americans, over thetist years ago, arguing the been able to envision themselves as alive, or invested.[39] West seems to have subjects moving and arranging their world. In this way, out of new structures, they have meaning within a world marked by no central undergirding old meaning.[30]   te gods using

Everything about African Americans as death has an underlyinthe former, of affirming as a right this grand narrative of white American life/mhe latter, There is a warped assumption that through zombification the zombie mat, and are able to harness reality, control it through a mode of prescience.[31] This ife the lot of the African American as undead, as zombie. African Americans are constructed as the embodiment and discourse of danger, destruction, and disorder whose very efforts to produce meaning result in contamination and chaos that must be controlled by naming it death—a push against ultimate meaning, against ultimate Unity.[32] Yet, oddly enough, this process is not without its weak points. For instance, to the extent that African Americans cannot be forgotten within the US narrative of white domination, the African American is immortal; dead to the extent as projected without meaning, but perpetually alive to the extent that the memory of him/her is essential for the safeguarding of the American narrative.

Hip hop's intervention

Some have recognized such weaknesses, and have worked to exploit them if by no other means than signifying them. From my perspective, this is the case with hip hop culture in general, and rap music in particular. Those who carry the bodies of symbolic death speak in haunting tones of their demise, and what it means for the larger structures of existential concern within the context of the United States.[33]

Hip hop culture is an intervention of sorts, marking a cultural shift—a change in the grammar and vocabulary of living in a way that acknowledges the presence of death's shadow. In this situation, meaning is me(an)ing—tension between the individual and frameworks of communality played out through and in the fragility of life. In some respects, hip hop, as with Nas at the start reject West's claim, they open themselves to other constructions of divinity. If West cannot stand next to God, what validates their status as next to God in knowledge and power? His act of rebellion exposes the larger system of corruption and the rather mundane justifications for the framing of the un/dead.[43] Through this epistemological turn a new self is produced, and it is one that pushes against and beyond the framing of the zombie. Even when West announces the "New Slaves," they are self-aware, and with the capacity to effect a reaction from those around them.[44]

This is more than the expansion of the self, the ego, alone; it instead entails a connection to others that is grand and determined outside the confines of what the zombie can achieve. "I know that we the new slaves." It is a statement of a collective present. There is something substantive (and perhaps rebellious) in West's proclamation. They are not simply zombies; they are more dangerous to the status quo than that because of their knowledge—familiarity with the structuring of the dominant narrative of life and meaning—and their actions (i.e., push against boundaries), even within the context of their condition. It's lucidity—awareness—of a kind. Turning to cultural critic Albert Murray, what he projects as the task of the blues is also present, I would argue, in certain modalities of rap music. One, for instance, could understand "New Slaves" and "I Am a God" in this way, in light of Murray's discussion of the blues:

> That kind of musical statement is a basic existential affirmation. And the musicians counterstate their problems; they counterstate the depression, despair, despondency, melancholia, and so forth. Blues music is a ritualistic counterstatement.[45]

This is not a push for liberation advocated by liberation theologians such as James Cone, nor is it the ethical approach championed by other advocates of theologies of liberation, but it is awareness of the geography and structures of life meaning.[46] It takes seriously movement possible within the world—a world that both needs and despises zombies. Perhaps there is something related to this framing of life/death, and the dismantling of the dominant narrative's Unity in Jay-Z's questioning of what the church can do for people, and whether or not Jesus can actually provide salvation. "Empire State of Mind" provides the answer: no, life is somewhere outside the confines of the Church's vision.[47] Chuuch!

By extension and implication, there are ways in which religion tries to cover-up this process of zombification, to redirect attention, through the assurance of an eternal logic and truth; but the flaws in religion's efforts are noteworthy and exposed: little can we gain, and nothing is certain, in that there is no overarching Unity binding all together. "No Church in the Wild," right?

schemes of absolutes and unities of ideas—the stuff from which zombies are constructed and maintained. By doing so, they seek to dismantle African Americans as death by exposing the logic of death (as a structuring of reality). Death is pulled out of a particular materiality—that is, embodied African Americans—and is resettled as a dimension of life rather than a type of meaninglessness that can be ontologically and epistemologically projected. The logic of the zombie is damaged, and in its place emerges the reestablished African. Again, whether its Tupac Shakur on a cross, or West claiming to be a god who constructs truth and demands a certain system of ethics, rap artists have, at times and in significant ways, troubled the logic of death that holds in place the nature and meaning of the African American as zombie. This work is important, but it is far from unproblematic, because what remains intact is the ability (if not desire) to create other zombies, to reconfigure other groups through a similar logic and structuring of reality.

The function of the zombie is to isolate misery and suffering, to isolate decay, and position it over and against life as represented by the population of "humans." Within the narrative offered in certain rap music quarters, this practice is challenged on a variety of fronts. Pain and misery are rendered human, not some type of epistemological and ontological virus, but rather dimensions of reality inseparable from living into death. In this way, rap music has the potential to disrupt this construction project by maintaining the presence of death as human—that is to say, endemic to all humanity, and not the structuring of any one group made for the purpose of warehousing death as meaninglessness, or, in a sense, history.

The altered ontology encourages some artists' ways of thinking about life in death, so as to hold them in creative tension, to recognize the contradictions but also similarities between them as markers of life's interior and borders— its exterior edges and interior spaces. This is a comfort with middle spaces, the vantage point from which both life and death are visible and blend into a common horizon of social, cultural, and artistic creation. Poetic representation and interrogation, in a broad sense, are what these artists have available to them. Perceived as "entertainment," even those considered zombies are allowed it. By these means, culture and cultural production, the artist challenges the making of zombies.

14

Real recognize real: Aporetic flows and the presence of New Black Godz in hip hop

Monica R. Miller

You make yourself art. That's amazing![1]

The above epigraph comes from a participant and spectator at the filming of Jay-Z's "Picasso Baby: A Performance Art Film" (2013), left in awe after having just been in the presence of a New Black God.

In 2010, renowned performance artist Marina Abramović blurred lines between artist, art, and world, by presenting herself in lieu of a traditional installation—*The Artist is Present* (MoMA—2010).[2] Abramović's performance piece brings into focus the absence of the artist in establishing the presence of the art in and through face-to-face engagement with the "Other"—the "stranger." Do we or can we see the artist behind art? Should we? In 2013, rapper Jay-Z took inspiration from Abramović and filmed a music video at Pace Gallery in New York City for his song "Picasso Baby"—remixing *The Artist is Present* into the presence of black recognition. In this essay, I discuss such remixing and sampling (i.e., the cultural borrowing of Jay Z's idea from Abramović à la the director of the music video behind "Picasso Baby") as an expression of aporetic flow—transformation of social nonpassages (i.e., black illegibility) into spaces of creative expression—and characterize such "flow" as a constituent building block of a "New Black God." I am particularly interested in charting and thinking further about the impact of the proliferation of New Black Godz (i.e., black hyper-legibility) in America through the lens of their construction in contemporary cultural expressions such as hip hop. In *Looking for Leroy: Illegible Black Masculinities* (2013), cultural critic Mark Anthony Neal argues that, "… Jay-Z/Shawn Carter serves as an entry point to examine, more concretely how black bodies (as constructed via the discourses of mainstream American hip hop) travel through the world, but also how the world travels through those bodies."[3] This essay takes up the task of examining Jay-Z's travels in and out of one world—the art world.

Tricia Rose suggests that effects of flow, layering, and rupture "at the level of style and aesthetics suggest affirmative ways in which profound social dislocation and rupture can be managed and perhaps contested in the cultural arena."[4] This suggests that hip hop offers a "blueprint" for learning how to "flow" with and against social ruptures, even "finding pleasure" in such ruptures, having trained oneself early on that "future survival" requires a dexterity of tactics and strategies.[5] In talking about the "story of the rapper and the story of the hustler," artist Jay-Z argues that variables such as "flow," among other effects, are endemic to how the rapper navigates life, by suggesting that flow is life: "If the beat is time, flow is what we do with that time, how we live through it."[6] For artists like Jay-Z, this "living" is often played out in the dusty and inhospitable landscape and corners of a fragmented postindustrial America, where "struggle" and flipping authority on its head have historically defined the rap game and black life, more generally. But what happens for those in hip hop for whom survival is seemingly no longer at stake? Can inherited flows and tactics (i.e, authenticity) be redeployed to address issues of hyper-legibility and illegibility—that is, questions of (black) presence and absence? Lastly, through a turn toward and reliance on the production of art and aesthetic appreciation, how do those once worried with survival reconstitute public and private racialized, gendered, and other social nonpassages into an aporetic flow transforming them into black authorities of presence—New Black Godz, where "god" becomes proxy for identity and recognition (presence), and "race" becomes understood through strategic practices of authority (i.e, by calling oneself "god," and forcing one's own legibility into spaces historically designed to not "see" you).

Aporetic flow and New Black Godz

Aporetic flow offers a means of capturing the social spaces where nonpassages are turned into creative expression. For example, such nonpassages are animated in hip hop's historical use of spinning, that is, taking their parents records, and alchemizing an ingenuity that would not offer a means of escape, but rather, new sonic travel and community while being stuck in the very concrete jungles that limited life options and opportunity for cultural exchange. More robust examples take focus in what follows below. "Flow" is inspired by hip hop culture and scholarship. By aporetic, I follow Jacques Derrida to the letter:

> ... *aporia*, which I chose a long time ago as a title for this occasion, without really knowing where I was going, except that I knew what was going to be at stake in this word was the "not knowing where to go." It had to be a matter of ... the nonpassage.... It should be a matter of ... what, in sum, appears to block our way or to separate us in the very place where *it would no longer be possible to constitute a problem....* There, in sum, in this place of aporia, *there is no longer any problem.*[7]

Aporetic flows, then, amount to the responses posed by those in social spaces "not knowing where to go," where such nonpassage can "no longer ... [be] constitute[ed] ... [as a] problem."[8] For instance, racially and ethnically marginalized groups, those seen as (or identified to be) politically oppressed, and legion others, make a practice of altering aporetic stasis into social and cultural movement and expression—that which I refer to as aporetic flow. Many marginal subjects are often left with living a life guided by a veritably omnipotent sense of their social impasse, the impossibility of getting ahead or even getting by.[9] For the purposes of this chapter, the progenitors of aporetic flow are often those who k(no)w where to go in turning illegibility into forced recognition.

If W. E. B. Du Bois asked so long ago about black life in America: "How does it feel to be a problem?"[10] Then, New Black Godz are those who seemingly flip the script on Du Bois and his legacy, shaking the epistemological, ethical, and ontological foundations upon which such a question is posed. Through aporetic flow, New Black Godz, simultaneously respond to "problem-status" and work to push against social parameters that make a question such as Du Bois's still relevant today. This chapter is born as much from my projection of such an identity onto them as from many of their own self-identification with "God-status" (that is, my concern here is not with intentionality, but rather the effects produced through such a rhetorical strategy for human recognition and capital). Through cultural hubris, or a connection to the esoteric religious movement known as the Nation of Gods and Earths, this chapter is a kind of brief ethnography of the impossible (or in Derrida's language, the nonpassage)—an exploration of social group differences—their mediations and movements—through the catalyst and prism of artistic expression. It is through art—be it visual, musical, literary, comedic, film, etc., that doubles consciousness and both binds yet recasts itself as an asset, reinforced because of its use, as such. All told, aporetic flows transmute artists into New Black Godz, a social status that comes with about as equally ironic and aporetic status as any traditional god. Such irony is captured by bars spit by one of these self-proclaimed Godz:

What's a king to a god?
What's a god to a nonbeliever who don't believe in anything?[11]

Listening to a New Black God flow

In the discourse of black religion, the "god" concept has served a social function, rhetorically demonstrating legibility and ritualistically undergirding recognition.[12] Listening to these New Black Godz, will we believe their cultural cries to witness black humanity?

Hip hop studies often rehearses the folk tale of hip hop's birth as being realized in US history on August 11, 1973 when DJ Kool Herc set up his speakers and PA system in the community room at 1520 Sedgwick Avenue in the South Bronx, arising out of a need for party music.[13] As much a product and effect as response to the racialized and classed fragmentations of postindustrialism and urban decay, hip hop also emerges as a need for pleasure—entertainment.[14] But some scholars of hip hop and African American religion might suggest that the story begins much earlier. A host of scholars gesture that hip hop culture was or is simply the logical outcome, the next step in the long and enduring lineage of black cultural production as a means by which to manage struggle in American life (i.e., from spirituals to blues to hip hop).[15] In other words, such narratives suggest that what is seen in and witnessed by hip hop culture is the expression of and struggle for black *survival*—thus, the twoness of black culture, as that which is caught between keeping it real and entertainment—an aporetic flow guided by the poles of individual integrity and social advance. In focusing on the effects and impact of individualized decision making—African American studies scholar Imani Perry argues that while something like color lacks meaning and is ultimately arbitrary—society places meaning automatically onto bodies— an inescapable reality. Thus, for Perry, this results in occupying a world where, "You grow and live in one, two, several, or many communities."[16] Thus, navigating black life becomes, for many, an automatic, everyday, and concurrent performance or practice of code shifting and switching between historical registers of constraint and possibility. Over and against this scene of structure/agency, crisis/possibility, survival/meaning—we often look to and think of "culture" as that which provides a blueprint for greater understanding of how individuals, groups, and communities live, respond, create, express, and so on.

Such an idea is poignantly captured in the work of Anthony B. Pinn, who argues that the study of black religions is the study of culture itself, and the ways in which black bodies seek increased agency and recognition through cultural production.[17] The black folkloric, literary, and musical traditions (especially the spirituals and the blues) have been major sources of scholarly reflection on the double meaning of black life as expressed in and through tricky and witty coded language. Songs such as "Canaan Land" and "Go Down Moses" were said to be manipulated among slaves to plan and plot secret meetings and to plan and plot escape to places like the North. In these songs, material culture is often thought to signify on religious rhetoric in an effort to say something more concrete about social life for African Americans. I too share in—and benefit from—the efficacy of such a "thick" description and approach. While such thick descriptions have been useful in making more out of what society often catalogues as less and illegible (i.e., black life)—I am also cautious of over-determining cultural reason as a determinant of actions, practices, the result of conflict and the production of meaning and novelty. French scholar Jean-Francois Bayart rightly reminds that our current constructions and (re)imaginings of culture are also, very much, fabrications of the past (i.e., we remember what we want to remember and how we want to remember)—culminating in competing origin narratives and the search for the "true" past.[18]

Culture becomes the cartography—and product—by which black bodies struggle for recognition of their humanity. Yet, with aporetic flow in mind (as a space reduced not to either struggle or progress but to the tension posed by manipulations and moldings of the two), how might we methodologically begin to rethink the manner in which "culture"—hip hop in particular—is discursively staged and assembled according to our (scholars) own self-interests? What happens when "it" studies us back? On this point, anthropologist John L. Jackson Jr. offers a thoughtful reconsideration and shift from the methodological excess of "thick" description toward "thin"—challenging the anthropological gaze to think "less" of its constructed "more," he writes, "Thick description, in a sense, has always been thin … we should recognize that there is thin and then there is thin. One tries to pass itself off as more than it is, as embodying an experience that simulates (and maybe even surpasses) any of the ways in which the people being studied might know themselves."[19] The grandness in our scholarly attempts to recover the expansive and immense narratives (i.e., retelling of history) we cite as retained and recuperated by culture—are always, in the end, about (our) seeing less.

From 3/5 a human to 5 percent
Poor Righteous Teachers

Thought of in the context of US history, the full humanity of black bodies was deemed by white others as 3/5s human. The constricting anthropological gaze of such violent historical actors (i.e., colonizers) with particular interests in mind (i.e., free labor, power) were quite strategic in making less out of the more of black bodies, among other marginalized groups—less productive were they in getting African Americans to believe "thick" myths of devaluation. Metaphorically speaking, for many blacks, cultural ingenuity and strategic manipulation helps to transform niggas (3/5s) into Godz (5/5s). That is, a certain sort of aporetic flow— the back-and-forthness—the twoness so emblematic of black life, enables the tactical repurposing of culture as creative strategy for recognition of presence and absence. The utility of the god idea or rhetorical strategy becomes mediated in and through culture, going back as far, at least, to Bishop Henry McNeal Turner's 1895 proclamation that "God is a negro," and likely much further. The cultural manipulation and recasting of "Godz" in black history have long covered the rhetorical gap between being 3/5s[20] and 5/5s human.[21]

For the Five Percent Nation (Nation of Gods and Earths—NGE), the "Black Man" is god, ALLAH incarnate, in the flesh—the black man's arm, leg, leg, arm, head literally spelling out their status as A.L.L.A.H.—creator and created, artist and art. Interviewed in Harlem ("Mecca" for the NGE) in 1967, one member makes clear the utility of "god":

> You see now we got our own rules and regulations, and we know that God is Allah, and he is black![22]

Within their mythos, 85 percent of the world is blind to the divinity of the black man, while 10 percent (the devils) actively work to keep the 85 percent blind to this fact. The 5 percent, also referred to as the Poor Righteous Teachers, not only claim their own status as "god" but also work to teach the 85 percent what is "right and exact" about the world.[23]

It comes as no surprise that the language of hip hop is so often imbued with such theological and religious signifiers in a search for embodied, sociopolitical authority, and respect, as both hip hop and its early influencer the NGE turn nonpassages into aporetic spaces of expression.[24] For instance, salutations such as "peace, god" and "what up, god" proliferate among marginal youth in urban spaces today that remain unaware—and seeming far removed—from the historical genealogy and context by which such usage emerged. Lyrical shout-outs to Godz—and the NGE—still heavily reverberate within and throughout hip hop culture today. In fact, the NGE and its claims to god-status are so vital to hip hop that "old school" artist and MC, Kool Moe Dee, titled his 2003 book, *There's a God on the Mic: The True 50 Greatest MCs* after this tradition. In the text, Kool Moe Dee registers MCs and MCing as mastery of language, and such mastery of language and body as the work of Godz. Striking, but not surprising, on this list is his selection of the second greatest, Rakim, who in hip hop circles is otherwise known as God MC, or just Rakim the God. Scoring Rakim's flow as 100, Kool Moe Dee suggests, "Rakim is basically the inventor of flow ... Rakim created flow!"[25] Suffice it to say, that which is understood as flow has a connection to recognition as a god, and thus to black presence and legibility.

In many ways, one might suggest that the success, fame, mobility, and global presence of hip hop culture has allowed and thus encouraged many African Americans to chart their legibility in America, as going from being created as god in the flesh to "niggas" (not fully human) and back to Godz, again (fully human and divine)—this logic also corroborates the often troped narrative and story of embodied excess and opulence to limitation—that black bodies went from being Kings and Queens (in Africa) to not even fully human (in the New World). Here, black life is seen as gaining legibility in and through cultural production itself. The "stuff of culture" provides both context and product for going from a nobody to something of a somebody in a world that either cannot see black bodies (illegibility) or can only see the black of black bodies (hyper-legibility).

Hip hop, like all cultures, becomes the terrain by which contests over self-identification and social recognition are waged. God talk and religious language are but mere rhetorical weapons—no less powerful ones—used in this contestation for/over identity making. Such thinking is evidenced in highly public and contested debates surrounding hip hop that often involve concerns over commodification, appropriation, market control, passive consumption, mainstream versus underground, and keeping it real and right, all of which rely upon and are driven by the fuel that is the illusion of authenticity.[26]

Old distinctions, new Godz

The denial of lower, coarse, vulgar, venal, servile—in a word, natural—enjoyment, which constitutes the sacred sphere of culture, implies an affirmation of the superiority of those who can be satisfied with the sublimated, refined, disinterested, gratuitous, distinguished pleasures, forever closed to the profane. That is why art and cultural consumption are predisposed, consciously and deliberately or not, to fulfill a social function of legitimating social differences.[27]

The movement between the contradictions constructed over and against hip hop—battles between the "new" and "old" and "blasphemous" and "political"—are not just matters of sheer taste and preference. Rather, as captured by the words of social theorist Pierre Bourdieu, they more aptly reflect, catalogue, and expose something of social group differences. According to Jay-Z, "Picasso Baby!" is ushering in—through hip hop—something new—in his words, "new venues, new energy, and new exchange."[28] But such a "new" in fact hinges on the "old." How is it that a black man rapping inside an upscale art gallery is "new," save historically, such bodies—the not yet godz—had no permission to be in such spaces? These rhetorical plays on words speak to the manner in which perception of the world is given new perspective in various historical moments according to particular needs and interests. New Black Godz come from an old heritage of transforming products and spaces into socially sustaining and marketed products of recognition. One of the aporias relied upon by Jay-Z for the video and song "Picasso Baby" is the distinction between high and low culture, or high and low art—the "sacred" and the "profane" of the art domain. Such binaries are indicative that something political is indeed at stake.[29]

For some, hip hop represents the continuation of black cultural genius, and for others, a reification and regression of black pathologies that many have historically fought to combat.[30] Such public and private expectations of black identity and the contentious debates over authenticity (that is, hip hop must represent and keep it real) suggest that hip hop struggles to represent the more (i.e, the space where black Godz are made) and less (i.e., art, pleasure, entertainment). According to some scholars of race, rap music and hip hop culture have been disproportionately critiqued and held to unfair expectations (compared to other musical genres), while being cast down as the othered step-sister of high culture.[31] Yet, a plethora of industries surrounding hip hop today proliferates across the globe. It is common now for rap artists to own their own clothing lines, businesses, record labels, nonprofit organizations, sports teams, perfume and shoe lines, and so on. If Andy Warhol's Soup Cans and Brillo Boxes indicated a final death-knell for a hard and fast distinction between high and low art, Jay-Z and other hip hop artists employ a kind of indigenous cultural capital, situating themselves as today's soup cans, in that their marketing prowess knows no bounds. What else can we make of Jay-Z's suggestion that he is the new Basquiat surrounded by Warhols, lest he is noting Warhol's final masterpiece/"soup can," Jean Michel Basquiat.[32] Hip hop, making use of a subjugated cultural capital, that is as suited to use in selling drugs, running numbers or rapping, as it is in pushing against the social confines truncating many options of constraint. Through such a practice as the use of indigenous cultural capital, Jay-Z constitutes himself both artist and art, underscoring in "Picasso

Baby" that the "Warhols" who surround Hova are his chosen "team."
As Jay-Z once famously spit, he is not just a "businessman" but also a
"business," "man!"[33] In other words, embrace of the market as artistic
venue frees up cultural resources to navigate the aporetic spaces offered
by a racist society. Such well-known words by Hova offer an initial—market
based—example of aporetic flow in practice. Overcoming the seemingly
insurmountable through forcible recognition of oneself as art and artist, as
business and business man, as object and subject. Through such a market
focus, form becomes content and content becomes form. Interestingly, and
providing rationale for the "indigenous" qualifier to such a practice, in the
light of history, content comes from a form marked as formless. Simply
put, black people historically have been illegible in spaces of high culture,
or, hyper-legible in spaces of "high" learning.[34] Rarely have black people
been registered as "high" art, or artists of "high" culture. Using oneself as
canvas and gallery, product and space, MCs like Jay-Z respond to very old
social challenges through creative manipulation of space and time through
the strategy of aporetic flow.

Jay-Z is in good company on this point. Artists like KRS-One and late rapper
Tupac Shakur have referred to this as the "good news"[35] of hip hop—that it's
gone from party music on the corner to one of the largest capitalistic endeavors
and money makers in the world—entertainment, like all entertainment, keeps
the wallets of many, thick. And yet, there is still a break—a point between
the recognition demanded and presupposed by the economic impact of hip
hop, and the recognition by many that hip hop is a "lesser" art, street art,
folk art, an art of the autodidact—the organic intellectuals—at best. Through
an indigenous identity-based artistic sleight-of-hand strategy employed by
Hova, listeners, viewers, and hip hop heads are allowed to do something
rarely socially sanctioned unless under the guise of death: reveal and revel in
blackness in its complexity, fullness, and ingenuity. The artist has transformed
himself into the art. And "that's amazing!"[36] Has Hova's *Blueprint Trilogy*
been all along a blueprint for building oneself a god, a New Black God, whose
presence is, quite simply, unavoidable?

God in the gallery: Recognition of presence
and the omnipresence of performance

In the gallery, Hova brings art to life by becoming the performance art *and*
artist. A cipher is formed around him by many who share a similar social
status—looking up, they wait for the beat and a word to drop from on high.
Things "get real," so to speak, as the absence of anything behind a word like

"god" gives way to the presence of artists as the embodiment of their art. Is not the "god" of a gallery, its art, the object of importance? Notions of absence and presence, as art, and questions of authenticity and recognition within art, offers a different angle for charting the "New Black Godz" of hip hop, highlighting the new frontiers of black recognition and exposing the not-so-new spectacle of black life, albeit with a twist. From street corners, to recreation rooms, to studios and, now, galleries—spaces of high art— context, form, style, all mediate and reflect changing positionalities of social group differences à la cultural production, process, and output. Technological advances and unsuspecting artistic collaborations power the desire for and manufacturing of the construction of New Black Godz in American culture. By "new," I mean "god-status" has transcended the sole purview of the NGE (where "building" often takes place on street corners), and has, instead, infiltrated and occupied "heaven-on-earth" spaces like galleries. Only now, such heavens are being marked by black (and white) bodies once out of place. The presences and absences are seen through and produced as hip hop culture takes over other artistic domains.

In the (lyrical) success of "Picasso Baby," the song (which comes before the performance art film version, hinting that he does not need the gallery to prove his Picasso status) works as an indication that "building" does not have to happen through traditionally defined "religious" rhetoric and lyrical shout-outs. What is religion, remember, save talk of the self, anthropologically reified through the stuff of culture? Jay-Z's "Picasso Baby" (the song) takes advantage of his social status to give a glimpse into the aporetic flow that helped him to arrive at such a new moniker (Picasso!). Quick to remind any detractors that what they are witnessing is made in and by America ("don't forget America this is how you made me"), Jay-Z's track came into clearer exhibit through its music video "Picasso Baby: A Performance Art Film" (2013). Through artistic flow, an aporetic flow is made possible, and he, as noted in the epigraph of this chapter, transforms himself into his own art, demonstrating in visual format what has already been his "blueprint" for god-status.

For decades now, Abramović has been one of the "most high" of the art world. Space precludes exploring her work in detail here. Suffice it to say, her work is radical, emotionally pregnant, and most often forces recognition of the recognition we give to ourselves and others through artistic, cultural, and social limitations. There's little wonder, then, that Abramović might inspire an artist, himself inspired to turn to "high" art for his own validation.

"Picasso Baby" begins with Jay-Z rapping that he wants to find a Picasso (painting) for his house. The song ends asking America how long it will take for them to see that he is the new Picasso, baby. What began as a story of searching for recognition gained through the procuring of pieces of "high" art, be it a Basquiat or Picasso, finds Hova acknowledging that recognition is awarded and earned from others by constituting oneself an object worth recognizing. In the widely formative text, *Terror and Triumph: The Nature of Black Religion* (2003), Anthony B. Pinn explores abstract expressionism and pop art for what they suggest as a model for exploring the form and content of African American religion, noting, that "art so conceived points to an underlying reality."[37] About this underlying reality, I have engaged Pinn elsewhere, suggesting that there is no essence or core at the center of such a reality.[38] Here, Jay-Z's blurring of distinctions exposes a significant feature of black religion, essences aside, and Pinn's turn to art, though the focus on inner impulse misplaced, does situate a connection between identity and aesthetics.[39] Any quest for complex subjectivity involves something of recognition.[40] To push his suggestion further, god-status might involve self-recognition made possible through external recognition—that the artist formally sought which has now arrived in the person of Jay-Z. His choice of artists is significant as well, fully embodying the break between high/low, form/content, black/white and other such aporetic paradoxes. Jay-Z's flow "swings the pendulum" of social possibility in the direction of black recognition and complex legibility through manipulations of illegibility and hyper-legibility—is an aporetic flow unto itself. He even stumbles over his flow while at the Chelsea gallery, and the flub is included in the finished product video for the song, suggesting that Godz are not perfect. Rather, they flow and for them, as Rose's work on flow indicates, "find pleasure" in such ruptures.[41]

What is the appeal for Jay-Z in mimicking an artist like Abramović whose works are so often marked by the exposure of limitation through artistic passivity (so, presence as absence)? Through her installations, audience members and viewers are forced to reckon with their own limits, most notably seen in her *Rhythm 0* 1974 piece in Germany, which she describes as an awful experience.[42] Most notably seen in this installation, the limits of art are used to expose the humanity of the artist and the audience. Her production of the presence of limits seems to expose the ubiquitous presence of "high" art artists, in the absence posed by their works hanging in galleries without them. The pieces amount to a proxy of omnipresence, of sorts, as artists achieve a god like presence through their works. Abramović's *The Artist Is Present*, then, is actually the absence of the omnipresence offered by the creative medium itself. That is, the presence of the artist prevents the omnipresence of the artist through a proxy. But Jay-Z is not just any artist. He is not just Picasso. He is the new Picasso, with newfangled tricks and techniques.

In contrast to Abramović's play with absence/presence as it exposes limits, Jay-Z adapts a similar artistic methodology as a means of divine recognition, an "I'm here, too, and I've always been here" ethos that belies its intent. If the presence of the artist (for Abramović) signals the absence of the omnipresence of those artists, then does the presence of Jay-Z do anything other than reinforce that he remains a "nigga" rather than a "god" in the eyes of the "high" art world from which he seeks recognition? Does his performance in the gallery short-circuit this process or change it? I would say so, here's how.

If we borrow from the NGE the political import of language, then Jay-Z's deployment of language within the space disrupts the silence imposed by the old Godz who historically excluded black voices. Abramović's performance art strategy of silence (as presence) reflects the reticence of the "old Godz" as the "New Black Godz" gain lyrical prominence in these new spaces. New Godz, although a residual of them, often do not play by the rules of the old Godz. Jay-Z gives up an effort at omnipresence so as to inculcate rhetorical dominance and power—power over others he now employs in the marketplace. Like Warhol before him, the artistic mentor to Basquiat, Jay-Z's hip hop god-status has found him blurring the lines between high and low to such an extent, his *Magna Carta Holy Grail* was promised immediate success, with a million copies purchased in advance by Samsung, evoking the sense that the entire album became an extended commercial.[43] This blurring of "high" and "low" dismantles the construct of the "gallery" as being able to provide the omnipresence it once offered the "old Godz" of high art. In its place, Jay-Z arrives as a New Black God, exuding omnipotence as his lyrical flow drowns the silence of the old Godz exposed in Abromovic's installation, *The Artist is Present*.

In an August 2013 interview with Bill Maher, around the time of Jay-Z's album, *Magna Carta Holy Grail* reached number 1, the conversation begins with a celebration of Jay's recent output as a mark of hip hop's future—as an envelope pusher—emblematic of the what's to come. Maher notes that, "… this album is a lot about art, and things kids would not necessarily be interested in." Jay responds by saying:

> The truth is that as far as hip hop and the arts, we were like cousins, if you think about those days when Fab Five Freddy was with Madonna and Basquiat … we all went to those clubs (that's when hip hop was more underground) … the arts and hip hop really partied together but once … when art started becoming part of the gallery it was this separation … but we pretty much came up together.[44]

Though Jay's history lesson might have a few loose ends, his position notes a shared connection and dislocation. He labels "the gallery" scene (of the 1980s) as the impetus for the separation, but the conversation about "cousins" notes the long history of high/low debates, ranging from Nietzsche's diatribe against Wagner to the pretense of many impressionist artists, to the abstract expressionist and pop-arts' breaking down of high and low.[45] Ostensibly, Jay-Z seems to suggest parallels between these two worlds of hip hop and art, and seeks to have his god-status validated by the remaining distinction of the constructed opposition. Are not such distinctions the very mechanisms that might prevent him from receiving such recognition? Does the presence of his body in the Chelsea gallery erase the absence of his (and most) black bodies from the gallery scene and the longer history of "high" art? In other words, is his chosen venue for validation actually keen to offer it?

Jay-Z, in his six-hour performance stint at Chelsea's Pace Gallery with art world luminaries, celebrities (including Picasso's granddaughter), and a host of random strangers, seems to register the space as his own, remixing the perceptions of hip hop, blackness, and artistic limitation (Abramović) into an aporetic flow (i.e., legibility vis-à-vis hyper-legibility à la illegibility via forced recognition). In the highly revered space of (the "high") art world, Jay-Z gains recognition of his (matured) success and arrival by demanding legibility and acceptance—even by Picasso's own family. Here, high art becomes a new mode of discourse for power and authority (a proxy for god itself), and a way of letting the world know that rappers are the new Warhols of the world today. No longer is it necessary to break down high from low, only to remind that the new Godz on the block are black!

I find it curious the manner in which Jay-Z conceptually subverts the approach to Abramović's *The Artist is Present*, one seemingly about limitation, allowing her already constituted "silent presence" to draw a changing cast of strangers to tears through recognition, being able to come face-to-face with the famous artist. No tears in sight, Jay-Z's performance garnered quite the opposite—hysteria, hype, and a vigilant security team to keep a flock of unwanted guests and unwelcome traffic at bay. The contradistinction between the performance (absence vs. presence) and social actors involved (strangers vs. celebrities) signal something about the rapper's desire for recognition and praise through a more structured and choreographed presence of the artist. The "difference" might hinge on Jay's expectation for a well-done final product, where his live "performance" art ultimately becomes technologically archived and mass-produced to sell more albums. In Abramović's case, her "wise" presence (to strangers) is the culmination of the installation of *The Artist is Present*, leaving little trace of the "event" itself. The final product for "Picasso Baby: A Performance Art Film," with Jay-Z at the center of the room, moving around and interacting with a range of participants, is one of celebration and worship. Here, Jay is the center of focus—the participants, visibly star struck, perform eclectic moves from ballet to break dancing, artistically paying homage to the one who calls himself J-Hova.

Director of the video Mark Romanek describes the project as exuding a humanistic vibe for something from an elitist New York art world. For the Picasso Baby project, Romanek had in mind something more sophisticated and "interesting" for the video than the "contrived" and "typical" rap video (as gestured in his words below). One might wonder what exactly Romanek has in mind. For if the lines between hip hop (as art and life) are indeed as separate as many rap artists claim (as do most entertainers), then what does the move from rapper from the projects to performance artist in a lower Chelsea gallery signal about progress, development, and arrival? The culmination of a true businessman? What would Picasso say? Do we need to ask?

Whether this space allowed for the continued making of New Black Godz or the recognition that rap Godz are here to stay, on whose authority do New Black Godz rest? Romanek states:

> When Jay said, "I'd like to do a music video for this song," … I wanted to work with him … but I didn't want to make a traditional music video because it felt uninteresting to me … and I presented this idea to Jay of this performance-art piece in the mode of *The Artist Is Present*. He loved the idea, but I felt immediately that we needed to get Marina's blessing, because it could seem like we were stealing her concept. So we contacted her and she couldn't have been more enthusiastic and open. She really felt flattered, actually, and she felt like it was part of a continuum of performance art, that all performance art has influenced other performance art.[46]

History of religion scholar Bruce Lincoln is correct that authority is not as much an entity as it is effect, an aspect of discourse and social performance that heavily relies upon credibility and the "trust" of an audience in its speaker.[47] Thus, the fine line separating executive authority from epistemic authority is the difference between something being an authority. A god is never a god without a certain sort of constitution. Here, Abramović plays an even bigger role than one might think—her input, thoughts, and agreement on Jay-Z sampling and (re)performing her installation weighs heavily on Romanek's uneasiness and anxiety (one could point out the interesting tension between a dominant notion of "stealing" (negative) and a long history of musical "sampling" (cultural sharing, borrowing, shout-out to one's greatness)). Metaphorically speaking, the question and resolution of Jay-Z's god-status is both the question and the answer here: the question of a rapper sampling someone like Abramović's work creates anxiety, and speaks to the long division between perceptions of the two (high art and low art form and content) and yet her resounding "Yes!" confirms what Jay has been saying about himself all along. This reappropriation of and recognition from Abramović herself speaks to both hip hop's (global) arrival and the long road to becoming an authority for itself. That is, for some, the desire for the omnipresence of black subjectivity through high art comes with a cost. Must hip hop seek recognition into and from such spaces to simply be registered as art? Was hip hop not, from its emergence in and through illegible brown and black bodies, already performance art?

"What's a God to a Nonbeliever?"

From Nation of Islam to the Five Percent Nation, scholars have long pointed out the enduring surveillance and suspicion of black religions.[48] Historically, black religion has provided rhetorical housing, and the civic space to organize, protest, and rebel. Indeed, black religion is the sum total of these activities. In a similar way to which scholars of African American religion have long debated the neglect of black religions as "proper objects of study" (for their perceived lack of orthodoxy, such as black Islams and black Judaisms), Jay-Z similarly poaches religious rhetoric to read and remake black recognition as and through an aporetic flow deployed as creative expression.[49] In the text *New Black Gods: Arthur Fauset and the Study of African American Religions* (2009), African American thought and religious studies scholar Sylvester Johnson asks, "What counts as data in the study of African American religions? How does one recognize real religion when one sees it?"[50] I might add, "How does one recognize New Black Godz, when our critical academic lenses do not 'see' Gods?" How does real recognize real?

The concerns and use of "high art" in the work of Jay-Z seem to be asking something similar—what counts as "proper" data in the study and doing of art? Can a world, which still witnesses a relative distance between black and white, conceive of the New Black Godz on the mic as artists that are just as good as the "Old" Picassos and Warhols? Are the New Black Godz, then, really, anything more than rare instances of an American and global culture wrestling with their own recognition of full black humanity? Perhaps they are, if, in achieving god-status, these New Black Godz force recognition that America—despite its rhetoric—has never fully believed (recognized) or taken seriously even old white Godz.

Might the public inability to register the cries of blasphemy lobbed at Jay-Z (by the religious), in claims that he is a devil worshipper and member of a secret society, as the dismissal of hip hop, highlight an internalized racist refusal to recognize—not Godz, or new godz—but black bodies, in the full complexity of "ALLAH?" That is, such god talk and the turn to art as validation force recognition of black arms, legs, legs, arms, and heads coming together, presented to the world in the vision of their full humanity. What I mean is that the market-driven indigenous cultural capital afforded by art meeting the market and expressed through a figure like Jay-Z as full recognition of his status requires an impossible task: his recognition by those who will not receive it. Artists like Jay-Z, Pusha T and Kanye West (i.e., "New God Flow"), among others, describe themselves with the language of god yet are quick to reinforce that being a god does not mean an end to problems. But it might just mean the transformation of problems into nonpassages, aporias, the opening up of new possibilities. The portrait of possibility and limit, frontier and horizon—painted here by the aurally and visually embodied aporetic brushstrokes of hip hop culture's New Black Godz recasts what it means to be human in the nonpassages of life.

Concluding thoughts: The future of the study of religion in/and hip hop

Monica R. Miller and Anthony B. Pinn

The well-known and critically acclaimed group The Roots, in their track "Understand," boast a provocative hook that, at face value, discusses a "traditional" transcendent deity:

People ask for God, 'till the day he comes, see God's face—turn around and run, God sees the face of a man, shaking his head, says "he'll never understand."

On another recently released track on the same album, "When the People Cheer," they (The Roots) claim to be on "their existential grind"—asserting they:

… live in a trap where things go crack, wake up in the boxes with a box of Apple Jacks, everybody acts like God is all that, but I got a feeling he aint neva coming back …[1]

The juxtaposition posed between these two songs—the first set of lyrics critiquing the social actors' wishy-washy epistemological limits in the face of rhetorical authority, and the second set, throwing the very symbol of authority posed in the first set under the rug of human skepticism, highlights just how tricky talk of religion in hip hop is. The warring ideals constituted in and through these two songs off the same album by the same band demonstrates, not so much linear belief, but rather highlights the slippery slope of human complexity and play at work in cultural production. The first epigraph criticizes the human inability to see the truth they so claim to desire—not truth with a capital "T" but rather the motivation to confront the very things they claim they want and yearn for (here exemplified in the face of God), the fundamental inability or fear to come to terms with, to square with the very thing many claim to desire. The second boasts a more cynical assertion focused not so much on human inability, but rather, a critique of the excess of overdetermined hope in something that is stuck in the "to come." Taken together, such a reorientation and re-presentation of the "religious" is one we strongly suggest hip hop culture "gets" with its altered linguistic heuristic of "both/and" and predilection for maintaining complexity and useful incoherence. While hip hop culture, from its very birth and inception, has more often than not done well to play up and play on themes of complexity, two-ness, narrativity, philosophy, existentialism, postmodernism, and much more, scholars have been slow to address the "thick" and "thin" of the complexity posed by this data and its contribution to academic study. So, what exactly do the contemporary mappings of hip hop culture necessitate of the new terrain of scholarship at such multifaceted intersections?

In *Religion in Hip Hop: Mapping the New Terrain in the US*, we have attempted to address this new reality, with an eye toward interdisciplinary methods and theories, and expansion of data. What are the formative features and stock materials of religion in hip hop scholarship? What does continued concern for the "Other" (broadly construed) in religion in hip hop studies suggest about new theoretical formulations and conceptual constellations of the "Other" in hip hop moving forward? How might we begin to map, plot, and address the "margins" of religion in hip hop scholarship in terms of the boundaries found within data—that is, marginal groups within hip hop, marginal data sets within religion in hip hop scholarship, and academic voices continuously deemed marginal in the broader intellectual arena? Indeed, as the demographic "look" of higher education and the academy grow continuously fluid, as to who finds themselves on the margins even while the margins are cast in new and ever more stringent ways, what, we ask, is the future of religion in hip hop scholarship? If, as much scholarship seems to suggest, religious studies is to thrive through an assessment of religion as some form of identity formation, then hip hop (as data) might hold a similar trajectory. As we more forcefully shift attention away from religion "and" hip hop scholarship (since the discursive score has indeed been settled among the manufactured battle between the sacred and profane) toward religion "in" hip hop scholarship, the precision with which arguments are crafted is strengthened, while the overlapping identitarian concerns of both hip hop culture and religion (as data) come into clearer focus. What may result from this attention is a greater ability on the part of scholars of religion in hip hop to offer insights about how identities are constructed, for whom such identities matter, and how those identities—competing for material, intellectual and affective resources in ever complicated ways—might begin to make sense of themselves and each other. What has remained constant among these essays is that there is something of deep value for the study of religion in the data of hip hop. What has shifted among these contributions, however, is "what happens" to such concepts when they meet up with new embodied, technological, metaphorical, creatively complex, ontological, virtual, and even posthumous concepts of what it means to be human, in life, and death, across the great gulf of hip hop culture.

This volume has tacked in many theoretical and methodological directions, appealed to a myriad of academic and popular cultural voices. One of the essays reclaims Frankfurt School ideas for the unpacking of data that Adorno and Horkheimer would find troubling, while others make use of postmodern-inflected critical approaches, phenomenology, as well as the philosophical analytical underpinnings of existentialisms (and moralisms), of such as Albert Camus and others. Perhaps, in these essays, we have offered a tacit explanation for why someone like Adorno would have been troubled by jazz, or why so much has been made of the distinction between high and low cultural forms, the sacred and the profane, or what attention to zombies and absurdity can offer to understanding more fully the manner in which black bodies are arranged and seen in time and space. To wit, such distinctions have been marked with assumptions about repetition, derivation, and the like. However, it seems the trouble with such "low" cultural products is not in form or medium, but, rather, in function and effect. Attention to these arenas marks a powerful intellectual awareness of why these distinctions matter to those who make them, and stands to mark a resonant "no" to assumptions about what matters, who matters, and why.

The many tools of analyses and analytical precision in hand—as this volume has advocated throughout—do not compete methodologically and theoretically, rather, they compliment and speak to the complex future of religion in hip hop studies and what'll be necessitated to attend to its kaleidoscopic assemblages. That is, the new terrain is anything but singular: how to manage such layered data might be found in the fields' continuous interrogation of intellectual, social, and rhetorical tools inherited from assumed "authorities," (e.g., God, Marx, Tupac) and a subsequent recasting and recalibration of "authority" as not so much an entity, as an effect.[2] That is, authority is made possible through an arrangement based on vocality, utility, and appreciation. As those most vocal, useful, and celebrated shift over time, often marked with a hip hop sensibility, then it stands that the "authorities" will too shift. In this volume, the posthumous presence of Tupac shows up alongside Adorno, Fiasco is placed in balance with Marx, rappers' oratorical skills with preachers,

Kanye West with Nietzsche, Zombies with Camus, Marcy Projects paralleled with esteemed art galleries that artists like Jay-Z have come to so love, West and Derrida over and against performance artists like Marina Abramović, the ritualizing of afterlife virtual holographic resurrections, engagement with the most controversial of ongoing conspiracy theories in hip hop, and the new centers of gravity they create, the new humanism in hip hop that challenges and rejects fundamentalisms and transforms anew this-worldly/otherworldly registers and appeals, the psychology of personal, creative, and collective selfhoods of artists, and much more. The authors of this volume, scholars and artists, journey alongside their intellectual predecessors and current conversation partners—lines blurred, knowledge contested—not abandoned, but challenged and challengeable.

The field of religion in hip hop studies, moving forward, will remain that space of epistemological and cultural contestation; a space of critical engagement, where ideas, linguistic formulations, and other modes of expression are confronted by and with the world, all with a certain swagger. The mapping of this new rugged terrain promises that this field will continue as a space where knowledge about the social world is produced, digested, sampled, and continuously remixed to meet the landscape of emergent academic and social enterprises. In this way, it gives proper attention to two of the most influential human developments—religion and hip hop (culture).

Afterword: An insider perspective

Bernard "Bun B" Freeman

The year 2014: we now see that things we thought were far apart are closer than we could've ever imagined. We now see that hip hop, which began as a small, regional movement in the 70s, has blossomed into a worldwide cultural phenomenon. Hip hop culture is not just a fad, but for many, a way of life and a means to contribute meaningfully to society, in general, and to communities in particular. Through hip hop, artists have grown and matured into caring human beings, who are not afraid to ask the hard questions to which many of us seek answers: Who are we? Why are we here? It is within the culture of hip hop, and those who conform to it, that we hope to find answers to these questions.

From the earliest days of hip hop, people like Melle Mel and Curtis Blow shared truth about the harsh realities of the world around them. Great men like Chuck D and KRS-One called upon us to search for knowledge of self and dared us to study our past and be more aware of the paths of our ancestors. Today, these same people are the forebears of new era of awareness and understanding of ourselves and those around us.

We see hip hop culture as a true contributing force in society today. We've seen the culture take the worst of us and help us mature into great thinkers and men and women of concern, compassion, and action.

As we looked to Ice Cube and the Geto Boys to share their search for their place in the physical and spiritual world while still dealing with the harsh realities of everyday life, so too do we see new members of this hip hop family coming to the culture. We have seen people like DMX share their own personal prayers with the masses. We have seen Common speak about finding a personal path to spiritual fulfillment. We have seen Brand Nubian use Islam as a way to "calm the savage beast" inside and find peace in a cruel and unforgiving world.

Now, a new generation has thoughtful figures like David Banner, from Mississippi. They have spiritual speakers like Lecrae. They have revolutionary rappers like Killer Mike. People who are not afraid to put their flaws on the table in an effort to help us all deal with our collective and individual struggles. People whose personal stories reflect ours. In the same way that many of the first several generations committed to hip hop benefited and grew as a consequence of this connection, so shall the generations to follow. As leaders of hip hop culture mature and have a better understanding of themselves and their roles, we will be able to communicate even more of our truths, in ways that bring us together and strengthen our connections as people.

Topics about personal beliefs and choices that were once considered taboo on radio or television are now part of a much-needed universal conversation, and they bring us together, as opposed to tearing us apart. And when we as members of the human family finally come together on a common accord of peace and unity, the world will see that hip hop, as a force as well as culture, was as necessary as any other factor in ushering in this new level of global humanity.

Time and time again hip hop has been used to bring people together. Whether it's the Stop The Violence campaign with "Self Destruction" or the gang situation with "We're All In the Same Gang," hip hop has used its platform to raise awareness and to push the culture and the world toward new levels of social consciousness and understanding. Hip hop has used its voice to call attention to global and regional humanitarian issues, as well as the individuals normally ignored by the powers that be. With the Vote or Die movement, for instance, hip hop called upon its own to help galvanize a voter registration initiative for those least active but most affected by the election process. Knowing its influence with those most affected by their social condition, it has spoken directly to and for the most oppressed.

Hip hop has also stood up against appointed authority figures who have used the power given to them by the tax-paying citizens of this country to restrict and confine the very people that they have sworn to protect. Where there are perceived instances of abuse, brutality, and civil rights violations by police, the hip hop community has helped make the issues at hand not only visualized, but vocalized. Hip hop has not stood by, but has gotten involved with, and in many instances initiated, the call to action. From Yusef Hawkins and Rodney King to Trayvon Martin and Michael Brown, hip hop has used its mighty voice to make the world aware that we have not evolved as a people or society as much as we believe. Hip hop has not been afraid to point the finger at those responsible for this condition and call them out when necessary. But when members of the black community are the perpetrators of crimes against our collective humanity, it has also been necessary for hip hop to "check" them.

At these times, when even hip hop has contributed to the existing condition, it has learned to point the finger at itself and admit its own culpability. Hip hop culture sees itself not as perfect or infallible but as an ever-learning community open to outside opinions and constructive criticism.

We, within hip hop culture, are constantly trying to learn more about the world around us, as well as our place and duties in it. This is necessary for self-improvement, and for the development of useful answers to the large and hard—even religious—questions of life: Who are we? Why are we here? It is only through this type of work that true growth can be achieved. Trill.

Notes

Introduction

1 W. E. D. Du Bois, *The Souls of Black Folk* (New York: Oxford University Press, 2007); John Lovett, *Black Song: The Forge and the Flame* (New York: Macmillan, 1972); James Cone, *The Spirituals and the Blues* (Maryknoll, NY: Orbis Books, 1972); Jon Michael Spencer, *The New Negroes and Their Music* (Knoxville, TN: The University of Tennessee Press, 1997); Spencer, *Theological Music: An Introduction to Theomusicology* (New York: Greenwood, 1991); Spencer, *Researching Black Music* (Knoxville, TN: The University of Tennessee Press, 1996); Spencer, *Sing a New Song* (Minneapolis: Fortress Press, 1995); Spencer, *Blues and Evil* (Knoxville, TN: The University of Tennessee Press, 1993); Spencer, ed., *Black Sacred Music: A Journal of Theomusicology*.

2 Monica Miller and Anthony Pinn, eds, *The Hip Hop and Religion Reader* (New York: Routledge Press, 2014).

Chapter One

1 "Erykah Badu Discusses Children, Love, and Life," by Ferrari Sheppard, stopbeingfamous.com, October 31, 2013, http://stopbeingfamous.com/2013/10/31/erykah-badu-discusses-children-love-and-life-with-stop-being-famous/_3308199.html.

2 "Exclusive Interview with Erykah Badu," billboard.com, June 10, 2010, http://www.billboard.com/video/exclusive-interview-w-erykah-badu-468824.

3 Charles Long, *Significations: Signs, Symbols, and Images in the Interpretation of Religion* (Aurora: The Davies Group, 1995), 7. Specifically, religion for Long "means orientation—orientation in the ultimate sense, that is, how one comes to terms with the ultimate significance of one's place in the world."

4 Felicia M. Miyakawa, *Five Percenters Rap: God Hop's Music, Message, and Black Muslim Mission* (Bloomington: Indiana University Press, 2005), 30.

5 "Erykah Badu," by Red Bull Academy Interviewer, redbullmusicacademy.com, 2011, http://www.redbullmusicacademy.com/lectures/erykah_badu_frother_of_the_month?template=RBMA_Lecture/transcript.

6 A more comprehensive presentation of Supreme Mathematics can be found in the Nation of Gods and Earths *Lessons*. Portions of these lessons can be found on the Internet (e.g., Assata Shakur Forums, "The Supreme Lessons," http://www.assatashakur.org/forum/watoto-wa-jua-children-sun/40408-supreme-lessons.html) or in scholarly treatments of the Five Percenters, see Miyakawa, *Five Percenter Rap*, ch. 2.

7 Lyrics for each of these songs can be accessed on the following website: http://www.azlyrics.com/b/badu.html.

8 See Miyakawa, *Five Percenter Rap*, 63; Michael Muhammad Knight, *The Five Percenters: Islam, Hip Hop and the Gods of New York* (Oxford: Oneworld Publications, 2007), 168, 218, 224. Both of these authors position the lyrics of Erykah Badu within a larger discussion of gender dynamics in the Nation of Gods and Earths. Specifically, Miyakawa use Badu's lyrics to examine the role of women in the family unit, while Knight employs the singer's lyrics to present an alternative image of women of the Five Percenters that is based on womanism.

9 Erykah Badu, "Ye Yo," on *Live*, Kedar/Universal, 1997, compact disc.

10 "Erykah Badu Interview," by Hip Online Staff Writer, hiponline.com, January 22, 2001, http://www.hiponline.com/219/erykah-badu-interview.html.

11 "Erykah Badu," thevine.com, January 26, 2011, http://www.thevine.com.au/music/interviews/erykah-badu-interview-20110126-239041.

12 "I Don't Vote: Interviewing Erykah Badu (unpublished interview)," by Alex Macpherson, alexmacpherson.tumblr.com, 2010, http://alexmacpherson.tumblr.com/post/927729043/i-dont-voting-interviewing-erykah-badu.

13 For a fuller discussion of the connection between humanism as an orientation, see Anthony B. Pinn, *Varieties of African American Religious Experience* (Minneapolis: Fortress Press, 1998), 154–84.

14 "Erykah Badu Vision of Visionaries Interview," YouTube video, 4:59, posted by "blacktreetv," September 1, 2011, http://www.youtube.com/watch?v=17oCkq_RrE4.

15 Joy Sewing, "Erykah Badu takes off the wraps and goes underground," *Houston Chronicle*, February 5, 2004.

16 Michael Roberts, "Q & A With Erykah Badu," *Westword*, May 28, 2008, http://blogs.westword.com/backbeat/2008/05/qa_with_erykah_badu.php (accessed on March 20, 2014).

17 See Erykah Badu's March 20, 2010 *tumblr.com* post concerning her religion.

18 "Erykah Badu Vision of Visionaries Interview," 2011. http://www.youtube.com/watch?v=17oCkq_RrE4.

19 "Erykah Badu," Red Bull Academy, 2011.

20 For an extensive discussion of the creative genius of J. Dilla, see Jordan Ferguson, *J Dilla's Donuts* (New York: Bloomsbury Publishing, 2014).

21 "Erykah Badu Discusses Children, Love, and Life," by Ferrari Sheppard, stopbeingfamous.com, October 31, 2013, http://stopbeingfamous.com/2013/10/31/erykah-badu-discusses-children-love-and-life-with-stop-being-famous/_3308199.html.

22 "Erykah Badu," Red Bull Academy, 2011.

23 Chloé A. Hilliard, "Arts & Crafts: Erykah Badu's Birthday Suit Performance for Window Seat," *Vibe*, June/July 2010.

24 Important to note that this poem is not found on the album version of "Window Seat." To hear the poem in its entirety see, "Erykah Badu Window Seat," YouTube video, 5:37, posted by "Vevo," April 2, 2010, http://www.youtube.com/watch?v=9hVp47f5YZg.

25 Irving L. Janis, *Groupthink: Psychological Studies of Policy Decisions and Fiascoes* (Boston: Houghton Mifflin, 1983).

26 Janis, *Groupthink*, 8.

27 Hilliard, "Arts & Crafts," 2010.

28 "Erykah Badu," YouTube video, 21:28, posted by "Out Da Box TV," August 25, 2011, http://www.youtube.com/watch?v=ghc9jTEBt_E.

29 "Window Seat: Erykah Badu's Explanation," YouTube video, posted by "Kalinda Productions," April 26, 2011, http://www.youtube.com/results?search_query=explanation+of+window+seat.

30 "Erykah Badu," Red Bull Academy, 2011.

31 "EMEK.net," https://www.emek.net/worx/covers.html (accessed April 9, 2014).

32 "Erykah Badu," Red Bull Academy, 2011.

33 Seana Moran and Vera John-Steiner, "How Collaboration in Creative Work Impacts Identity and Motivation," in *Collaborative Creativity: Contemporary Perspectives*, eds. Dorothy Miell and Karen Littleton (London: Free Association Books, 2004), 11.

34 "Erykah Badu to Release 'New Amerykah Part Two: The Return of the Ankh,'" by Hip Online Staff Writer, hiponline.com, March 20, 2010, http://www.hiponline.com/9571/erykah-badu-to-release-new-amerykah-part-two-return-of-the-ankh.html.

35 "Erykah Badu to Release 'New Amerykah Part Two: The Return of the Ankh,'" by Hip Online Staff Writer, hiponline.com, March 20, 2010, http://www.hiponline.com/9571/erykah-badu-to-release-new-amerykah-part-two-return-of-the-ankh.html.

36 Moran and John-Steiner, "How Collaboration in Creative Work Impacts Identity and Motivation," 14.

37 Lyrics for "Window Seat" are available at "Lyrics A-Z Universe," http://www.azlyrics.com/lyrics/erykahbadu/windowseat.html.

38 For a detailed explication of the "dynamical self," see Margarita Simon Guillory, "Creating Selves: An Interdisciplinary Exploration of Self and Creativity in African American Religion" (PhD dissertation, Rice University, 2011).

39 Margarita Simon Guillory, "Creating Selves: An Interdisciplinary Exploration of Self and Creativity in African American Religion" (PhD dissertation, Rice University, 2011).

Chapter Two

1 KRS-One has said this in many interviews, but the one that is most noted is in the documentary *Rhyme & Reason* (1997) at the introduction of the film.

2 This method borrows from ethnohistory, Philip Dark, "Methods of Synthesis in Ethnohistory," *Ethnohistory* 4, no. 3 (1957), and event history analysis, Kazuo Yamaguchi, *Event History Analysis*, Applied Social Research Methods Series, vol. 28 (Newbury Park, CA: Sage Publications, 1991), but focuses primarily on qualitative data.

3 Ethnolifehistory, while still very young in its development, has room for a quantitative perspective.

4 Themes and memes which arose from various interviews in my own work.

5 While still an important aspect to the artist and study, music becomes a component in the study and not the main focus.

6 Ethnolifehistory involves a trinary approach to research and allows the researcher to utilize a multi-method (that is, its utilization of interviews [active, structured, semi-structured], case studies, ethnographic processes, discourse analysis) approach in gathering data.

7 From interviews to E.D.I and Noble from the rap group The Outlawz, viewed Tupac as a sort of "Black Jesuz" with the letter "Z" in place of "S" to reflect a more contextual image of a Jesus figure.

8 These were writings (either poetry, rhymes, journal entries, or handwritten letters) given to me from interviewees, archivally reproduced letters/writings from Tupac in Jamal Joseph, Cox Gloria, Monjauze Molly, and Shakur Tupac, *Tupac Shakur Legacy* (New York: Atria Books, 2006), Book; Sound Recording, p. 64, notes copied from manager Lelia Steinberg (Tupac's former manager), and his writings found in Jacob Hoye and Karolyn Ali, eds, *Tupac Resurrection 1971-1996* (New York, NY: Atria Books, 2003).

9 Daniel White Hodge, *Heaven Has a Ghetto: The Missiological Gospel & Theology of Tupac Amaru Shakur* (Saarbrucken, Germany: VDM Verlag Dr. Muller Academic, 2009); "Baptized in Dirty Water: Locating the Gospel of Tupac Amaru Shakur," in *Secular Music and Sacred Theology*, ed. Tom Beaudoin (Collegeville, MN: Liturgical Press, 2013).

10 Peter Spirer (Director), *Tupac Shakur – Thug Angel (The Life of an Outlaw)* (DVD, Image Entertainment, April 2, 2002).

11 Telephone interview with an unknown interviewer from a local Oakland radio station given around 1990.

12 Given in a 1990 interview for the Bay Area radio station KMEL.

13 Daniel White Hodge, *Heaven Has a Ghetto: The Missiological Gospel & Theology of Tupac Amaru Shakur* (Saarbrucken, Germany: VDM Verlag Dr. Muller Academic, 2009) 152–89.

14 Charles Murray, *Losing Ground: American Social Policy, 1950-1980* (New York, NY: Basic Books, 1984), ch. 4.

15 Taken from an early manuscript of this poem.

16 Tupac's writings are now at the Tupac Amaru Shakur Foundation located in Atlanta Georgia.

17 Taken from an interview given to me on CD circa 1987 while living with Shock G from Digital Underground.

18 Taken from an interview in June 2005.

19 It was noted by many of the interviewees that Tupac spent a considerable amount of time during this era attempting to gain support, both spiritually and financially, from black churches and was met with "closed doors" as both Leila and "Maurice" confirmed to me.

20 This was shown in the film *Tupac Resurrection* (2003) and also quoted in Hoye and Ali, *Tupac Resurrection 1971-1996*, 70.

21 Some of his roommates said, later in Tupac's life, that he was haunted by God and that God himself cursed Tupac to see life as it really was; something that Tupac later admitted to Ed Gordon in an interview in 1995.

22 This was taken from an interview with Tupac's bodyguard Frank, who worked closely with Pac, and told me his sister had finally "come to her damn senses and heeded Tupac's warning to her in the song."

23 As noted in his journaling at the time and confirmed with radio interviews he gave in the summer of 1992; this was also noted in homemade films taken of Tupac at Thug Life fundraisers in local communities throughout California (mainly the Bay Area and Los Angeles).

24 Hodge, *Heaven Has a Ghetto*.

25 Micheal Eric Dyson in Ken Peters, "Tupac Vs.," (DVD, USA: Dennon Entertainment, 2001).

26 See Anthony B. Pinn, *The Black Church in the Post-Civil Rights Era*, in which he discusses the effects of the civil rights movement, post soul creations, and postrevolutionary elements for the black church and Black theology.

27 See Mark Anthony Neal, *Soul Babies: Black Popular Culture and the Post-Soul Aesthetic* (New York: Routledge, 2002); *New Black Man* (New York, NY: Routledge, 2005).

Chapter Three

1 Nietzsche states that "A living thing seeks above all to discharge its strength—life itself is *will to power*; self-preservation is only one of the indirect and most frequent results" (Nietzsche 1966, 21). Furthermore, "The influence of 'external circumstances' is overestimated by Darwin to a ridiculous extent: the essential thing in the life process is precisely the tremendous shaping, form-creating force working from within which utilizes and exploits 'external circumstances' ..." (Nietzsche WP s.647). The key to will to power is to keep in mind that it should not be seen as a form of nihilism, in the sense of being an absolute rejection of value. Despite it's strong criticism of traditional morals and Judeo-Christian value, Nietzsche's notion entails a *vitalism* of sorts, a reification of life beyond the body/mind separation.

2 I strongly encourage readers to also read Jean-Paul Sartre, *Nausea* (London: Penguin Books, 2000), a book that changed my life and my view of the world.

3 Whether consciously or not may not be of such relevance as may seem at first. One should keep in mind Derrida's text on *citation* and *citationality* and ask, like he does, whether a claim to authorship can, in fact, be absolutely made.

4 Jean-Paul Sartre, *Existentialism is a Humanism*, trans. Carol Macomber (New Haven: Yale University Press, 2007), 17.

5 Friedrich Nietzsche, *The Gay Science*, trans. Watler Kaufmann (New York: Vintage, 1974), 181 ·

6 Sam Cooke, "A Change is Gonna Come," *Ain't That Good News* (Hollywood: RCA Victor, 1964).

7 Just as Tupac reaffirms his faith at the end of the Vibe interview, asserting, "I believe in God," he includes in "Blasphemy" an un-ironic recitation of the Lord's Prayer at the end of the song.

8 Makaveli (Tupac Shakur), "Blasphemy," *Don Killuminati: The 7 Day Theory* (Los Angeles: Death Row, 1996).

9 Makaveli, "Blasphemy," *Don Killuminati*, 1996.

10 See Holy Bible Matthew 17:20 or Psalms 31:24.

11 Tupac Shakur, "Vibe.com—Tupac Shakur—The Lost Interview, Pt. 6," YouTube video, 6:00, posted by "Vibe.com" October 1, 2009, http://www.youtube.com/watch?v=Un-leJT1jTs.

12 Recently I was invited to speak to the youth ministry at a large Baptist ministry in Springfield, Ohio. While the pastor "shouted me out" on my recent Kanye publication, the Youth Pastor admonished me with an oft-cited critique of Jay-Z. He asked "how can we do our jobs as Christian stewards, and appreciate Kanye and Jay-Z when messages like 'Jesus can't save you … life starts when the church ends." I reminded him of the line prior where Jay-Z warns that Mary is a virgin to the city and the devil(s) are omnipresent, so whatever heavenly euphoria experienced at church on Sunday is going to be met with hell on Sunday night.

13 See Julius Bailey, "When Apollo and Dionysus Clash: A Nietzschean Perspective on the Work of Kanye West," in The *Cultural Impact of Kanye West*, ed. Julius Bailey (New York: Palgrave, 2014).

14 Nietzsche, *The Gay Science*, 81.

15 Rick Ross and Jay-Z (Shawn Carter), "The Devil is a Lie," *Mastermind* (Miami: Maybach, 2013).

16 A full discussion of the role of Supremacy in hip hop can be found in Rumination (chapter 2) "Firebrands and Battle Plans: Jean-Paul Sartre, Friedrich Nietzsche, and GWF Hegel," in *Philosophy and Hip Hop: Ruminations on Postmodern Cultural Form* (New York: Palgrave-Macmillan, 2014).

17 Jay-Z (Shawn Carter), "Lyrical Exercise," in *The Blueprint* (New York: Roc-A-Fella, 2001).

18 Jay-Z, *The Blueprint*, 2001.

19 Kanye West and Jay-Z (Shawn Carter), "No Church in the Wild," *Watch the Throne* (New York: Roc-A-Fella, 2011).

20 It is Foucault more than any other contemporary thinker, who has most explored the structural character of Victorian sexuality. Given Foucault's closeness to Nietzsche, the former plays an important complimentary role in the developing argument on the importance of self-creation and social critique.

21 Hedonism as a way of life characterized by the constant search for pleasure is not reconcilable with Nietzsche's will to power—for him the search for pleasure can be emptied of meaning and can be nothing but a reactionary response to traditional or Victorian morality.

22 See these pop culture reference accessed on March 29, 2014, http://www. mirror.co.uk/3am/celebrity-news/kanye-west-monster-says-simon-2331178; http://www.spin.com/articles/kanye-west-yeezus-album-title-june-18/; http:// edition.cnn.com/2013/06/20/showbiz/music/kanye-west-god-complex-yeezus/.

23 This may not hold to the Five Percent Nation who associates the "god" term with an enlightenment, a separation from the masses of folk in need of *Righteous Teachers*.

24 "The term is the name given by Sigmund Freud to the process whereby an instinctual representative that has been repressed from the conscious mind [a traumatic experience, although not only] goes back from the unconscious in a distorted form, which is the result of a compromise between the forces of repression and what has been repressed. It is a fundamental logic of Freudian psychoanalysis." Columbia Dictionary of Modern Literary & Cultural Criticism, p. 262, 1995.

25 Rahiel Tesfamariam, "Tupac's 'Thug Life', White-Washed Jesus and the Black Church," *The Washington Post*, last modified September 13, 2012, http:// www.washingtonpost.com/blogs/therootdc/post/tupacs-thug-life-white--washed-jesus-and-the-black-church/2012/09/13/b5aa1080-fde7-11e1-a31e-804fccb658f9_blog.html.

26 Bakari Kitwana, *The Hip Hop Generation: Young Blacks and the Crisis in American Culture* (New York: Basic Civitas, 2002), 4.

27 Eddie S. Glaude Jr., Anthea Butler, Fredrick Harris, Obery M. Hendricks Jr., Eboni K. Marshall, Otis Moss, III, Josef Sorett, "Is the black church Dead? A Roundtable on the Future of Black Churches," Youtube video, 2:02:05, posted by "Columbia university," January 13, 2012, http://www.youtube. com/watch?v=7r8Djfxu1Bk.

28 Manning Marable, *Beyond Black and White: Transforming African American Politics* (New York: Verso, 2009), 213.

29 Pew Research, "A Religious Portrait of African-Americans," last modified, January 30, 2009, http://www.pewforum.org/2009/01/30/a-religious-portrait-of-african-americans/.

30 Pew Research, "A Religious Portrait of African-Americans," last modified January 30, 2009, http://www.pewforum.org/2009/01/30/a-religious-portrait-of-african-americans/.

31 The hypermasculine public image of hip hop does not come across as locus which has addressed issues like same sex relationships. We must not forget the type of art and work that rapper/activists like "Tim'm West" (Chicago) and "Invincible" (Detroit) do that bucks the norms of the conservative and heterosexist binary imagination. My favorite read is Adreana Clay (2008), "'Like an Old Soul Record': Black Feminism, Queer

Sexuality, and the Hip Hop Generation." Certainly Earnest Winborne (2013), "Unsolved Black LGBT Murders: Where is the Outrage?" December 1, 2013, http://www.huffingtonpost.com/earnest-winborne/unsolved-blacklgbt-murde_b_4098430.html (accessed December 11, 2013).

32 Glaude, Butler, et al.

33 Makaveli (Tupac Shakur), "Blasphemy," *Don Killuminati: The 7 Day Theory* (Los Angeles: Death Row, 1996).

34 Martin Luther King, Jr., "Letter from Birmingham Jail," in *Blessed are the Peacemakers*, ed. S. Jonathan Bass (Baton Rouge: Louisiana State University Press, 2001), 253.

35 Ralph C Watkins, "Rap, Religion, and New Realities: The Emergence of a Religious Discourse in Rap Music," in *Noise and Spirit: The Religious and Spiritual Sensibilities of Rap Music*, ed. Anthony Pinn (New York: New York University Press, 2003), 190.

36 Monica Miller, *Religion and Hip Hop* (New York: Routledge, 2013), 84.

37 See, for instance, Nas's video for "Hate me Now," Kanye's February 2006 *Rolling Stone* cover, and the Game's album cover for *Jesus Piece*.

38 Ebony A. Utley, *Rap and Religion: Understanding the Gangsta's God* (Santa Barbara: ABC-CLIO, 2012), 58.

39 Bakari Kitwana, *The Hip Hop Generation: Young Blacks and the Crisis in American Culture* (New York: Basic Civitas, 2002), 6.

40 Michael Eric Dyson, "Prosperity Gospel," *Religion and Ethics Newsweekly* last modified August 17, 2007, http://www.pbs.org/wnet/religionandethics/2007/08/17/august-17-2007-prosperity-gospel/21321/.

41 Shakur, "Vibe.com—Tupac Shakur—The Lost Interview, Pt. 6."

42 Watkins, in *Noise and Spirit*, 191.

43 Watkins, in *Noise and Spirit*, 1.47.

44 See Rumination 5, "Lost in the City and Lost in the Self: Sin and Solipsism in Hip Hop's Dystopia" in my book, *Philosophy and Hip Hop: Ruminations on Postmodern Cultural Form* (New York: Palgrave-Macmillan, 2014).

Chapter Four

1 This essay is based on a keynote lecture delivered by Dr. Michael Eric Dyson at The CUNY Graduate Center in November 2011, hosted by The Committee for the Study of Religion, as part of the Black American Popular Religion Conference. Section headings have been added by the coeditors of this volume for conceptual organization.

2 Albert J. Raboteau, *A Fire in the Bones* (Boston, MA: Beacon Press, 1996), 141–51.

3 Lenard C. Bowie, *African American Musical Heritage: An Appreciation, Historical Summary, and Guide to Music Fundamentals* (Xlibris Corporation, 2012), 246.

4 Gardner C. Taylor, *How Shall They Preach* (Elgin, IL: Progressive Baptist Publishing House, 1977).

5 Jay-Z, "Where I'm From," *In My Lifetime Vol. 1* (Island Def Jam, 1997).

6 Max Weber, *The Protestant Ethic and the Spirit of Capitalism* (New York: Merchant Books, 2013) (originally 1930 by Allen & Unwin).

7 C. H. Dodd, *Coming of Christ* (Cambridge: Cambridge University Press, 2008).

8 William Ronald Jones, *Is God a White Racist?: A Preamble to Black Theology* (Boston, MA: Beacon Press, 1997).

9 Jay-Z, "December 4th," *The Black Album* (Island Def Jam, 2003).

10 Martin Luther King, Jr., "I May Not Get There With You." Qtd in Michael Eric Dyson, *April 4 1968: Martin Luther King, Jr.'s Death and How It Changed America* (New York: Basic Civitas Books, 2009).

11 Michael Eric Dyson, *April 4 1968: Martin Luther King, Jr.'s Death and How It Changed America* (New York: Basic Civitas Books, 2009).

12 Robin D. G. Kelley, *Race Rebels: Culture, Politics, And The Black Working Class* (New York: Simon and Schuster, 1996); James C. Scott, *Domination and the Arts of Resistance: Hidden Transcripts* (New Haven, CT: Yale University Press, 2008), 183.

Chapter Five

1 In a billboard.com article, just days after the virtual performance, Jason Lipshutz captures these dual sensibilities (April 16, 2012 7:25p), http://www.billboard.com/articles/columns/the-juice/494288/opinion-the-problem-with-the-tupac-hologram.

2 In *The Hip Hop Generation: Young Blacks and the Crisis in African-American Culture* (Basic Civitas, 2002), Bakari Kitwana argues that the Hip Hop generation consists of those constituents of the culture who were born between 1965 and 1984.

3 James W. Perkinson, "Rap as Wrap and Rapture: North American Popular Culture and the Denial of Death," in *Noise and Spirit: The Religious and Spiritual Sensibilities of Rap Music*, ed. Anthony Pinn (New York: New York University Press, 2003), 134.

4 Unfortunately the photo still circulates on the World Wide Web. On CelebrityMorgue.com they claim that the photo was leaked by the Las Vegas Police Department and posted by Cathy Scott in 1997. http://www.celebritymorgue.com/tupac-shakur/.

5 Lindon Barrett, "Dead Men Printed: Tupac Shakur, Biggie Small [sic], and Hip hop Eulogy," *Callaloo* 22, no. 2 (Spring 1999): 306–32 (p. 306).

6 Monica Miller, *Religion and Hip Hop* (New York: Routledge, 2013), p. 87.

7 2 Pac. *2Pacalypse Now.* "Trapped" (California: Interscope Records, 1991).

8 Michael Eric Dyson, *Holler If You Hear Me: Searching for Tupac Shakur* (New York: Basic Civitas, 2001), 202–3.

9 The Estate of Tupac Shakur, *The Rose that Grew from Concrete* (New York: MTV Books/Pocket Books, 1999), 32–3.

10 Ralph C. Watkins, "Rap, Religion, and New Realities: The Emergence of a Religious Discourse in Rap Music," in *Noise and Spirit: The Religious and Spiritual Sensibilities of Rap Music*, ed. Anthony B. Pinn (New York: New York University Press, 2003), 184.

11 Martin Heidegger, *Being and Time*, trans. John Macquarrie and Edward Robinson (New York: Harper Perennial, 2008) (originally 1962 by Harper & Row), 30.

12 Jonathan Elderfield, "Tupac's 'Fuck You' to a Cop and the Best Last Words," *The Daily Beast*, May 27, 2014, http://www.thedailybeast.com/articles/2014/05/27/tupac-s-f-ck-you-to-a-cop-and-the-best-last-words.html (last accessed).

13 From a 1997 New Yorker interview.

14 Thug Life, "How Long Will They Mourn Me?" *Thug Life: Volume One* (Los Angeles: Interscope Records, 1994).

15 I discuss my experience seeing the play "Holler if You Hear Me" and my dialogue with the performers, in another chapter/essay on Tupac Shakur.

16 The intentional fallacy is a conventional literary term used to describe the phenomena whereby readers/critics make assumptions about an artistic text based upon the perception of the author/writer and his/her life.

17 Miller, 88.

18 David Papineau, *Philosophy* (New York: Oxford University Press, 2009), p. 12.

19 Papineau, *Philosophy*, 12.

20 Papineau, *Philosophy*, 12.

21 While there is absolutely no credible evidence that Tupac Shakur lives in Cuba, the fact that his "god mother," Assata Shakur, miraculously escaped prison and has been a "most-wanted" fugitive in the country of Cuba for nearly thirty years, only serves to deepen the mythos that shapes Tupac's posthumous legacy and the possibility that he is in exile with another revolutionary member of the Shakur family.

22 Ebony Utley, *Rap and Religion: Understanding the Gangsta's God* (Santa Barbara, CA: Praeger, 2012), 63.

23 Dave Chappelle, "Tupac is Alive," *Chappelle Show* (New York: Comedy Central [television network], 2006).

24 Bikari Kitwana (2002) coins the phrase "Hip Hop Generation." He defines it as those born between 1965 and 1984 and who situate their life's experiences within a context of watershed moments and social justice issues (such as the LA Riots in response to the Rodney King verdict and police brutality).

25 Forbes, NPR, MTV, Billboard and a wide range of media outlets reported on the Tupac "Hologram" almost immediately. The one common element in most of this reporting was that uncomfortable experience that audience members reported and the fact that the Tupac "hologram" was actually not a hologram.

26 David Thier, "Tupac 'Hologram' Wasn't a Hologram at All," Forbes.com, posted April 17, 2012, http://www.forbes.com/sites/davidthier/2012/04/17/tupac-hologram-wasnt-a-hologram-at-all/ (last accessed June 8, 2014).

Chapter Six

1   S. Craig Watkins, Hip Hop Matters: Politics, Pop Culture, and the Struggle for the Soul of a Movement (Boston, MA: Beacon Press, 2005).

2   See Smith 1998; McCutcheon 1997; Weibe 1981.

3   Monica R. Miller, Religion and Hip Hop (New York: Routledge, 2013).

4   Miller, Religion and Hip Hop, 11.

5   Miller, 12.

6   TDGvideos. TDGvideos (True Disciple of God) Channel, YouTube, April 1, 2009, https://www.youtube.com/user/TDGvideos (accessed July 10, 2014).

7   TDGvideos. About page—TDGvideos (True Disciple of God) Channel, YouTube, April 1, 2009, https://www.youtube.com/user/TDGvideos/about (accessed July 10, 2014).

8   For more information on Five Percent Nation teachings, see Felicia M. Miyakawa, Five Percenter Rap: God Hop's Music, Message, and Black Muslim Mission (Bloomington: Indiana University Press, 2005).

9   TDGvideos. Hip hop Is A Religion (8 of 8)—The Heart of Disciples, YouTube, December 13, 2010, https://www.youtube.com/watch?v=IO11h9XMOik&list =UUIaH7Hu0F5K-MyH349wEZeQ (accessed July 10, 2014).

10 Heidi A. Campbell, "Understanding the relationship between religious practice online and offline in a networked society," Journal of the American Academy of Religion 80, no. 1 (2012): 64–93.

11 The Church of Yeezus/Yeezianity is not to be confused with Church of Yeezus/ Boston University. See Laycock 2014.

12 Yeezianity. 2014, http://www.Yeezianity.com (accessed July 4, 2014).

13 Lauriel Cleveland, The Kanye God complex, CNN.com, June 21, 2013, http:// www.cnn.com/2013/06/20/showbiz/music/kanye-west-god-complex-yeezus/ (accessed August 15, 2014).

14 Kanye West, "I am a God," Yeezus. 2013.

15 BBC Radio 1. Kanye West. Zane Lowe. Part 2. Zane Lowe chats to Kanye West in the 2nd of a special 4 part interview. Contains the strongest possible language, September 24, 2013, https://www.youtube.com/watch?v=nx3X4r-eCYQ#t=116 (accessed July 21, 2014).

16 BMAN. Beats and Booty Calls, September 2013, http://bmanmakesmusic. com/ (accessed June 4, 2014).

17 Samantha Grossman, "We're Gonna Let You Finish, Christianity, But Yeezianity Is The Best Religion OF ALL TIME," Time.com (accessed July 22, 2014).

18 Huffington Post Staff. Yeezianity, A Religion Based On Kanye West, Is A Thing That Exists (UPDATE), Huffington Post, January 25, 2014, http://www. huffingtonpost.com/2014/01/15/yeezianity-religion-kanye-west_n_4602708. html (accessed July 8, 2014).

19 BET Staff. Yeezianity: Anonymous Group Starts Kanye West Religion. The Church of Yeezus believes rapper was sent by God to "usher in a New Age of humanity," BET.com, January 15, 2014.

20 Jessica Marinez, "Yeezianity" Religion Founder Revealed; Says Kanye West Is "a Stepping Stone to Jesus," Christian Post, January 27, 2014, http://www.christianpost.com/news/yeezianity-religion-founder-revealed-says-kanye-west-is-a-stepping-stone-to-jesus-113440/ (accessed July 16, 2014).

21 Vincent Funaro, Kanye West Religion? Yeezianity Created Based on Rapper's "Yeezus" Persona, Christian Post, January 15, 2014, http://www.christianpost.com/news/kanye-west-religion-yeezianity-created-based-rappers-yeezus-persona-112718/ (accessed August 15, 2014).

22 Marinez, "Yeezianity" Religion Founder Revealed; Says Kanye West Is "a Stepping Stone to Jesus," Christian Post, January 27, 2014, http://www.christianpost.com/news/yeezianity-religion-founder-revealed-says-kanye-west-is-a-stepping-stone-to-jesus-113440/ (accessed July 16, 2014).

23 Peter Weber, No, Yeezianity is not a real Kanye West–worshipping religion: Sometimes a story is too good to ... read all the way through, January 17, 2014, http://theweek.com/article/index/255245/no-yeezianity-is-not-a-real-kanye-westndashworshipping-religion (accessed July 10, 2014).

24 See Turkle 1995; Papacharissi 2012; Lövheim 2005; and Campbell 2012.

25 Ervin Goffman, *The Presentation of Self in Everyday Life* (New York: Doubleday, 1959).

26 Judith Butler, *Gender Trouble: Feminism and the Subversion of Identity* (New York: Routledge, 1990).

27 Ervin Goffman, *The Presentation of Self in Everyday Life* (New York: Doubleday, 1959).

28 Judith Butler, *Gender Trouble: Feminism and the Subversion of Identity* (New York: Routledge, 1990).

29 *Yeezianity*. About page, http://yeezianity.com/about/.

30 *Yeezianity*. Dogma Page, 2014, http://yeezianity.com/dogma/ (accessed July 4, 2014).

31 *Yeezianity*. Declaration of Faith Page, 2014, http://yeezianity.com/declarations-of-faith/.

32 Zizi Papacharissi, "Without you, I'm nothing: Performances of the self on Twitter," *International Journal of Communication* 6 (2012): 1989–2006.

33 Richard Schechner, *Performance Studies: An Introduction* (New York: Routledge, 2002), 42–3.

34 See Clay 2009; Miller 2009, 2013.

35 Elonda Clay, "These Gods Got Swagger: Avatars, Gameplay, and the Digital Performance of Hip Hop Culture in Machinima," *Bulletin for the Study of Religion* 40, no. 3 (2011): 4–9.

36 Stewart M. Hoover and Nabil Echchaibi, "The 'Third Spaces' of Digital Religion," in *Finding Religion in the Media* (Boulder, CO: The Center for Media, Religion, and Culture, 2012).

37 Pinn, *Noise and Spirit: The Religious and Spiritual Sensibilities of Rap Music* (New York: New York University Press, 2003), 99.

38 Pinn, *Noise and Spirit*, 96.

39 For a satirical example of a Ye'ciples digital performance, see Mimi Ace. Yeezus and Jesus. Vimeo, May 4, 2014, http://vimeo.com/93559662 (accessed August 15, 2014).

Chapter Seven

1 Anthony B. Pinn, *Noise and Spirit: The Religious and Spiritual Sensibilities of Rap Music* (New York: New York University Press, 2003), 86.

2 Bernard Schwarze, "Religion, Rock, and Research," in *Sacred Music of the Secular Society: From Blues to Rap*, a special issue of *Black Scared Music: A Journal of Theomusicology* 6, no. 1 (Spring 1992): 85. Quoted in Anthony B. Pinn, *Noise and Spirit: The Religious and Spiritual Sensibilities of Rap Music* (New York: New York University Press, 2003), 85.

3 Anthony B. Pinn, *Embodiment and the New Shape of Black Theological Thought* (New York: New York University Press, 2010), 5.

4 Phil Hubbard, "Space/Place," in *Cultural Geography: A Critical Dictionary of Key Concepts*, ed. David Atkinson (London: I.B. Tauris, 2005), 41.

5 Thomas F. Gieryn, "A Space for Place in Sociology," *Annual Review of Sociology* 26 (January 1, 2000): 465.

6 Hubbard, "Space/Place," 41.

7 Gieryn, "A Space for Place in Sociology," 465.

8 Rashad Shabazz, "Masculinity and the Mic: Confronting the Uneven Geography of Hip-Hop," *Gender, Place & Culture: A Journal of Feminist Geography* 21, no. 3 (2014): 370.

9 See Murray Forman, *The 'Hood Comes First: Race, Space, and Place in Rap and Hip-Hop* (Middletown, CT: Wesleyan University Press, 2002).

10 Maco L. Faniel, *Hip Hop in Houston: The Origin & the Legacy* (Charleston, SC: The History Press, 2013), 24.

11 Scarface (Brad Jordan), "On My Block," *The Fix* (Def Jam South, 2002).

12 Murray Forman, "Visualizing Place, Representing Age in Hip-Hop: Converging Themes in Scarface's 'My Block,'" *Continuum* 28, no. 3 (2014): 306.

13 Forman, "'Represent': Race, Space and Place in Rap Music," *Popular Music* 19, no. 1 (January 2000): 75.

14 Bun B (Bernard Freeman) featuring Rick Ross (William Leonard Roberts II), David Banner (Lavell Crump), 8Ball (Premro Smith) and MJG (Marlon Jermaine Goodwin), "You're Everything," *II Trill*, Rap-A-Lot Records, 2008.

15 Lil Keke (Marcus Edwards), *A Screwed Up History: DJ Screw and the Screwed Up Click*, 2012, http://www.youtube.com/watch?v=tT9e8r9-bYo&feature=youtube_gdata_player.

16 Geto Boys, "The World is A Ghetto," *The Resurrection*, Rap-A-Lot Records, 1996.

17 War, "The World Is A Ghetto," *The World is a Ghetto*, United Artists Records, 1972.

18 See Loic Wacquant's definition of the ghetto in Loic Wacquant, "The New 'Peculiar Institution': On the Prison as Surrogate Ghetto," *Theoretical Criminology* 4, no. 3 (2000): 377–89.

19 Pete T., "Review- Geto Boys: The Resurrection," *Rap Reviews "Back to the Lab" Series*, March 23, 2010, http://www.rapreviews.com/archive/BTTL_getoresurrection.html.

20 "Recompense evil for evil" is a play on a bible verse in Romans. See Romans 12:17 (King James Version).

21 Tricia Rose, *Black Noise: Rap Music and Black Culture in Contemporary America* (Hanover: University Press of New England, 1994), 21.

22 Howard Beeth and Cary D. Wintz, eds, *Black Dixie: Afro-Texan History and Culture in Houston* (College Station, TX: Texas A & M University Press, 1992), 4.

23 See Thurman W. Robins, *Requiem for a Classic: Thanksgiving Turkey Day Classic* (Bloomington, IN: Authorhouse, 2011).

24 Robert D. Bullard, *Invisible Houston: The Black Experience in Boom and Bust* (College Station: Texas A & M University Press, 1987), 7, 33.

25 Loic Wacquant, "The New 'Peculiar Institution': On the Prison as Surrogate Ghetto," *Theoretical Criminology* 4, no. 3 (2000): 377–89.

26 Geto Boys, "Mind Playing Tricks On Me," We Cant Be Stopped, Rap-A-Lot Records, 1991.

27 Lil' Keke (Marcus Edwards) featuring DJ Screw (Robert Earl Davis, Jr.), "Still Pimping In The Pen (Screwed)," Don't Mess Wit Texas, Jam Down Records, 1997; Slim Thug (Stayve Thomas), "The Intro," *Already Platinum*, Geffen Records, 2005.

28 K-Rino (Eric Kaiser) interview with Lance Scott Walker in Lance Scott Walker and Peter Beste, *Houston Rap Tapes* (Los Angeles: Sinecure Books, 2013), 80.

29 Ghetto Boys, "Do it Like a G.O.," *Grip It! On That Other Level*, Rap-A-Lot Records, 1989.

30 Faniel, 84.

31 Michael Hall, "The Slow Life and Fast Death of DJ Screw," *Texas Monthly*, April 2001, http://www.texasmonthly.com/story/slow-life-and-fast-death-dj-screw.

32 Lil Keke, "Pimp Tha Pen," *3 "N The Mornin" (Part Two)*, Big Tyme Records, 1995.

33 Sheila Whiteley, Andy Bennett, and Stan Hawkins, *Music, Space and Place: Popular Music and Cultural Identity* (Aldershot, Hants, England; Burlington, VT: Ashgate, 2004), 4.

34 Julie Grob quoted in Faniel.

35 See Fat Pat (Patrick Hawkins), "Ghetto Dreams," *Ghetto Dreams*, Wreckshop Records, 1997; Michael Hall, "The Slow Life and Fast Death of DJ Screw," *Texas Monthly*, April 2001, http://www.texasmonthly.com/story/slow-life-and-fast-death-dj-screw.

36 See Shorty Mac interview with Lance Scott Walker in Lance Scott Walker and Peter Beste, *Houston Rap Tapes* (Los Angeles: Sinecure Books, 2013), 22.

37 Grob quoted in Faniel, 133.

38 Lil Keke, "Pimp Tha Pen."

39 Swangas are "distinctive wire wheels were originally created for 1983 and '84 Cadillacs. They went out of production for years until a California company called Texan Wire Wheel started making them again." *Swangers On ABC13 News Part 1of 2 - HD*, 2010, http://www.youtube.com/watch?v=N9MHfl77 OGo&feature=youtube_gdata_player; Yungstar, "Knocking Pictures Off The Wall," *Throwed Yung Playa*, Straight Profit Records, 1999.

40 *Swangers On ABC13 News Story Part 2 of 2 - HD*, 2010, http://www.youtube.com/watch?v=FZqe-SMaGD8&feature=youtube_gdata_player.

41 Ortega, "Houston's First SLAB Parade Rolls through Town on Sunday," *Houston Chronicle*, October 18, 2013, http://blog.chron.com/rantandrave/2013/10/houstons-first-slab-parade-rolls-through-town-on-sunday/.

42 Big Tiger, "Drank Up in My Cup," *I Came To Wreck*, SwishaBlast Entertainment, 2001.

43 Ronald J. Peters, Yacoubian GS, Rhodes W, Forsythe K, Bowers K, Eulian V, Mangum C, O'Neal J, Martin G, Essien EJ, "Beliefs And Social Norms About Codeine And Promethazine Hydrochloride Cough Syrup (Cphcs) Onset And Perceived Addiction Among Urban Houstonian Adolescents: An Addiction Trend In The City Of Lean," *Journal of Drug Education* 33, no. 4 (September 1, 2007): 415–25, doi:10.2190/NXJ6-U60J-XTY0-09MP.

44 Ron Kenner, "Lean With It: Rap's Deadly Dance With Syrup," *Complex.com*, http://www.complex.com/music/2013/03/lean-with-it-raps-deadly-dance-with-syrup (accessed June 9, 2014).

45 Ronald Peters quoted in Kenner.

46 Ron Kenner, "Lean With It: Rap's Deadly Dance With Syrup," *Complex.com*, http://www.complex.com/music/2013/03/lean-with-it-raps-deadly-dance-with-syrup (accessed June 9, 2014).

47 Kiese Laymon, "Hip-Hop Stole My Southern Black Boy," in *How to Slowly Kill Yourself and Others in America: Essays* (Chicago, IL: Bolden Press, 2013), 64.

Chapter Eight

1 Adam Smith, *The Wealth of Nations* (Blacksburg, VA: Thrifty Books, 1937), book IV, ch. 11, 423.

2 Karl Marx, *Capital: A Critique of Political Economy*, vol. 1, ed. F. Engels, trans. S. Moore and E. Aveling (New York: International Publishers, 1967), 360.

3 Michael Taussig, *Shamanism, Colonialism, and the Wild Man: A Study in Terror and Healing* (Chicago and London: The University of Chicago Press, 1987), 129.

4 Cf. Tricia Rose's classic academic treatment of hip hop that outlines and analyses the four basic elements of hip hop culture (Rose, 38–9).

5 Cf. Imani Perry's argument that whatever the phenotypical appearances of its now global adherents and practitioners, hip hop remains evocative especially of black experience in postindustrial North America, in a black aesthetic form, with black audiences as its primary reference point (Perry, 12–13).

6 George Leonard, *The Silent Pulse: A Search for the Perfect Rhythm That Exists in Each of Us* (New York: E. P. Hutton, 1978), 30–4, 38, 77.

7 Thomas Dumm, "The New Enclosures: Racism in the Normalized Community," in *Reading Rodney King/Reading Urban Uprising*, ed. Robert Gooding-Williams (New York: Routledge, 1993), 178, 184–7.

8 Michael Davis, "Uprising and Repression in L.A.: An Interview with Mike Davis by the *Covert Action Information Bulletin*," in *Reading Rodney King, Reading Urban Uprising*, ed. R. Gooding-Williams (New York: Routledge, 1993), 142–56 (149).

9 Dumm, 182–3.

10 Frank Wilderson, "Blackness and the Imaginative Labor of Policing," Talk given at the "Confronting Racism Conference," University of Colorado, Denver, October 9, 2003, 13–14, 17–18, 23; Frank Wilderson, "Gramsci's Black Marx: Whither the Slave in Civil Society?" *We Write*, January 2005, 2:1, 1–17, 10, 13–16.

11 Orlando Patterson, *NY Times*, March 26, 2006, 26.

12 Cf. The way Michel Foucault uses Ernst Kantorowitz's analysis of "The King's Body" in his book *Discipline and Punish* to discuss a related point on the production of the modern "soul" through the means of power brought to bear on the body, giving rise to an interior eye of supervision and surveillance (Foucault, 28–9).

13 Stephen Bender, "Propaganda, Public Relations, and the Not-So-New Dark Age," *LiP* (Winter 2006): 25–31 (26).

14 The first wildly popular (though technically the second recorded rap record) hip hop release, "Rapper's Delight," kicked out by the Sugar Hill Gang in 1979, entailed a studio remake of Chic's "Good times," and reflected much of the original ambiance of the Old School ethos deriving from the warehouse and block parties convened by the likes of Africa Bambaataa, DJ Kool Herc, and Grandmaster Flash.

15 Obviously apparent in Grandmaster Flash's early 1980s release "The Message," but also evident more generally, as indicated in the comments of Chuck D of Public Enemy to the effect that unique and compelling feature in rap was the "anger that was in it," even though too often directed at other rappers rather than at those responsible for the inner-city conditions out of which rap grew (Chuck D, quoted in Perkins, 21).

16 As was the case with the way the Los Angeles disturbances of 1992 were foreshadowed by rap "soundings" for more than a decade prior to the eruption of South Central, so too with the situation in the immigrant *banlieus* ("ghettos") of Paris that rappers were characterizing and caricaturing since 1990 (Baker, 46, 48; Williams, A29).

17 Both Houston Baker and Imani Perry characterize the function of rap as "prophetic"; Baker and Tricia Rose are not averse to articulating its effects as those of spirituality; Michael Eric Dyson and Philip Royster pose the medium as shamanic; and Jon Michael Spencer will exegete its rhythmic knowledge as insurrectionary and utopia (Baker 46, 48; Perry, title page; Rose, xii; Dyson, 22; Royster, 62; Spencer, 6, 10).

18 Paul Gilroy, *The Black Atlantic: Modernity and Double Consciousness* (Cambridge, MA: Harvard University Press, 2000), 23, 36, 52.

19 The category is that Michel Mafesoli, arguing that sociology has need to account for the entire history of contradictory values and erotic energies that, no matter how rigorously repressed in the name of Promethean productivity or bourgeois propriety, continually animate everyday life and collectively return in one or another form of Dionysian "orgy" as the "true" polymorphic character of human vitality, channeled by and giving shape to society (Mafesoli, 4–5, 11, 35, 41, 82, 85, 95).

20 Cf. Stephen Bender's summary of the history of manipulation of mass habit that, under tutelage to Sigmund Freud's nephew Edward Bernays, gave rise to the Public Relations industry from the 1920s forward in the United States, and after World War II's encounter with Nazism, was subsequently galvanized into serious political use (Bender, 27, 29).

21 Norbert Elias, *The Civilizing Process, Vol. 2: State Formation and Civilization* (Oxford: Basil Blackwell, 1982), 238–9.

22 Elias 1982, 238–9; 1978, 257; Norbert Elias, *The Court Society* (Oxford: Basil Blackwell, 1983), 243.

23 Norbert Elias, *The Civilizing Process, Vol. 1: The History of Manners* (New York: Pantheon Books, 1983), 90–1.

24 Elias 1978, 140.

25 Pierre Bourdieu, "The Forms of Capital," in *Readings in Economic Sociology*, ed. Nicole Woolsey Biggart (New York: Blackwell, 1986 [2002]), 280–91 (283, 286).

26 Michel Foucault, *Discipline and Punish: The Birth of the Prison*, trans. A. Sheridan (New York: Vintage, 1979), 200–5; Michel Foucault, *Power/Knowledge: Selected Interviews and Other Writings, 1972-1977*, ed. C. Gordon, trans. C. Gordon (Brighton, Sussex: Pantheon Books, 1980), 92–100.

27 Elias 1982, 242.

28 Cf. Elias and Dunning's 1986 work entitled *Quest for Excitement: Sport and Leisure in the Civilizing Process*.

29 Mikhail Bahktin, *Rabelais and His World*, trans. H. Iswolsky (Bloomington: Indiana University Press, 1984), 11, 27, 32, 84.

30 David Roediger, *The Wages of Whiteness: Race and the Making of the American Working Class* (London; New York: Verso, 1991), 95–111.

31 This is a contemporary form of the medicalizing and pathologizing of resistance whose earlier constructs included (in 1851) the discovery of "drapetomania"—the disease causing slaves to flee captivity—and "dysaesthesia aethiopis"—the disease causing slaves "to pay insufficient attention to the master's needs." Cf Bruce Levine, "Depathologizing the Spirit of Resistance," *Z Magazine* (October 2005): 26–7 (26).

32 C. S. Lewis, "The Abolition of Man," in *From Christ to the World: Introductory Readings in Christian Ethics*, eds. Wayne G. Boulton, Thomas D. Kenedy, Allen Verhey (Grand Rapids, MI: Eerdmans Publ. Co., 1978 [1994]), 157–63 (158).

33 The danger of rendering human beings in the image of the genetic "goofies" loosed on the world by the domestication of plants and animals in a project of control that is now 10,000 years old and giving evidence on all sides of its likely destiny in disaster, without a significant re-visioning of what a "human being" is in relationship to what "nature" is (Shepard 1998a, xxvi, 16, 278; 1998b, 103).

34 Paul Shepard, "The Abolition of Man," in *From Christ to the World: Introductory Readings in Christian* Ethics, eds. Wayne G. Boulton et al. (Grand Rapids, MI: Eerdmans Publ. Co., 1998), 5, 27, 34, 83–5, 94, 131 ff., 157–63; Gary Snyder, *The Practice of the Wild: Essays by Gary Snyder* (San Francisco: North Point Press, 1990), 7, 15–17; David Abram, *The Spell of the Sensuous: Perception and Language in a More than Human World* (New York: Vintage Books, 1996), 25–7.

35 Rudolph Otto, *The Idea of the Holy*, trans. John W. Harvey (London: Oxford University Press, 1950), 13; Charles Long, *Significations: Signs, Symbols, and Images in the Interpretation of Religion* (Philadelphia: Fortress Press, 1986), 123, 137–9, 142, 165, 196–97.

36 Adam Krims, *Rap Music and the Poetics of Identity* (Cambridge: Cambridge University Press, 2000), 74, 134; Adam Krims, "The Hip-Hop Sublime as a Form of Commodification," in *Music and Marx: Ideas, Practice, Politics*, ed. Regula Burckhardt Qureshi (New York: Routledge, 2002), 70, 72.

37 Krims 2002, 70–1; 2000, 54, 73–4.

38 Immanuel Kant, *Critique of Judgment*, trans. Werner S. Pluhar (Indianapolis: Hackett Publishing Co., 1987), 101, 105, 124–5.

39 Kant, 100–1, 112, 138.

40 Fredric Jameson, *Postmodernism: Or, The Cultural Logic of Late Capitalism* (Durham: Duke University Press, 1991), 49, 54.

41 Jameson, 38–9.

42 Jean-Francois Lyotard, "The Sublime and the Avant-Garde," In *The Polity Reader in Cultural Theory* (Cambridge, MA: Polity Press, 1994), 284–8 (287–8); Jameson, 6, 16, 34.

43 Gilroy, *The Black Atlantic*, 37, 38, 131.

44 Gilroy, 37, 203, 215, 218.

45 Lewis, 158–60.

46 Cf. Shepard for the idea of the hunt and the encounter with large game as the quintessence of "meaning" that is recapitulated in religious ritual (Shepard 1998b, 58, 60, 61, 65, 96–7; Snyder, 183–5).

47 Cf. Jensen for a deep philosophical and political probing of the cyborg ideal we are fast rushing into and its effects on the planet and "the human being" alike in *Welcome to the Machine*. More specifically Shepard notes the changes as humans from finding their primary "other" in oracular and numinous animal species to the agriculturalists' "Great Mother Goddess" and the pastoralists' "Sky Father," to the city now festishized as the "Great Machine" and the (disastrous) attempt to escape from the body they reflect and license (Shepard 1998b, 77, 96, 111, 120). Cf. also David Abram's concern about the same thing (Abram, 22, 270–3).

48 Long, 123, 137–9; Shepard 1998, 88–9, 93.

49 Cf. for instance, Snyder's reflections on the experience of the Spanish conquistador, Alvar Núñez Cabeza de Vaca, who after being stranded and stripped of companions by a terrifying killer storm in 1527 on the coast of Louisiana, spent eight years wandering, learning from indigenous tribes, enduring having nothing, facing death numerous times, but also solicited and embraced by those tribes as a "healer" during that time (Snyder, 7, 13, 22–3). Cf. also, Long's description of a certain profound "formation" of African American culture under similar tutelage to terror (Long, 138–9, 153, 169–1, 197).

50 Cf. Shepard's idea that percussive music is primordial and conducive, if not necessary to human well-being (Shepard 1998, 29, 40, 56). Cf. also, Thompson's identification of the primacy of the percussive in African and Afro-diasporic modes of living and probing reality—I call "percussive epistemologies" (Thompson, xiii–xiv).

Chapter Ten

1 I would like to offer my sincerest thanks to Monica Miller and Anthony Pinn, both of whom provided extensive and detailed feedback throughout the process. I am deeply thankful to both.

2 Mark Anthony Neal, *Soul Babies: Black Popular Culture and the Post-Soul Aesthetic* (New York: Routledge, 2003); Bakari Kitwana, *The Hip Hop Generation* (New York, Basic Books, 2003).

3 Stathis Gourgouris, "Transformation, Not Transcendence," *boundary 2* 31, no. 2 (2004): 57.

4 Gourgouris 2004, 79.

5 Malise Ruthven, *Fundamentalism* (New York: Oxford, 2007).

6 Ruthven 2007, 5–6.

7 Arjun Appadurai, *Fear of Small Numbers* (Durham: Duke University Press, 2006).

8 Ruthven 2007, 10.

9 Arjun Appadurai, *Modernity at Large* (Minnesota: University of Minnesota Press, 1996).

10 Paul Gilroy, *Postcolonial Melancholia* (New York: Columbia University Press, 2006).

11 Ruthven 2007, 22.

12 Arjun Appadurai, *The Future as Cultural Fact* (London: Verso, 2013), 243.

13 Manfred Steger, *Globalization* (New York: Oxford University Press, 2003).

14 Manfred Steger, *Globalization* (New York: Oxford University Press, 2009).

15 Ruthven 2007, 22.

16 Monica Miller, *Religion and Hip Hop* (New York: Routledge, 2013).

17 Anthony Pinn, *The End of God Talk?* (New York: Oxford University Press, 2012), 6.

18 Edward Said, *Humanism and Democratic Criticism* (New York: Columbia University Press, 2004), 22.

19 Said 2004, 26.

20 Said 2004, 22.

21 Pinn 2012, 7.

22 Pinn 2012, 5.

23 Amiri Baraka, *Blues People* (New York: Harper, 1964).

24 Baraka 1964, 29.

25 Imani Perry, *Prophets of the Hood* (Durham: Duke University Press, 2004), 88.

26 http://www.hiphopdx.com/index/news/id.25252/title.big-boi-remembers-outkast-getting-booed-at-source-awards-calls-idlewild-movie-classic-.

27 See Murray Forman and Mark Neal, eds, *The Hip Hop Studies Reader* (New York: Routledge, 2012).

28 Roni Sarig, *Third Coast* (New York: Da Capo Press, 2007), xiv.

29 Said 2004, 22.

30 Said 2004, 26.

31 Pinn 2012, 15.

32 Pinn 2012, 21.

33 Pinn 2012, 7.

34 Pinn 2012, 57.

35 Mark Lamont Hill, *Beats, Rhymes, and Classroom Life* (New York: Teachers College Press, 2009), 127.

36 Pinn 2012, 21.

37 Ruthven 2007, 23.

38 Appadurai 2006, 7.

Chapter Eleven

1 For a discussion of how Robert Moses helped to redesign public space in the city, see Robert A. Caro, *The Power Broker: Robert Moses and the Fall of New York* (Vintage, 1974), a book that shows how much Moses actually underdeveloped Bedford Stuyvesant in the 1930s and 1940s.

2 I bring up the Barclay Center (which is located in downtown Brooklyn, not Bed-Stuy), because Jay-Z was a very public advocate for that site and has rhymed about the sightline between one of his old weed-stashing spots and that new concert/sports arena. Also, some of the more "venerable" and famous hip hop locales range from midtown Manhattan nightclubs like Latin Quarter (cited in songs by KRS-One in the 1980s) and Harlem World on Lenox Avenue (where DJs and MCs battled for the crowds) to swaths of entire neighborhoods such as Queensbridge Houses and the South Bronx.

3 Spillers would share this argument with my former colleagues and me at Duke University during her year-long visiting professorship there in 2005–6.

4 In many ways, hip hop is the latest entry into a long traditional of black popular forms engaging existential questions. For example, Anthony B. Pinn, ed., *Noise and Spirit: The Religious and Spiritual Sensibilities of Rap Music* (New York: New York University, 2003) begins with a convincing discussion of the blues and spirituals as earlier iterations of such existential engagement. Also see Monica R. Miller, *Religion and Hip Hop* (New York: Routledge, 2013), both for its specific take on the aesthetics of pop-cultural practice (including certain dance genres and their filmic representation) and its critique of how scholarly assumptions about religiosity unfairly and categorically exclude hip hop. Lewis R. Gordon, *Existentia Africana* (New York: Routledge, 2000) does a masterful job of providing the conceptual/philosophical scaffolding for any substantive understanding of hip hop's existential/ist longings.

5 Michael Taussig, *Beauty and the Beast* (Chicago: University of Chicago Press, 2012).

6 Taussig, *Beauty and the Beast*, 2.

7 Taussig, *Beauty and the Beast*, 3.

8 *Can't Truss It* is a 1991 song from the hip hop group Public Enemy. Their "minister of information," Professor Griff, would later become a major proponent of the theories linking hip hop acts to the Illuminati. Hip hop's most prominent figures, including Jay-Z, Kanye West, Rihanna, Nikki Minaj and Eminem are most often invoked as key culprits in a fascinating contemporary—and age-old—conspiracy theory.

9 There is a long list of hip hop acts that are unintelligible without recourse to their religious commitments. For instance, "gangsta rapper" DMX spends as much time praying to God on his albums as he does describing his sexual exploits or homicidal tendencies. Ma$e and Run-DMC, emcees from two different eras of hip hop, both decided to become religious leaders in their respective Christian faiths.

10 See Felicia M. Miyakawa, *Five Percenter Rap: God Hop's Music, Message and Black Muslim Mission* (Bloomington: Indiana University Press, 2005). Many historical treatments of hip hop do not spend a lot of time on the Illuminati (if any time at all), but some do discuss the Five Percent Nation of Gods and Earths as well as the Nation of Islam.

11 Since Public Enemy's Professor Griff is such a key player in these Illuminati conspiracy theories, I will just use that group to flag how political claims are voiced in spiritual/religious registers in hip hop. Just two examples: The group begins its most critically acclaimed album, *It Takes a Nation of*

Millions To Hold us Back, with an explicit "Countdown to Armageddon," the Judeo-Christian articulation of the end of human existence. In "Don't believe The Hype," they frame their critiques of racist social exclusion and public ostracism by claiming to be "a follower of Farrakhan" and calling out those that "hope to the Pope," a distinction duly marked between the mildness of Catholicism and the Nation of Islam's racially conscious religious radicalism.

12 Using the Bible as an explicit model for the its structure, KRS-One, *The Gospel of Hip Hop: The First Instrumental* (Brooklyn, NY: powerHouse Books, 2013) attempts to argue for how and why "Hiphoppas" (adherents to "Hip Hop Kulture") can learn from a careful reappraisal of philosophical positions intrinsic to hip hop. For the video to that Nick Minaj song, see https://www.youtube.com/watch?v=2mwNbTL3pOs.

13 Manning Marable, *Malcolm X: A Life of Reinvention* (New York: Viking, 2011); Jared Ball and Todd Steven Burroughs, eds, *A Lie of Reinvention: Correcting Manning Marable's Malcolm X* (Baltimore: Black Classic Press, 2012).

14 John L. Jackson, Jr., *Racial Paranoia: The Unintended Consequences of Political Correctness* (New York: Basic Civitas, 2008).

15 These conspiracies are some of the most prominent today: Mexico plotting to attack America and reclaim its land; the UN's "Agenda 21" as an attempt to operationalize its plan to seize southern states and transform them into communist oases; Common Core as a federal plot to turn young test-takers into anti-Christian and anti-American homosexuals; and even this internet-fomented talk of Jay-Z actively working for Satan.

16 Illuminati conspiracy theories read these alter egos as examples of demonic spirit possession. Moreover, the deaths of pop singer Aaliyah and of Kanye West's mother, Donda, are interpreted as purposeful sacrifices demanded of would-be initiates before they can become members of the Illuminati. Donda West's death as a function of plastic surgery is even further complicated by the fact that Kanye West subsequently married the so-called queen of plastic surgery, Kim Kardashian. I want to thank Monica Miller for informing me of the interesting comments Kanye West made when describing his attempt to post Instagram photos linked to his wedding. His comments speak to fine-grained aesthetic preoccupations that Taussig would want us to note: "Can you imagine telling someone who wants to just Instagram a photo, who's the No. 1 person on Instagram, 'We need to work on the color of the flower wall,' or the idea that it's a Givenchy [wedding] dress, and it's not about the name Givenchy, it's about the talent that is [its designer] Riccardo Tisci—and how important Kim is to the Internet," he said. "And the fact the No. 1 most-liked photo [on Instagram] has a kind of aesthetic was a win for what the mission is, which is raising the palette." Retrieved from http://www.okayplayer.com/news/kanye-west-speaks-cannes-lions-creativity-conference-quotes-video.html.

17 Anthony T. Browder, *From the Browder Files: 22 Essays on the African American Experience* (Washington, DC: The Institute of Karmic Guidance, 1989).

18 I cannot even begin to list all the many interrelated and cross-referencing titles that traffic in such claims, two (very different) places to begin interrogating claims about Freemasonry's links to Satanism are A. Ralph Epperson, *The New World Order* (Tuscon: Publius Press, 1990), a part of the canon within this literature, and a more recent version of this kind of analysis, linking these discussions more directly to hip hop, Rebecca Scott, *Hip-Hop Illuminati: How and Why the Illuminati Took Over Hip-Hop* (CreateSpace Independent Publishing Platform, 2012). This essay is not a book about the history of Illuminati and Freemason linked global conspiracy theories, which others have written about, including Daniel Pipes, *Conspiracy: How the Paranoid Style Flourishes and Where It Comes From* (New York: Simon and Schuster, 1997). Pipes, a rather controversial figure for his activist work with the site Campus Watch, links the founding of these conspiracies to early nineteenth-century Europe while making a case for their constitutive ties to anti-Semitism.

19 For this discussion of such conspiratorial claims, see John L. Jackson, Jr., *Real Black: Adventures in Racial Sincerity* (Chicago: University of Chicago Press, 2005).

20 Illuminati claims would also highlight the eagle's symbolic connection to sun-worship (as an animal, the argument goes, that can stare directly into the sun) as well as the assortments of (unlucky/evil) thirteen positioned throughout the bill (arrows, leaves, stars, even the number of steps on the pyramid).

21 More specifically, Rockefella Records is ostensibly named after New York State's infamous Rockefeller Drug Laws signed into law by Governor Nelson Rockefeller in the early 1970s.

22 For a canonical anthropological argument about how the modern world is overdetermined by such magical, uncanny, and apocalyptic thinking/longing, see Jean Comaroff and John L. Comaroff, "Millennial Capitalism: First Thoughts on a Second Coming," *Public Culture* 12, no. 2 (2000): 291–343.

23 There are, admittedly, plenty of political scientists and other social scientists who do more than just dismiss conspiracy theories as obstructions to real political action. For a discussion of how such theories speak to concerns about the lack of global transparency (which things like the wikileaks scandal and Edward Snowden's leaked files help to foment), see Harry G. West and Todd Sanders, eds, *Conspiracy and Transparency: Ethnographies of Suspicion in the New World Order* (Durham: Duke University Press, 2003). Also see a discussion of the performance of "cultural paranoia" in Patrick O'Donnell, *Latent Destinies: Cultural Paranoia and Contempoary U.S. Narrative* (Durham: Duke University Press, 2000). One of the newest (and more high-profile) entries into the study of conspiracy theories is an attempt to argue for the problematic and self-destructive nature of contemporary conspiracy theories as an alternative to actual political action/analysis: Cass R. Sunstein, *Conspiracy Theories and other Dangerous Ideas* (New York: Simon and Schuster, 2014).

24 Stokely Carmichael with Ekwueme Michael Thelwell, *Ready for Revolution: The Life and Struggles of Stokely Carmichael* (New York: Scribner, 2003), 752. And see Jawanza Kunjufu, *Countering the Conspiracy to Destroy Black Boys* (Sawk Village, IL: African American Images, 1985). Also, for a discussion of black masculinity as a specific kind of social "cool pose," see Richard Majors and Janet Mancini Billson, *Cool Pose: The Dilemmas of Black Manhood in America* (New York: Touchstone, 1992).

25 For Baudrillard, language often misleads us in our attempt to accurately analyze social life. For one version of this argument (linked to his long-standing claims about the kinds of "simulacra" that pass for reality in the contemporary moment), see Jean Baudrillard, *The Gulf War Did Not Take Place* (Bloomington: Indiana University Press, 1995).

26 This is a lyric from a Public Enemy song, "Louder Than a Bomb," which starts with a critique of Christian demonizations of Africana subjects and recounts several accusations of secret governmental spying on politically radical citizens.

27 Felicia M. Miyakawa, *Five Percenter Rap: God Hop's Music, Message and Black Muslim Mission* (Bloomington: Indiana University Press, 2005).

28 Robert Christgau, "The Shit Storm: Public Enemy," LA Weekly, 1989. Retrieved June 17, 2014.

29 Professor Griff, *The Psychological Covert War on Hip Hop: The Illuminati's Take Over of Hip Hop* (Atlanta, GA: Hierz to the Shah, 2011).

30 Griff, *Psychological Covert*, 77.

31 For a discussion of the government's counter-intelligence history through original documents, see Ward Churchill and Jim Vander Wall, *The COINTELPRO Papers: Documents from the FBI's secret Wards against Dissent in the United States* (Boston: South End Press, 1990).

32 Jay-Z, *Decoded* (New York: Spiegel and Grau, 2011), 289.

Chapter Twelve

1 When the term "Frankfurt School" is used, people usually have in mind the early twentieth-century group of thinkers—Theodor Adorno, Erich Fromm, Max Horkheimer, Leo Lowenthal, Herbert Marcuse, and Franz Neumann— that combined philosophy, sociology, psychology, and cultural theory to make sense of the pernicious/horrific developments and tendencies within the twentieth century (Fascism, Soviet communism, world wars, exploitative capitalism). For a helpful book on this group of thinkers, see Martin Jay, *The Dialectical Imagination: A History of the Frankfurt School and the Institute of Social Research, 1923-1950* (Berkley: University of California Press, 1996). In addition to the aforementioned, other thinkers, like Ernst Bloch and Walter Benjamin, are often associated with the Frankfurt School since their ideas and writings influenced authors like Adorno or Horkheimer. In this article, I will focus on Adorno and Benjamin's ideas and contributions to cultural and critical theory. For a helpful text that focuses on the relationship between Benjamin and Adorno, see Susan Buck Morss, *The Origin of Negative Dialectics: Theodor Adorno, Walter Benjamin, and the Frankfurt Institute* (New York: Free Press), 1977.

2 Seem for instance, Adorno, "Perennial Fashion—Jazz," in *Prisms*, trans. Samuel and Shierry Weber (Cambridge, MA: MIT Press, 1983), 121–32.

3 Walter Benjamin, *The Origin of German Tragic Drama*, trans. John Osborne (New York: Verso, 1985), 34.

4 See, for instance, Habermas, *Moral Consciousness and Communicative Action*, trans. Christian Lendardt and Shierry Weber Nicholsen (Cambridge, MA: MIT Press, 1990), 7.

5 Adorno, *Negative Dialectics*, trans. E. B. Ashton (New York: Continuum, 1973), 162.

6 Adorno, *Negative Dialectics*, 166.

7 See Romand Coles, *Rethinking Generosity* (Ithaca: Cornell University Press, 1997), 115.

8 Adorno, *Aesthetic Theory*, trans. Robert Hullot-Kentor (Minneapolis: University of Minnesota Press, 1997), 6.

9 See Rose, *Black Noise: Rap Music and Black Culture in Contemporary America* (Middleton: Wesleyan University Press, 1994), 21–61.

10 See Imani Perry, *Prophets of the Hood: Politics and Poetics in Hip Hop* (Durham: Duke University Press, 2004). Robin Kelley also addressed this issue in his classic essay on early gangsta rap, "Kickin Reality, Kickin Ballistics: 'Gangsta Rap' and Postindustrial Los Angeles," in *Race Rebels: Culture, Politics, and the Black Working Class* (New York: The Free Press, 1996), 183–228.

11 Adorno, *Aesthetic Theory*, 135.

12 Adorno, *Aesthetic Theory*, 173.

13 Adorno, *Aesthetic Theory*, 83.

14 See Benjamin, "Theses on the Philosophy of History," in *Illuminations*, trans. Harry Zohn (New York: Schocken Books, 1973), 255.

15 Lupe Fiasco, "American Terrorist," *Food and Liquor* (Atlantic Records, 2006).

16 Benjamin, 258.

17 Adorno and Horkheimer, *Dialectic of Enlightenment*, ed. Gunzelin Noerr, trans. Edmund Jephcott (Stanford: Stanford University Press, 2002), 25.

18 For a brilliant use of Adorno's ideas and reflections to complicate the notion of gift-giving and generosity, see Coles, 75–137.

19 Adorno, *Negative Dialectics*, 5.

20 Adorno, "Notes on Kafka," in *Prisms*, trans. Samuel and Shierry Weber (Cambridge, MA: The MIT Press, 1983), 257.

21 See Pinn, "'Handlin My Business': Exploring Rap's Humanist Sensibilities," in *Noise and Spirit: The Religious and Spiritual Sensibilities of Rap Music*, ed. Anthony Pinn (New York: New York University Press, 2003), 85–104.

22 See Miller, *Religion and Hip Hop* (New York: Routledge, 2013), chs 3 and 4.

23 For a helpful volume on the religious dimensions of the Frankfurt School, see Eduardo Mendieta (ed.), *The Frankfurt School on Religion: Key Writings by the Major Thinkers* (New York: Routledge, 2005).

Chapter Thirteen

1 W. E. B. Du Bois, *The Souls of Black Folk* (Chicago: A. C. McClurg & Co., 1903), 8.

2 Du Bois, *The Souls of Black Folk*, 8.

3 "Stay Black and Die? African American Theism, Cultural Production, and the Nature of Death," to be included in my book, *The Meaning of Things*, under contract with Oxford University Press; "The End: Thoughts on Humanist Theology, Rap Music, and Death," invited essay to appear in *Dialog*; and, "When It's Over: Humanism, Rap Music and the Culture of Death," to be included in my book, *Humanism: Essays in Race, Religion, and Culture Production*, under contract with Bloomsbury Academic.

4 Much of the anxiety in the United States in recent decades revolves around the threat of infection, contamination, whereby death imposes on the grand narrative of privileged life and meaning. Globalization imposes this potential for meaningless by pointing out the porous and vulnerable nature of USA's modalities of protection—economic superiority, educational status, political certainty (i.e., a certain positioning of democracy as ideally "American"). And on the domestic front, public advancement of African Americans (perhaps best represented in/by the presidency of Barack Obama) heightens fear that African Americans may not be so easily captured and reified as zombies but rather have range and a modality of life long denied.

5 It is the case that I attempt to describe zombies and zombification in numerous ways in the first few sections of the chapter. And, while this puts me at risk of redundancy, these two concepts are essential and, therefore, it is vital that readers have clarity regarding what I have in mind.

6 Sharon Patricia Holland, *Raising the Dead: Readings of Death and (Black) Subjectivity* (Durham: Duke University Press, 2000), 15; Toni Morrison, *Beloved* (New York: Vintage, 2004).

7 Holland, 23.

8 Nas, "Black Zombies," *The Lost Tapes* (New York: Columbia Records, 2002).

9 http://www.azlyrics.com/lyrics/nas/blackzombie.html.

10 I give more attention to Trayvon Martin in "Do Atheist Understand and Appreciate Black Bodies?" First posted on the Richard Dawkins Foundation Website (May 4, 2012). See: http://old.richarddawkins.net/articles/645837-do-atheists-understand-and-appreciate-black-bodies.

11 See Cornel West, "Nihilism in Black America," in *Black Popular Culture*, ed. Gina Dent (New York: The New Press, 1998), 37–47.

12 See Gary Laderman, *Rest in Peace: A Cultural History of Death and the Funeral Home in 21st Century America* (New York: Oxford University Press, 2003).

13 Elizabeth Hallam, Jenny Hockey, and Glennys Howarth, *Beyond the Body: Death and Social Identity* (London: Routledge, 1999), ch. 1.

14 Elizabeth Hallam, Jenny Hockey, and Glennys Howarth, *Beyond the Body: Death and Social Identity* (London: Routledge, 1999), ch. 1.

15 In some ways, the same could be said of the portrait as in the case of Dorian Gray, particular as Gray's effort is to stop this process of fragility. See: Oscar Wilde, *The Picture of Dorian Gray* (Franklin Park, IL: World Library Publications, 2009).

16 Russ Castronovo, *Necro Citizenship: Death, Eroticism, and the Public Sphere in the Nineteenth-Century United States* (Durham: Duke University Press, 2001), 1.

17 Russ Castronovo, *Necro Citizenship: Death, Eroticism, and the Public Sphere in the Nineteenth-Century United States* (Durham: Duke University Press, 2001), 4–5.

18 Orlando Patterson, *Slavery and Social Death: A Comparative Study* (Cambridge, MA: Harvard University Press, 1985).

19 Castronovo, 10, 40–4.

20 Wade Davis, *The Serpent and the Rainbow: A Harvard Scientist's Astonishing Journey into the Secret Societies of Haitian Voodoo, Zombis, and Magic* (New York: Touchstone, 1997).

21 I read this meaning in many of his works such as those referenced throughout.

22 Albert Camus, *Resistance, Rebellion, and Death: Essays* (New York: Vintage International, 1995), 222.

23 Camus uses the phrase in reference to the logic behind capital punishment— the death penalty. Speaking against the usefulness of it, he argues "capital judgment" rather than aiding actually harms our most fundamental human solidarity, that against death. See Camus, *Resistance, Rebellion, and Death*, 222.

24 These are categories of exchange mentioned by Camus. See, for instance, *The Plague* (New York: Vintage International, 1991).

25 Keep in mind the content and description of sermons given by the priest, Father Paneloux, in *The Plague*. See Albert Camus, *The Plague* (New York: Vintage International, 1991).

26 My earlier work, particularly the idea of "rituals of reference" found in *Terror and Triumph: The Nature of Black Religion* (Minneapolis: Fortress Press, 2004) speaks to the realization that African Americans have been "othered." The auction block and lynching pointed out to African Americans that they were not perceived to have the same ontological importance as white Americans. There are ways in which this current discussion of death is an extension of that earlier discussion. Hence, what rituals of reference might be said to affirm for African Americans is the manner in which they are zombies: they are ontologically and epistemologically dead. In latter work, I plan to further unpack this relationship between the terror and dread of rituals of reference and my current sense of zombies.

27 Lewis Gordon (ed.), *Existence in Black: An Anthology of Black Existential Philosophy* (New York: Routledge, 1996).

28 My assertion here runs contrary to many others who claim there is an effort within society to destroy death. See, for example, Clive Seale, *Constructing Death: The Sociology of Dying and Bereavement* (Cambridge: Cambridge University Press, 1998), ch. 1.

29 Think about this in relationship to Trayvon Martin and George Zimmerman. Trayvon was a zombie attempting to be human, and to extend itself beyond the confines of death and it had to be resettled within its proper epistemological and ontological geography. Zimmerman's action—the killing of Martin—was an effort to restore a bizarre and damning sense of meaning—to embody death—in ways that safeguarding white Americans through Zimmerman with protection from death. Killing sought to confine death by protecting a particular unity of ideas around the nature and meaning. On the surface this was the protection of white privilege, but on a more fundamental level it was the restoration of death's confinement by disciplining a zombie. Martin is not the first, nor will he be the last, graphic example of how fissures in zombification are addressed. So important is the work done by the classification of zombies that the United States, among other societies, will kill (bodies, ideas, meaning) to maintain it. The strategies of "law and order" provide the justification as well as outline the most product techniques.

30 Camus, "Fourth Letter," *Resistance, Rebellion, and Death*, 28.

31 See http://www.nytimes.com/2013/07/14/us/george-zimmerman-verdict-trayvon-martin.html?pagewanted=all&_r=0 (accessed December 21, 2013).

32 Genesis 10–11. See Anthony B. Pinn and Allen D. Callahan (eds), *African American Religious Life and the Story of Nimrod* (New York: Palgrave Macmillan, 2008).

33 This statement could be read through the work of various rap artists, such as Ice Cube, "My Skin Is My Sin," *Bootlegs & B-Sides* (Los Angeles: Priority Records, 1994).

34 I give this normalization of death more attention in "When It's Over: Humanism, Rap Music, and the Culture of Death," a chapter in *Humanism: Essays on Race, Religion, and Cultural Production*, under contract with Bloomsbury Academic.

35 I offer a discussion of Tupac Shakur in relationship to notions of death in another piece: "The End: An Essay on Humanist Theology, Rap Music, and Death," submitted to a special issue of *Dialog: A Journal of Theology*.

36 Jay-Z, "Crown," and "Heaven," *Magna Carta* (New York: Roc-A-Fello Records, 2013).

37 West argues his song "I Am a God," was motivated by his experiences at Fashion Week. See: http://www.wmagazine.com/people/celebrities/2013/06/kanye-west-on-kim-kardashian-and-his-new-album-yeezus/; http://www.huffingtonpost.com/2013/06/24/kanye-west-i-am-a-god-fashion-week-diss_n_3490688.html (accessed January 29, 2014).

38 Kanye West, "I Am a God," *Yeezus* (New York: Def Jam Recordings, 2013).

39 Readers will find his Temple of Hip Hop of interest: http://www.krs-one.com/temple-of-hip-hop/ (accessed January 29, 2014).

40 Kanye West, *Yeezus* (New York: Def Jam Recordings, 2013).

41 I want to thank Monica Miller, my coeditor, for introducing me to the Church of Yeezus: http://yeezianity.com/, and "Yeezus Wept: LA Street Mural Shows Kanye West As Christ Crucified, Just In Time For Easter," http://www.inquisitr.com/1219780/yeezus-wept-la-street-mural-shows-kanye-west-as-christ-crucified-just-in-time-for-easter/#Ot6fuTCqeMbiy2FM.99.

42 http://rapgenius.com/Kanye-west-i-am-a-god-lyrics.

43 Camus, *The Rebel*, 55.

44 Kanye West, "New Slaves," *Yeezus* (New York: Def Jam Recordings, 2013).

45 Albert Murray, "An All-Purpose, All-American Literary Intellectual," in *From the Briarpatch File: On Context, Procedure, and American Identity* (New York: Pantheon, 2001), 195.

46 James Cone, *A Black Theology of Liberation* (Maryknoll, NY: Orbis Books, 1989). See, for instance, Gayraud Wilmore, *Black Religion and Black Radicalism* (Maryknoll, NY: Orbis Books, 1973).

47 Jay-Z, "Empire State of Mind," *The Blueprint 3* (New York: Roc Nation, 2009).

48 http://www.assatashakur.org/forum/open-forum/9011-code-thug-life.html; http://www.tupac.be/various/code.php (accessed December 19, 2013).

49 Albert Camus, *The Myth of Sisyphus and Other Essays* (New York: Vintage International, 1991); and Camus, *The Rebel.*

50 Camus, *The Rebel*, 101.

51 Camus, *The Rebel*, 250.

52 Camus, *The Rebel*, 101.

53 Camus, *The Rebel*, 102.

54 Camus, *The Rebel*, 262.

Chapter Fourteen

1 Participant at the filming of Jay-Z's "Picasso Baby: A Performance Art Film" (2013).

2 For a video presentation of "The Artist is Present," see: http://www.youtube.com/watch?v=YcmcEZxdlv4ent.

3 Neal, Mark Anthony, *Looking for Leroy Illegible Black Masculinities* (New York: New York University Press, 2013), 39.

4 Tricia Rose, *Black Noise: Rap Music and Black Culture in Contemporary America*, 1st edn (Middletown: Wesleyan, 1994), 39.

5 Rose, *Black Noise*, 39.

6 Jay-Z, *Decoded* (New York: Spiegel & Grau, 2010), 4.

7 Jacques Derrida, *Aporias* (Stanford: Stanford University Press, 1993), 12.

8 Derrida, 12.

9 Michelle Alexander, *The New Jim Crow: Mass Incarceration in the Age of Colorblindness*, 1st edn (The New Press, 2010); and, Sudhir Alladi Venkatesh, *Off the Books: The Underground Economy of the Urban Poor* (Cambridge, MA: Harvard University Press, 2006), are but two works that bring to bear these social realities.

10 W. E. B. Du Bois and William Edward Burghardt Du Bois, *The Souls of Black Folk* (Unabridged. Dover Publications, 1994), 1.

11 Kanye West and Jay-Z, feat. Frank Ocean, "No Church in the Wild," *Watch the Throne* (New York: Def Jam, 2011), http://rapgenius.com/Kanye-west-no-church-in-the-wild-lyrics.

12 See Anthony Pinn's discussion of the significance of dress in African American religion. Anthony Pinn, *Terror and Triumph : The Nature of Black Religion* (Minneapolis, MN: Fortress Press, 2003).

13 Jeff Chang and D. J. Kool Herc, *Can't Stop Won't Stop: A History of the Hip-Hop Generation* (New York: Picador, 2005), 76–7.

14 Rose, 21, 30.

15 Anthony Pinn, *Noise and Spirit: The Religious and Spiritual Sensibilities of Rap Music* (New York: New York University Press, 2003).

16 Imani Perry, *More Beautiful and More Terrible: The Embrace and Transcendence of Racial Inequality in the United States* (New York: New York University Press, 2011), 35.

17 Pinn, *Noise and Spirit*, 22.

18 Jean-Francois Bayart, *The Illusion of Cultural Identity* (Chicago: University of Chicago Press, 2005), 69, 80–94.

19 John L. Jackson Jr., *Thin Description* (Cambridge, MA: Harvard University Press, 2013), 14.

20 For the text of the 3/5 Compromise, see: http://www.heritage.org/constitution/#!/articles/1/essays/6/three-fifths-clause.

21 Of course, African Americans accomplished this through diverse and varied means—including legal avenues, assimilationist tendencies and separatist visions. The varieties of strategies of social protest challenged/es the perceived homogeneity of black culture and the productive fragmentation of black life.

22 Interview found on Youtube. See: http://www.youtube.com/watch?v=-oOm7mSka0A.

23 Felicia M. Miyakawa, *Five Percenter Rap: God Hop's Music, Message, and Black Muslim Mission* (Bloomington: Indiana University Press, 2005), 32. See "Chapter 2: The Five Percent 'Way of Life'" for more background.

24 Josef Sorett, "'Believe Me, This Pimp Game Is Very Religious': Toward a Religious History of Hip Hop," *Culture and Religion* 10, no. 1 (March 1, 2009): 11–22.

25 Kool Moe Dee, *There's a God on the Mic: The True 50 Greatest MCs* (New York City: Da Capo Press, 2003), 328.

26 Jeff Chang and D. J. Kool Herc, *Can't Stop Won't Stop: A History of the Hip-Hop Generation* (New York: Picador, 2005), xiii.

27 Pierre Bourdieu, *Distinction: a Social Critique of the Judgement of Taste* (Cambridge, MA: Harvard University Press, 1984), 7.

28 Jay-Z, "Picasso Baby: A Performance Art Film," 2013. Video.

29 For more on this perspective on the sacred and the profane, see: William Edward Arnal and Russell T. McCutcheon, *The Sacred Is the Profane: The Political Nature of Religion* (Oxford: Oxford University Press, 2012).

30 At the time of this writing, the United States awaits hearing whether or not Florida resident Michael Dunn will be convicted in the shooting death of seventeen-year-old African American Jordan Davis, a confrontation that is said to have begun because Dunn did not like the rap music blaring from the car in which Davis sat as passenger, http://www.firstcoastnews. com/story/news/local/2014/02/13/jordan-davis-family-verdict-michael-dunn/5459417/.

31 For background on this treatment of hip hop, see: Tricia Rose, *The Hip Hop Wars: What We Talk About When We Talk About Hip Hop—and Why It Matters* (New York: Basic Civitas Books, 2008), "Chapter 2: Hip Hop Reflects Black Dysfunctional Ghetto Culture."

32 Jay-Z, "Picasso Baby!"

33 Jay-Z. In Kanye West's "Diamonds from Sierra Leone (Remix)." On Kanye West, *Late Registration* (New York: Def Jam, 2005). See: http://rapgenius. com/Kanye-west-diamonds-from-sierra-leone-remix-lyrics#note-17918.

34 The Hottentot Venus offers one such example. For more information, see: Clifton C. Crais and Pamela Scully, *Sara Baartman and the Hottentot Venus: A Ghost Story and a Biography* (Princeton: Princeton University Press, 2009).

35 Monica R. Miller, *Religion and Hip Hop* (New York City: Routledge, 2012), 45–6, 86–92.

36 "Picasso Baby" film participant.

37 Pinn, *Terror and Triumph*, 193.

38 Miller, 2012.

39 Pinn, 194.

40 Pinn, 173.

41 Rose, *Black Noise*, 39.

42 For more on this piece, see: http://www.moma.org/explore/multimedia/ audios/190/1972.

43 http://www.businessinsider.com/jay-zs-5-million-samsung-deal-2013-7.

44 See: http://www.youtube.com/watch?v=QsPFYIVNIqc.

45 Friedrich Wilhelm Nietzsche, *The Case Against Wagner* (Honolulu, Hawaii: University Press of the Pacific, 2003).

46 http://www.vulture.com/2013/08/jay-z-picasso-baby-video-mark-romanek-hbo.html.

47 Bruce Lincoln, *Authority: Construction and Corrosion* (Chicago: University of Chicago Press, 1994), 10–11.

48 See the following for three of many examples: Gerald McKnight, *The Last Crusade: Martin Luther King, Jr., the FBI, and the Poor People's Campaign* (Boston: Westview Press, 1998; Contributor); Alex Haley (Interviewer), Attallah Shabazz (Foreword) Malcolm X (Primary), *The Autobiography of Malcolm X: As Told to Alex Haley* (1987); Edward E. Curtis and Danielle Brune Sigler, *The New Black Gods: Arthur Huff Fauset and the Study of African American Religions* (Bloomington: Indiana University Press, 2009).

49 Sylvester Johnson, "Religion Proper and Proper Religion: Arthur Fauset and the Study of African American Religions," in *The New Black Gods: Arthur Huff Fauset and the Study of African American Religions*, ed. Curtis and Sigler (Bloomington: Indiana University Press, 2009), 145–70.

50 Curtis and Sigler, 146.

Conclusion

1 The Roots, *And Then You Shoot Your Cousin* (Audio CD. Def Jam, 2014).

2 Bruce Lincoln, *Authority: Construction and Corrosion* (Chicago: University of Chicago Press, 1994).

Select bibliography

Abello, Janus A. *The Portrayal and Frequency of Religion in Secular Rap Music.* M.A. Thesis, University of Missouri-Columbia, 2012.

Abram, David. *The Spell of the Sensuous: Perception and Language in a More than Human World.* New York: Vintage Books, 1996.

Adorno, Theodor and Max Horkheimer. *Dialectic of Enlightenment.* Translated by Edmund Jephcott. Stanford: Stanford University Press, 2002.

Adorno, Theodor. *Aesthetic Theory.* Translated by Robert Hullot-Kentor. Minneapolis: University of Minnesota Press, 1997.

Adorno, Theodor. *Negative Dialectics.* Translated by E. B. Ashton. New York: Continuum, 1973.

Adorno, Theodor. *Prisms.* Translated by Samuel and Shierry Weber. Cambridge, MA: MIT Press, 1983.

Appadurai, Arjun. *Fear of Small Numbers.* Durham: Duke University Press, 2006.

Appadurai, Arjun. *The Future as Cultural Fact.* London: Verso, 2013.

Bailey, Julius. "When Apollo and Dionysus Clash: A Nietzschean Perspective on the Work of Kanye West." In *The Cultural Impact of Kanye West.* Edited by Julius Bailey. New York City: Palgrave, 2014, 149–166.

Bailey, Julius. *Philosophy and Hip Hop: Ruminations on Postmodern Cultural Form.* New York City: Palgrave, 2014.

Baker, Houston. "Scene ... Not Heard." In *Reading Rodney King, Reading Urban Uprising.* Edited by R. Gooding-Williams. New York: Routledge, 1993, 38–50.

Bakhtin, Mikhail. *Rabelais and His World.* Translated by H. Iswolsky. Bloomington: Indiana University Press, 1984.

Baraka, Amiri. *Blues People.* New York: Harper, 1964.

Barkun, Michael. *Culture of Conspiracy: Apocalyptic Visions in Contemporary America.* Berkeley, CA: University of California Press, 2013.

Beckford, James. *Cult Controversies: The Societal Response to the New Religious Movements.* London: Tavistock, 1985.

Bender, Stephen. "Propaganda, Public Relations, and the Not-So-New Dark Age." *LiP*, Winter (2006): 25–31.

Benjamin, Walter. *Illuminations.* Translated by Harry Zohn. New York: Schocken Books, 1973.

Benjamin, Walter. *The Origin of German Tragic Drama.* Translated by John Osborne. New York: Verso, 1985.

Bonilla-Silva, Eduardo. *Racism without Racists: Color-Blind Racism and the Persistence of Racial Inequality in the United States.* Lanham: Rowman & Littlefield Publishers, 2006.

Bourdieu, Pierre. *Distinction: A Social Critique of the Judgment of Taste.* London: Routledge, 1984.

Bourdieu, Pierre. "The Forms of Capital." In *Readings in Economic Sociology.* Edited by Nicole Woolsey Biggart. New York: Blackwell, 2002 (1986), 280–91.

Buck-Morss, Susan. *The Origin of Negative Dialectics: Theodor Adorno, Walter Benjamin, and the Frankfurt Institute.* New York: Free Press, 1977.

Butler, Judith. *Gender Trouble: Feminism and the Subversion of Identity.* New York: Routledge, 1990.

Campbell, Heidi A. *When Religion Meets New Media.* Abingdon: Routledge, 2010.

Clay, Elonda. "These Gods Got Swagger: Avatars, Gameplay, and the Digital Performance of Hip Hop Culture in Machinima." *Bulletin for the Study of Religion* 40, no. 3 (2011): 4–9.

Clay, Elonda. "Two Turntables and a Microphone: Turntablism, Ritual and Implicit Religion." *Culture and Religion* 10, no. 1 (2009): 23–38.

Coles, Romand. *Rethinking Generosity.* Ithaca: Cornell University Press, 1997.

Cook, "Davey-D". "The Meeting with a President and a 'King'." In *Jay Z: Essays on Hip Hop's Philosopher King.* Edited by Julius Bailey. Jefferson, NC: McFarland, 2011, 52–66.

Cowan, Douglas E. *Cyberhenge: Modern Pagans on the Internet.* New York: Routledge, 2004.

Dark, Philip. "Methods of Synthesis in Ethnohistory." *Ethnohistory* 4, no. 3 (1957): 231–78.

Davis, Michael. "Uprising and Repression in L.A.: An Interview with Mike Davis by the *Covert Action Information Bulletin.*" In *Reading Rodney King, Reading Urban Uprising.* Edited by R. Gooding-Williams. New York City: Routledge, 1993, 142–56.

Dawson, Lorne L. and Douglas E. Cowan (eds), *Religion Online: Finding Faith on the Internet.* New York City: Routledge, 2004.

Deleuze, G. and F. Guattari. *A Thousand Plateaus: Capitalism and Schizophrenia.* Translated by Brian Massumi. London: The Athlone Press Ltd., 1988.

Derrida, Jacques. *Of Grammatology.* Translated by G. Spivak. London: John Hopkins University Press, 1998.

Dyson, Michael Eric. "Performance, Protest, and Prophecy in the Culture of Hip-Hop." In *The Emergency of Black and the Emergence of Rap* (A special issue of *Black Sacred Music: A Journal of Theomusicology*). Edited by Jon Michael Spencer. Durham: Duke University Press, 1991, 12–24.

Elias, Norbert. *The Civilizing Process, Vol. 1: The History of Manners.* New York City: Pantheon Books, 1978 (1939).

Elias, Norbert. *The Civilizing Process, Vol. 2: State Formation and Civilization.* Oxford: Basil Blackwell, 1982 (1939).

Elias, Norbert. *The Court Society.* Oxford: Basil Blackwell, 1983.

Elias, Norbert and E. Dunning. *Quest for Excitement: Sport and Leisure in the Civilizing Process.* Oxford: Basil Blackwell, 1986.

Fenton, William N. "Ethnohistory and Its Problems." *Ethnohistory* 9, no. 1 (1962): 1–23.

Ferguson, Jordan. *J Dilla's Donuts.* New York City: Bloomsbury Publishing, 2014.

Forman, Murray and Neal, Mark (eds), *The Hip Hop Studies Reader.* New York City: Routledge, 2012.

Foucault, Michel. *Discipline and Punish: The Birth of the Prison.* Translated by A. Sheridan. New York City: Vintage, 1979.

Foucault, Michel. *The History of Sexuality Vol. 1: An Introduction*. Translated by Robert Hurley. New York: Random House Inc., 1990.

Foucault, Michel. *Power/Knowledge: Selected Interviews and Other Writings, 1972-1977.* Edited by C. Gordon. Translated by C. Gordon et al. Brighton, Sussex: Pantheon Books, 1980.

Gadamer, H. G. *Truth and Method.* Translated by Joel Weinsheimer and Donald G. Marshall, 2nd edn. New York City: Continuum, 2004.

Gilroy, Paul. *The Black Atlantic: Modernity and Double Consciousness.* Cambridge, MA: Harvard University Press, 1993.

Gilroy, Paul. *Postcolonial Melancholia.* New York City: Columbia University Press, 2006.

Glaude, Eddie S. *In a Shade of Blue: Pragmatism and the Politics of Black America.* Chicago and London: University of Chicago Press, 2007.

Goffman, Ervin. *The Presentation of Self in Everyday Life.* New York City: Doubleday, 1959.

Goldstein, Warren S., Roland Boer, and Jonathan Boyarin. "Editorial." *Critical Research on Religion* 1, no. 1 (April 2013): 3–8.

Gosa, Travis L. "Counterknowledge, Racial Paranoia, and the Cultic Milieu: Decoding Hip Hop Conspiracy Theory." *Poetics* 39, no. 3 (2011): 187–204.

Gourgouris, Stathis. "Transformation, Not Transcendence." *Boundary 2* 31, no. 2 (2004): 57.

Grayson, Kent. "The Dangers and Opportunities of Playful Consumption." In *Consumer Value: A Framework for Analysis and Research.* Edited by Morris B. Holbrook. New York: Psychology Press, 1999, 105–25.

Habermas, Jürgen. *Moral Consciousness and Communicative Action.* Translated by Christian Lendardt and Shierry Weber Nicholsen. Cambridge, MA: MIT Press, 1990.

Hagin, Kenneth. *New Thresholds.* Tulsa: Faith Library, 1980.

Heidegger, Martin. *Being and Time.* Translated by John Macquerrie and Edward Robinson. New York: Blackwell Publishing, 2007.

Helland, Christopher. "Religion Online/Online Religion and Virtual Communitas." In *Religion on the Internet: Research Prospects and Promises.* Edited by Jeffrey K. Hadden and Douglas E. Cowan. Hadden: JAI, 2000, 205–24.

Hill, Mark. *Beats, Rhymes, and Classroom Life.* New York City: Teachers College Press, 2009.

Hodge, Daniel White. "Baptized in Dirty Water: Locating the Gospel of Tupac Amaru Shakur." In *Secular Music and Sacred Theology.* Edited by Tom Beaudoin. Collegeville: Liturgical Press, 2013.

Hodge, Daniel White. *Heaven Has a Ghetto: The Missiological Gospel & Theology of Tupac Amaru Shakur.* Saarbrucken: VDM Verlag Dr. Muller Academic, 2009.

Hodge, Daniel White. *The Hostile Gospel: Exploring Socio-Relgious Traits in the Post-Soul Theology of Hip Hop.* Critical Studies in Religion. MA: Brill Academic, 2015 (Forthcoming).

Hodge, Daniel White. *The Soul of Hip Hop: Rimbs Timbs & a Cultural Theology.* Downers: Inner Varsity Press, 2010.

Hofstadter, Richard. *The Paranoid Style in American Politics.* New York: Random House LLC, 2012.

Hojsgaard, Morten and Margrit Warburg (eds). *Religion in Cyberspace.* London: Routledge, 2005.

Hoover, Stewart M. and Nabil Echchaibi. "The 'Third Spaces' of Digital Religion." In Finding Religion in the Media. Boulder: The Center for Media, Religion, and Culture, 2012.

Howard, R. G. Digital Jesus: The Making of a New Christian Fundamentalist Community on the Internet. New York City: New York University Press, 2011.

Hoye, Jacob and Karolyn Ali (eds). Tupac Resurrection 1971-1996. New York, NY: Atria Books, 2003.

Ignacio, E. N. Building Diaspora: Filipino Cultural Community Formation on the Internet. New Brunswick: Rutgers University Press, 2005.

Jackson Jr, John L. Racial paranoia: The Unintended Consequences of Political Correctness. New York City: Basic Books, 2010.

Jameson, Fredric. Postmodernism: Or, The Cultural Logic of Late Capitalism. Durham: Duke University Press, 1991.

Janis, Irving L. Groupthink: Psychological Studies of Policy Decisions and Fiascoes. Boston: Houghton Mifflin, 1983.

Jay, Martin. The Dialectical Imagination: A History of the Frankfurt School and the Institute of Social Research, 1923-1950. Berkeley: University of California Press, 1996.

Jensen, Derrick. Welcome to the Machine: Science, Surveillance, and the Culture of Control. White River Junction, VT: Chelsea Green Publishing Co., 2004.

Joseph, Jamal, Cox Gloria, Monjauze Molly, and Shakur Tupac. Tupac Shakur Legacy. New York City: Atria Books, 2006.

Kant, Immanuel. Critique of Judgment. Translated by Werner S. Pluhar. Indianapolis: Hackett Publishing Co., 1987.

Kantorowicz, Ernst. The King's Two Bodies: A Study in Medieval Political Theology. Princeton: Princeton University Press, 1957.

Karaflogka, A. "Religious Discourse and Cyberspace." Religion 32, no. 4 (2002): 279–91.

Kelley, Robin. Race Rebels: Culture, Politics, and the Working Class. New York City: The Free Press, 1996.

King Jr., Martin Luther. "Letter from Birmingham Jail." In Blessed are the Peacemakers. Edited by S. Jonathan Bass. Baton Rouge: Louisiana State University Press, 2001, 237–56.

Kitwana, Bakara. The Hip-Hop Generation: Young Black and the Crisis in American Culture. New York City: Basic Civitas, 2003 (2002).

Knight, Michael Muhammad. The Five Percenters: Islam, Hip Hop and the Gods of New Islam, Hip Hop and the Gods of New York. Oxford: Oneworld Publications, 2007.

Kolko, Beth E., Lisa Nakamura, and Gilbert B. Rodman (ed.). Race in Cyberspace. New York and London: Routledge, 2000.

Krell, David Farrell. Infectious Nietzsche. Bloomington: Indiana University Press, 1996.

Krims, Adam. "The Hip-Hop Sublime as a Form of Commodification." In Music and Marx: Ideas, Practice, Politics. Edited by Regula Burckhardt Qureshi. New York City: Routledge, 2002.

Krims, Adam. Rap Music and the Poetics of Identity. Cambridge: Cambridge University Press, 2000.

KRS-One (Lawrence Parker). The Gospel of Hip Hop: First Instrument. New York City: Powerhouse, 2009.

Leonard, George. *The Silent Pulse: A Search for the Perfect Rhythm that Exists in Each of Us.* New York: E. P. Hutton, 1978.

Levine, Bruce. "Depathologizing the Spirit of Resistance." *Z Magazine* (October 2005): 26–7.

Lewis, C. S. "The Abolition of Man." In Wayne G. Boulton, Thomas D. Kennedy, Allen Verhey (eds), *From Christ to the World: Introductory Readings in Christian Ethics.* Grand Rapids, MI: Eerdmans Publishing Co., 1978 (1994), 157–63.

Lincoln, Eric C. and Lawrence H. Mamiya. *The Black Church in the African American Experience.* Durham and London: Duke University Press, 1990.

Linton, Ralph. *The Study of Man; an Introduction.* New York: London, D. Appleton-Century Co., 1936.

Long, Charles. *Significations: Signs, Symbols, and Images in the Interpretation of Religion.* Aurora: The Davies Group, 1995.

Lövheim, Mia and Alf G. Linderman. "Constructing Religious Identity on the Internet." In *Religion and Cyberspace.* Edited by Morten Hojsgaard and Margrit Warburg. London: Routledge, 2005, 121–37.

Lyotard, Jean-Francois. "The Sublime and the Avant-Garde." In *The Polity Reader in Cultural Theory.* Cambridge, MA: Polity Press, 1994, 284–8.

Mafesoli, Michel. *The Shadow of Dionysius: A Contribution to the Sociology of the Orgy.* Translated by Cindy Linse and Mary Kristina Palmquist. New York: State University of New York Press, 1993.

Marable, Manning. *Beyond Black and White: Transforming African American Politics.* New York City: Verso, 2009.

Marx, Karl. *Capital: A Critique of Political Economy,* vol. 1. Edited by F. Engels. Translated by S. Moore and E. Aveling. New York: International Publishers, 1967.

McCloud, Sean. "From Exotics to Brainwashers: Portraying New Religions in Mass Media." *Religion Compass* 1, no. 1 (2007): 214–28.

McCutcheon, Russell T. "Critical Trends in the Study of Religion." In *New Approaches to the Study of Religion.* Edited by Peter Antes, Armin W. Geertz, and R. R. Warne. Berlin: Walter de Gruyter, 2005.

McCutcheon, Russell T.. *Manufacturing Religion: The Discourse on Sui Generis Religion.* New York/Oxford: Oxford University Press, 1997.

McKim, Donald K. *Westminster Dictionary of Theological Terms* [in English], 1st edn. Louisville: Westminster John Knox Press, 1996.

Mendieta, Eduardo (ed.). *The Frankfurt School on Religion: Key Writings by the Major Thinkers.* New York City: Routledge, 2005.

Miller, Monica R. "The God of the New Slaves or Slave to a Religion and a God?" In *The Cultural Impact of Kanye West.* Edited by Julius Bailey. New York City: Palgrave-Macmillian, 2013, 167–79.

Miller, Monica R. "Humanist Outlaws: Thinking Religion/Living Humanism." In *What is Humanism, and Why Does it Matter?* Edited by Anthony B. Pinn. Cambridge: Cambridge University Press, 2013, 77–92.

Miller, Monica R. "'The Promiscuous Gospel': The Religious Complexity and Theological Multiplicity of Rap Music." *Culture and Religion* 10, no. 1 (2009): 39–61.

Miller, Monica R. *Religion and Hip Hop.* New York City: Routledge, 2013.

Miyakawa, Felicia M. *Five Percenter Rap: God Hop's Music, Message, and Black Muslim Mission.* Bloomington: Indiana University Press, 2005.

Moran, Seana and Vera John-Steiner. "How Collaboration in Creative Work Impacts Identity and Motivation." In *Collaborative Creativity: Contemporary Perspectives*. Edited by Dorothy Miell and Karen Littleton. London: Free Association Books, 2004, 11.

Murray, Charles. *Losing Ground: American Social Policy, 1950-1980*. New York: Basic Books, 1984.

Nakamura, Lisa. *Cybertypes: Race, Ethnicity, and Identity on the Internet*. New York City: Routledge, 2002.

Nakamura, Lisa. *Digitizing Race: Visual Cultures of the Internet*. New York City: Routledge, 2008.

Nakamura, Lisa and Peter Chow-White. *Race After the Internet*. New York City: Routledge, 2012.

Nancy, Jean-Luc. *La Création du Monde ou la Mondialisation*. Paris: Galilée, 2002.

Neal, Mark Anthony. *New Black Man* [in English]. New York City: Routledge, 2005.

Neal, Mark Anthony. *Soul Babies: Black Popular Culture and the Post-Soul Aesthetic*. New York City: Routledge, 2002.

Nietzsche, Friedrich. *Ecce Homo: How one becomes What One Is*. Translated by Thomas Wayne. New York: Algora Publishing, 2004.

Nietzsche, Friedrich. *The Will to Power*. Edited by Walter Kaufmann. Translated by Walter Kaufmann and R. J. Hollingdal. New York City: Random House, 1967.

Oosterling, Henk. "From Interest to Interesse: Jean-Luc Nancy on Deglobalization and Sovereignty." *Substance* # 106, 34, no. 1 (2005): 97.

Parker, D. and M. Song. "New Ethnicities Online: Reflexive Racialisation and the Internet." *Sociological Review* 54, no. 3 (2006): 575–94.

Perkins, William Eric. "The Rap Attack: An Introduction." In *Droppin' Science: Critical Essays on Rap Music and Hip-Hop Culture*. Edited by William E. Perkins. Philadelphia: Temple University Press, 1996, 1–45.

Perkinson, James W. *Shamanism, Racism and Hip-Hop Culture: Essays on White Supremacy and Black Subversion*. New York City: Palgrave Macmillan Press, 2005.

Perkinson, James W. *White Theology: Outing Supremacy in Modernity*. New York City: Palgrave Macmillan Press, 2004.

Perry, Imani. *Prophets of the Hood: Politics and Poetics in Hip Hop*. Durham: Duke University Press, 2004.

Peters, Ken. "Tupac Vs." 90 minutes. DVD, USA: Dennon Entertainment, 2001.

Pinn, Anthony B. *The End of God Talk*. New York City: Oxford, 2012.

Pinn, Anthony B. (ed.). *Noise and Spirit: The Religious and Spiritual Sensibilities of Rap Music*. New York: New York University Press, 2003.

Pinn, Anthony B. *Varieties of African American Religious Experience*. Minneapolis: Fortress Press, 1998.

Rasmussen, Birgit Brander, Irene J. Nexica, Eric Klinenberg, Matt Wray. *The Making and Unmaking of Whiteness*. Durham: Duke University Press, 2001.

Richardson, James T. and Barend van Driel. "Journalists' Attitudes Toward New Religious Movements." *Review of Religious Research* 39 (December 1997): 116–36.

Roediger, David. *The Wages of Whiteness: Race and the Making of the American Working Class*. London and New York: Verso, 1991.

Rose, Tricia. *Black Noise: Rap Music and Black Culture in Contemporary America*. Middletown: Wesleyan University Press, 1994.

Roster, Philip M. "The Rapper as Shaman for a Band of Dancers of the Spirit; 'U Can't Touch This'." *The Emergency of Black and the Emergence of Rap* (A special issue *of Black Sacred Music: A Journal of Theomusicology).* Edited by Jon Michael Spencer. Durham: Duke University Press, 1991, 60–7.

Ruthven, Malise. *Fundamentalism: The Search for Meaning.* New York City: Oxford, 2005.

Said, Edward. *Humanism and Democratic Criticism.* New York City: Columbia University Press, 2004.

Said, Edward. *Orientalism.* New York City: Vintage, 2003.

Sarig, Ronig. *Third Coast.* New York City: Da Capo Press, 2007.

Sartre, Jean-Paul. *Existentialism Is a Humanism.* Translated by Carol Macomber. New Haven: Yale University Press, 2007.

Schechner, Richard. *Performance Studies: An Introduction.* New York City: Routledge, 2002.

Shepard, Paul. *"The Abolition of Man."* In *From Christ to the World: Introductory Readings in Christian Ethics.* Edited by Wayne G. Boulton et al. Grand Rapids: Eerdmans Publishing Co., 1998a (1973), 157–63.

Smith, Jonathan Z. "Religion, Religions, Religious." In *Critical Terms for Religious Studies.* Edited by Mark C. Taylor. Chicago: University of Chicago Press, 1998, 269–84.

Smith, Leslie Dorrough. *Righteous Rhetoric: Sex, Speech, and the Politics of Concerned Women for America.* Oxford: Oxford University Press, 2014.

Snyder, Gary. *The Practice of the Wild: Essays by Gary Snyder.* San Francisco: North Point Press, 1990.

Spencer, Jon Michael. "Introduction." In *The Emergency of Black and the Emergence of Rap* (A special issue *of Black Sacred Music: A Journal of Theomusicology).* Edited by Jon Michael Spencer. Durham: Duke University Press, 1991, 1–11.

Steger, Manfred. *Globalization,* 2nd edn. New York City: Oxford University Press, 2009.

Taussig, Michael. *Shamanism, Colonialism, and the Wild Man: A Study in Terror and Healing.* Chicago and London: The University of Chicago Press, 1987.

Thompson, Robert Farris. *Flash of the Spirit: African and Afro-American Art and Philosophy.* New York City: Vintage Books, 1983.

Turkle, Sherry. *Life on the Screen: Identity in the Age of the Internet.* New York City: Simon & Schuster, 1995.

Utley, Ebony A. *Rap and Religion: Understanding the Gangsta's God.* Santa Barbara: ABC-CLIO, 2012.

Waldenfels, Bernhard. "Levinas and the Face of the Other." In *The Cambridge Companion to Levinas.* Edited by S. Critchley and R. Bernasconi. Cambridge: Cambridge University Press, 2002.

Watkins, S. Craig. *Hip Hop Matters: Politics, Pop Culture, and the Struggle for the Soul of a Movement.* Boston, MA: Beacon Press, 2005.

Watkins, S. Craig. *The Young and the Digital: What the Migration to Social-Network Sites, Games, and Anytime, Anywhere Media Means for Our Future.* Boston, MA: Beacon Press, 2009.

West, Cornel. *Democracy Matters: Winning the Fight Against Imperialism.* New York City: Penguin, 2004.

West, Cornel. "On Afro-American Music: From Bebop to Rap." In *The Cornel West Reader.* New York City: Basic Civitas, 1990, 474–84.

Wiebe, Donald. *Religion and Truth*. Hague: Mouton Publishers, 1981.

Wilderson, Frank. *"Blackness and the Imaginative Labor of Policing."* Talk given at the "Confronting Racism" Conference, University of Colorado, Denver, October 9, 2003.

Wilderson, Frank. "Gramsci's Black Marx: Whither the Slave in Civil Society?" *We Write* 2, no. 1 (January 2005): 1–17.

Williams, Rhys H. and Thomas J. Josephsohn. "North American Sociology of Religion: Critique and Prospects." *Critical Research on Religion* 1, no. 1 (April 2013): 62–71.

Yamaguchi, Kazuo. *Event History Analysis*. Applied Social Research Methods Series, 28. Newbury Park: Sage Publications, 1991.

Index